DAVID CRUISE & ALISON GRIFFITHS

# WILD HORSE ANNIE

### AND

## THE LAST OF
## THE MUSTANGS

### THE LIFE OF
### *Velma Johnston*

*Scribner*

NEW YORK   LONDON   TORONTO   SYDNEY

Scribner
A Division of Simon & Schuster, Inc.
1230 Avenue of the Americas
New York, NY 10020

First Scribner hardcover edition March 2010

SCRIBNER and design are registered trademarks of The Gale Group, Inc., used under
license by Simon & Schuster, Inc., the publisher of this work.

For information about special discounts for bulk purchases, please contact
Simon & Schuster Special Sales at 1-866-506-1949
or business@simonandschuster.com.

The Simon & Schuster Speakers Bureau can bring authors to your
live event. For more information or to book an event, contact the
Simon & Schuster Speakers Bureau at 1-866-248-3049
or visit our website at www.simonspeakers.com.

Manufactured in the United States of America

1   3   5   7   9   10   8   6   4   2

ISBN 978-1-4165-5335-9
ISBN 978-1-4391-6846-2 (ebook)

Photo credits: 8, 22, 29, 32, 37, 62, 102, 115, 125, 139, 140, 152, 179, 249, 257 courtesy of Private
Family Collection; 68 by Charles Herbert, Western Ways Features Company, courtesy of
the Arizona Historical Society; 82–83 courtesy of the Gus Bundy Collection, Special
Collections, University of Nevada Reno Library; 209, 217 by Hope Ryden.

*To our own remuda, past and present, Honey, Irish, Tenny, Fogerty, Hoodoo, Maverick, and Destry—all great trail horses who have taken us on many adventures coast to coast.*

# CONTENTS

# ONE

# *Velma*

RENO, NEVADA, SPRING 1917

BUNDLES OF DRIED sagebrush clung to the fencing of the corral behind Joe and Trudy Bronn's small clapboard house. When the wind picked up, as it always did in west central Nevada, the spiny branches played a scritchy tune against the wire. In time they blew free and tumbled away, but the gusts always brought replacements. Sagebrush shrubs, some ground-hugging, others tall enough to shred a rider's pants from ankle to hip, were the most common natural features of Nevada, after rock and sand.

The corral was round, a shape easier to construct than a square or rectangle, which required heavy bracing in the corners. Joe had fashioned it of mismatched posts and barbed wire with a short stretch of wood railing beside the gate. On a clear day—there could be two hundred such days every year in Reno—it seemed possible to stretch out and touch the heavily wooded foothills of the Sierra Nevada Mountains on the western horizon. Yet timber was scarce. A team and wagon needed a week or more to reach the forests, cut the timber, and haul it back to Reno, making wood far too valuable to lavish on fencing.

Five-year-old Velma Bronn loved to perch on the lower wooden rail of the corral, watching her father train horses. Joe telegraphed his displeasure with stony silences or penetrating glares, but his affection had no easy outlet. The precious section of wood fencing he'd built for his curious daughter was a way of showing his love. Joe was a drover and he allowed Velma to groom the teams used for pulling his wagon and the buggy her mother, Trudy, drove well and often too fast through the streets of Reno. After a training session she helped clean tack and hang up bits, bridles, and ropes. Her father liked things just so and insisted Velma loop the ropes an exact number of times, hang the bridles so the bits were level, and line up brushes precisely on the edge of the shelf.

In the spring of 1917 Joe worked Apache, a mustang he'd caught in the Virginia Range to the southeast, near Virginia City. In the first days of capture some wild horses were apathetic with the shock of separation from their herd and the unaccustomed confinement, but most were like Apache, repeatedly testing their prisons, wheeling in one direction, then another, storming around the corral as if expecting the wire to collapse before their frenzy. Joe's small, round pen was safer than a square or rectangle since the horse could not back into a corner, and it was no more than fifty feet across, to prevent escape. Mustangs were smaller than most ranch horses, under fifteen hands, but they had powerful hind ends and could make short work of fences five or six feet high after a run up of only a few strides.

When her father wasn't busy carting goods for local businesses, Velma slipped out of the house at every opportunity to watch him take the wild out of a mustang. The process varied little. First he slowly took over the authority of the leader, the herd stallion, by controlling the horse's movements. He drove the animal around the pen, pushing it on with his voice, long whip, and lariat. When he had it moving consistently in one direction, he flicked the lariat, turning the horse to run in the opposite direction. Once he was in command of direction he worked on pace, walk to trot to canter and stop. There was always an element of danger; most horses will avoid colliding with a human but a terrified mustang will run over anything to get free. Threatened, they can strike out with their front feet, or deliver a cannonlike kick with rear hooves. And a stallion's bite is strong enough to break an arm.

Most ranchers and wranglers of the nineteenth and early twentieth centuries preferred traditional horse-breaking techniques. It was easier and quicker to lasso the animal, tie him to a snubbing post, and let him fight against the rope until exhaustion brought surrender. Then came a blindfold, stiff hobbles, a tightly cinched saddle, and a ferocious display of bucking when the animal was turned loose. But snubbing didn't work for the wildest mustangs, which had to be foot-roped, yanked to the ground, and hog-tied. Once safe from the dangerous hooves, the horse breakers let the animal struggle up before putting on the saddle. Then the horse was pulled to the ground again, allowing a man to mount. Freshly caught wild horses could dispatch their riders with one or two heaving bucks, so the animal would have to be roped and thrown until there was no more fight left. As many as one in three mustangs died or were damaged so severely in the breaking process that they had to be shot.

Joe Bronn took a slower, gentler route, in part because he couldn't afford the waste. But he also knew that patience and time produced a better horse. Still, he never let Velma anywhere near the wild horses he was training to sell on as green broke, mostly to ranchers for working stock. They were far too unpredictable, even after the worst of their fear had been replaced by wary acceptance.

Despite his caution Velma knew, just as well as she knew her own name, that no mustang would ever harm her or her father, because wild horses were in the Bronn blood.

----

VELMA'S GRANDPARENTS BEN and Mary settled in the mining town of Ione, Nevada, in 1877 just as they were expecting their first child. Thirty-seven-year-old Ben, a carpenter,[*] was an affable sort, but it was Mary, twenty-three, who made a permanent impression. A striking figure at six feet tall, she had no truck with any kind of foolishness. Even family members described her as "starched" in demeanor and somewhat intimidating. Children came quickly, Rena, a daughter,[†] in 1878, Ella a year later, and Ben Junior in 1881. Mary was "fixy" and could make something out of next to nothing, a critical talent in the middle of Nevada where a few yards of woven tricot from San Francisco or St. Louis cost a month's wages and even rough homespun was literally worth its weight in silver.

----

[*] Ben is listed as a carpenter on the 1880 census, though Velma referred to him as a millwright.

[†] Velma thought her name was Rena, but the census records show her as Reno.

In the early 1880s Ione suffered a rapid decline as the ore ran out, forcing closure of three of Ione's four saloons, the school, and all but one store. In 1883, a fire destroyed the hoisting works in the Shamrock Canyon mine.[1] That same year, five-year-old Rena succumbed to a fever.

More than 525 people fled Ione in the months following the mine closure, but Ben, by then superintendent, hung on waiting for the paymaster, who was scheduled to arrive after Christmas with back wages. When the unpaid miners began agitating, Ben made the ruinous decision to advance the money out of his own pocket. The paymaster never showed up, leaving Ben and Mary almost penniless, with two children to support and another on the way.

They planned to head for Lake County in central California, mining country where Mary's uncle had a ranch, but they couldn't leave until Mary gave birth. There was no ideal time to make the three-hundred-mile wagon trek west across the desert, through the rocky foothills at the California border and over the Sierra Nevada range. Every season had its challenges, but the urgency to leave, despite the appalling summer heat they would face during the first half of the trip, was acute. If they lingered in Ione too long, snow in the mountains might stop them from reaching California.

Ione's population shrank every month until Joe was born in August 1884, temporarily raising the count to twenty-nine. The Bronns left shortly after in a covered spring wagon pulled by two domestic horses with a mustang mare Ben had captured tethered to the back, her weanling foal trotting loose behind. The mustang mare was their insurance. Wild horses have iron-tough feet, tremendous endurance, and the ability to go without food or water far longer than domestic horses.

Mary, still weak from childbirth and exhausted during the first arduous days, found her milk giving out, and Joe failed visibly, growing more fretful with every mile. In desperation, Ben hobbled the still-wild mare and gingerly squeezed her teats, teasing out a precious amount of thin white liquid that Mary spooned into Joe's mouth.

Velma never tired of hearing the family story about how mustang milk saved her father's life. She always giggled to hear her tall, strong father described as "the sickliest, cryingest, puniest baby ever."

The Bronns finally reached Nevada City, California, where Mary's uncle invited Ben to work for him in his brewing business. Another child, Mae, was born in 1894, but five years later, just-married Ella died at the age of twenty, followed in 1902 by Ben at twenty-one. Once-sickly Joe grew into a handsome man with deep set blue eyes. Curly, dark brown hair escaping from beneath his felt hat set off unusually high cheekbones. He was particular about his appearance, almost vain, and precise about everything in his life. Joe knew exactly how many steps it took to get to the butcher or the blacksmith. He had inherited his mother's taciturn nature and never said two words when one would do.

In California Joe courted the eldest daughter of Frank Clay, a nearby rancher, but it was her younger sister who ultimately captured his attention. Not only was she lovely, with dark, luxuriant hair, fine skin, and regular features, but she was the only one besides Joe who dared ride his fiery saddle horse, a stallion. Sixteen-year-old Gertrude (Trudy) Clay and Joe Bronn, twenty-four, were married on Christmas Day, 1910.

In 1912 Ben and Mary moved to Reno, population six thousand, which offered a different kind of opportunity than most Nevada towns. The new money flowing into the high desert community came not from gold or silver but divorce. Most states in the union granted divorces to petitioners after a year of residency. With a waiting period of only six months, Nevada cut the time in half. In the words of a hit song from 1910, "My wife and I don't get along / We simply fight and fight. / I married her to win a bet / it really serves me right. / The love she once declared was mine / has simply turned to hate. / So I've made up my mind / to visit old Nevada State."[2] Temporary citizens, many of them well-off or downright rich, generated a surge of jobs and revenue for Reno—dubbed the Divorce Capital—as they partied in furnished houses and apartments until they'd established their legal residency.

Joe and Trudy also left California in 1912, stopping briefly in Reno before heading to the town of Joe's birth. Ione had been revitalized once more by the demands of an expanding industrial economy. Their first child, Velma Ione, was born on March 5, 1912. When Britain declared war on Germany in 1914, the young family returned to Reno to live with Ben, Mary, and Mary's unmarried sister, Mae, a practical nurse. Two-year-old Velma basked in the attention of five doting adults.

"In the eyes of my family, I had been endowed with the greatest intelligence, the best disposition and the most beautiful features and was no less than a candidate for Miss America."[3]

The Bronns' Washington Street home sat on the western outskirts of the city, not far from Virginia Street, the main route connecting the Truckee River with the Comstock Lode mines near Virginia City. A few unpaved streets separated the house from the fields of scrub stretching west. The narrow porch had an unobstructed view of the foothills and beyond them the slopes of the eastern Sierra Nevada Mountains. A white picket fence enclosed the front yard and in summer supported a riot of sweet peas that perfumed the air. Near the standpipe where a watering hose was fastened grew a thick patch of mint. Velma picked leaves all summer, rolling them between her fingers to release the scent.

Like most men of his time, Joe yearned for a son, and after two stillbirths Trudy presented him with Jack in 1915. Jack proved to be no competition for Velma, who jealously stuck close to her father, especially when he had a wild horse to train.

Joe earned a spare living, in part because his stiff manner and unyielding temperament weren't the best combination for entrepreneurial success. He referred to the mustangs in the hills as his bank account, dipping into it when he was short. By 1915 his bank account began to pay dividends. After the outbreak of World War 1, the demand for horses escalated dramatically. By the time the United States entered the conflict in 1917, seven million horses had died on the battlefields of Europe. Fewer than 23,000 horses were exported from the United States to Europe in 1914, but by 1916 the number had leaped to over 357,000 annually. Before the war, the top price paid for a green broke mustang, one that would take a saddle and bridle quietly and had been worked for a few weeks, was $20. But as the troops dug in across France, buyers for the Allied armies were offering up to $40 and didn't care if the animals had not yet seen a saddle or harness.

Joe usually caught his own mustangs but to meet the war demand he bought additional head from the Paiute tribe at the Pyramid Lake reservation thirty-five miles northeast of Reno. It was a long ride but four dollars got him a horse, and for fifty cents more, one of the older boys or young men would ride the bucking animal to a lathered stand-still, pacifying it enough for the return trip home.

There were dozens of herds within a few hours of Reno, but catching them single-handedly was a formidable task. Few saddle horses, burdened with two hundred pounds or more of man and tack, could keep up with a wild herd for long. Most mustangers worked in relays with fresh horses and riders substituting at regular intervals. A chase could last several days with as many as half a dozen men and a dozen replacement mounts. Even so, the mustangers often came back empty-handed.

A lone wild horse chaser could be successful, especially if he rode a mustang himself, as Joe did. Old Baldy, Joe's favorite mount, was a balky stallion, small and unimpressive at first glance.[4] But when Joe set off out into the hills around Reno he rarely came back without another horse in tow.

Joe trusted Old Baldy, despite his fractious nature, to carry Velma. Every now and then, Joe would lean down from the saddle and lift the little girl onto Old Baldy's back, wedging her between his body and the saddle horn. The mustang moved out at the slightest pressure from Joe's legs and Velma couldn't wait until she felt her father's arm tighten around her ribs and the stallion lift softly out of a slow jog and into a rocking lope. Mustangs are born in the wind, her father explained; they drink it; that's why they can run so fast. Velma knew nothing moved as fast as Old Baldy when her father clucked his tongue.

After one such ride, Velma readied herself to be dropped lightly to the ground. "Stay there," her father commanded. He slid off, gathered the reins in one hand, and directed Velma to hang on to Old Baldy's sparse mane, which was more bristle than silk. At that instant, Joe unexpectedly sneezed, an explosion so loud it seemed to freeze time. Velma and Old Baldy parted company, the horse starting one way, then another, but coming to a trembling stop when Velma rolled beneath his feet. Later, Velma explained to her mother and Aunt Mae that Old Baldy just "forgot" she was on his back and she declared that he was far too smart to trample the daughter of the only human he cared about.

Velma grew into early adolescence, tall for her age and slender. Her mother had been more striking as a young woman, but with big round eyes and an impish smile, Velma had a wholesome attractiveness and plenty of charm when she overcame her shyness. Though she had a tomboy's outdoorsy ways, she was also very much the feminine girl, with dress-up her favorite game. She inherited her grandmother's fixy nature and could turn lace, fabric remnants, and other scrounged bits into elaborate costumes. In 1918 three-year-old Jack broke his hip and was never able to walk properly again. When Loreene, born in 1922, joined the family, Velma played horses with her father, hospital with her brother, and house with the baby.

School came close behind her family and horses in Velma's affections. She adored the exactitude of penmanship exercises, the game of matching words and meanings, and the quiet time spent listening as the teacher read stories and poems aloud. Her quick mind made schoolwork a breeze; her only unhappy moments came when she was called on to answer questions in front of the class. Words stuck in her

*Trudy and Joe Bronn in front of their*
*Washington St. home in Reno*

throat, her tongue refused to move, and hot flushes of embarrassment left her nearly paralyzed and miserable.

———

DISEASE HELD THE greatest terror for the parents of Velma's generation. Before the discovery of sulfa drugs and penicillin and the introduction of various preventative vaccines, viruses and bacteria carried by contaminated drinking water and unpasteurized milk killed 10 percent of all infants in America before their first birthdays. In some regions the infant mortality rate surged to 30 percent. Nationally, 25 percent of children died before the age of twelve. Velma sidestepped scarlet fever, Spanish flu, tuberculosis, diphtheria, and typhus but her luck ran out when poliomyelitis swept through Nevada.

Originally called infantile paralysis, polio is an ancient, highly infectious virus, incubated in human feces, which enters the body orally and invades the central nervous system. Outbreaks typically occurred in the summer and fall when heat overwhelmed sanitation efforts. Polio was difficult to diagnose because its symptoms—headache, vomiting, and constipation—were indistinguishable from those of many other illnesses. Though not confined to children, the disease overwhelmingly afflicted them. During the epidemics some recovered unscathed, but hundreds of thousands were stricken by some form of paralysis or left with shriveled limbs.

The first recorded polio outbreak in the United States was in Vermont in 1894, with 132 cases; the first epidemic struck New York City in 1916, with 9,000 affected. By the time it abated, 2,343 victims, mostly children, were dead. The panic was so great that towns ringing New York posted signs forbidding the entry of children. "Many inspectors," reported the *Los Angeles Times* in August 1916, "stationed themselves at the railway stations, ferries and boat landings along the Delaware River . . . to bar all children under sixteen years of age who attempted to cross into [Pennsylvania] without certificates of health."[5] A crippler and a killer, polio also carried the stigma of being a lower-class disease, originating in poverty, ignorance, and poor sanitation. If a well-bred child contracted it, parents blamed contact with someone lacking the education or desire to keep themselves or their households clean. The disease crested again and again in the decades following until the mid-1950s when Salk and Sabin developed their separate vaccines that eliminated polio from the list of modern scourges.

Velma was eleven in 1923 when she came down with a fever. Within days an ache crept into her joints and muscles; the pain concentrated most intensely in her back, neck, and shoulders. Then tremors developed in her limbs and swallowing became painful. Soon Velma had to be carried to the bathroom, and her mother, aunt, and grandmother spoon-fed her with tiny amounts of soft food.

Young Jack's medical bills had already put a financial strain on the Bronns. A multitude of antipolio serums, potions, and other treatments popped up in the wake of the 1916 New York City epidemic, but Joe and Trudy couldn't afford any of them. They tried other treatments promoted to alleviate the twisting, paralysis, and pain, from hot towels, cold baths, and mud rubs to vigorous massage and manipulation of the limbs, an early and torturous form of physiotherapy. But nothing worked, and when Velma worsened, Joe and Trudy somehow scraped together enough money to take her to Children's Hospital in San Francisco, which offered care to poorer victims of the disease.

Cavernous, dark, and full of sad echoes, the Infectious Diseases Pavilion was more terrifying to Velma than the polio, and the treatment was almost as horrific as the affliction itself—a three-quarter body cast, from the top of her head to below her hips, with holes drilled in various places so her skin could breathe. "It is better than nothing and the best we have at the moment," the kindly but firm doctor told her distressed parents. "She can move somewhat. If we don't do it life will become . . ." the doctor might have paused in his attempt to describe the indescribable, "difficult."[6]

The cast was little more than the application of brute force to halt the contortion of her back and limbs. But it also interfered with a child's normal growth. Still, the doctor warned Trudy and Joe that without being restrained, Velma's body would eventually twist completely to one side. Walking would be impossible and she would lose bladder control. The doctor also hinted that if the disease did not slow, Velma would not be able to breathe. The invention of the iron lung was still four years in the future.

Velma didn't know what was worse: the itching, the immobility, the wretched smell of her body when the plaster cast was changed, or the loneliness. There is no record of how long she lived in the cast but six months was the norm. During those months of hospitalization she learned not to cry. Each tear made a track of misery down her face and into the gauze dressing between her body and the plaster, one more discomfort to her skin, which felt thinner than the delicate membrane on the underside of a bird's wing.

At first, though, everything made her cry, especially the fear that her parents, who couldn't afford to stay with her in San Francisco, would not come back, that she would never again see her house, tease Jack, play with Loreene, or sit on the fence rail and watch her father tame a wild horse. Eventually, the interminable pain taught Velma to adapt to its ebb and flow. She learned to avoid any movement that brought on the stabbing needles and lingering aches and to find the positions that kept them at bay. At long last the doctor declared that the cast could be removed.

Joe Bronn went cold when the nurses cut the plaster away from Velma's face. A pale gargoyle peered back at him. The force of Velma's natural growth, coupled with the twisting caused by the polio, had pushed her body against the immovable wall of the plaster. The left side of her face seemed deflated, like a hand imprinted on a soft cushion; her eye drooped alarmingly. Her jaw was displaced, the teeth no longer aligning top and bottom, leaving her not with a smile but with a grimace. One shoulder rode significantly higher than the other and behind it her back bulged. Her legs were spared the paralysis that afflicted many survivors, but scoliosis of the spine, a curvature wrought by both the polio and the restraint, gave her a tilted posture, as if she was forever on her way somewhere even while standing still. Already slender, Velma emerged from the cast emaciated.

Joe couldn't summon the words to comfort the daughter who had clung to him like his shadow. To outsiders, Joe appeared to be the formidable core of the family, but it was Trudy who possessed the grit. Over her long life she shrugged off physical infirmities and personal tragedies that might have incapacitated a weaker personality, all the while carrying the heavy workload of a wife and mother who had to count every penny in order that her family be properly fed and decently clothed. Trudy had more than most mothers' share of woes, but she accepted them as "the price you pay for having a family. There's bound to be some things that go wrong."[7]

If Trudy ever allowed regret or despair to get the better of her, none of her children saw it. She said the secret to living was "to stay as happy as you can . . . remember there's a lot of happy things that go on in your life."[8] Trudy was also a mother of unusual patience who listened sympathetically to the woes of her children and grandchildren, never breaking a confidence or passing judgment. Trudy did her best to compensate for her husband's reaction with her fervent optimism. "When you get down to the wire," she often told Velma, "you tighten your belt, hold your head high and squarely face whatever is in store."[9] Trudy and Aunt Mae had stripped the house of mirrors before Velma came home. They had been prepared for some disfigurement, though not to the extent that Velma suffered, and they couldn't bear to let her see the ravages wrought by the cast. Driven by curiosity, Velma hunted until she found a mirror hidden in her parents' bedroom. When she peered into the glass, another girl's face, like a reflection in a warped surface, looked back.

Once home in the spring of 1924, Velma faced months of recuperation. Aside from the damage inflicted by the polio and the cast, her muscles were atrophied. The continuous pain was eased slightly by the only medication available, Bayer Aspirin. She underwent manual therapy at Reno's Saint Mary's Hospital where nurses manipulated her back and limbs, and the doctor ordered periodic traction for her back, an agonizing procedure. The days in bed became more tedious as Velma recovered, but Aunt Mae kept her busy reading, talking, and playing memory games to fill time and distract her from the discomfort.

Clouding everything was her father's inexplicable reticence. The warmth between them had been replaced by a chill Velma never completely understood or accepted. If that wasn't enough, she developed an allergy to horses. Her eyes watered and her nose ran, her breath rasped and her throat tickled whenever she came close.

Velma was stricken at the beginning of grade six. When she returned to class in the late spring of 1924, graduation to middle school was only weeks away. The teacher advised against attempting the final examinations, fearing the work would be too hard on the still-frail child. Velma pleaded for permission. The teacher relented, and after passing a special test, Velma was allowed to advance with her classmates. But much of Velma's joy in school was gone. Her earlier shyness in front of the class became absolute dread as the cruelty of children carved deep wounds.

"Hey! Which way you headed?" the boys hollered while playing pitch penny. "You coming or going?"

"Here comes humpy!" they jeered as she walked past.[10]

Even the Bronns' annual summer family picnic, the highlight of the hot days before school began, became an ordeal. The other children didn't invite Velma to play the games she once excelled at and she hid when one of the adults brought out a Brownie box camera. "The years that followed made a little girl grow up very fast. Of this period, I remember mostly the hurting. And not ever being able to play with the other kids.... There was always the pain. And the adults who discussed my 'pitiful' condition and wondered what on earth would ever become of me, as though I was deaf, too, and not able to wonder myself what would become of me, since they mentioned it."[11]

Polio transformed Velma from a popular girl with friends into a near recluse. In all her voluminous correspondence, there is no mention of a single friend from those years except for Walter Baring, a gregarious boy of the same age who lived across the river. His father owned a furniture store and Joe Bronn likely delivered pieces for them from time to time. The social isolation brought her even closer to her younger brother, Jack, while her mother and aunt did their best to fill the void.

In 1927 a fresh tragedy struck. Jack, then thirteen, contracted meningitis, a cousin of the virus that causes polio. Death was swift but excruciating as the disease traveled up the spinal column with the speed of a flame consuming a taper, invading, then swelling the meninges membrane surrounding his brain. Trudy kept their day-to-day lives together with her stoicism and energy, but Joe, already subdued by Velma's bout with polio, was flattened. The loss of his only son blanketed each day with a grief that never left him. In time he came to lavish his love on Loreene and was besotted by the newest born, Betty Jo, who grew into a cheerful, devil-may-care child with the gift of making people forgive her any transgression. But even they were touched by their father's solemnity and a little afraid of him.

The change in her father devastated Velma as much as the change in her body and face. To compensate, she conjured elaborate fantasies of what her future might be rather than accept what others deemed inevitable. Her father firmly believed a woman's place was in the home, but Velma imagined herself as a professional secretary. "Not just an ordinary one—but a private, confidential secretary to an important man. My job would be the envy of all who knew me, and I would be an inspiration to other career seekers." For a disfigured young woman of modest means, being the private secretary to a senior executive was a near-impossible aspiration.

Velma dreamed also of a happily-ever-after life with a tall, handsome husband "who loved horses only slightly less than he loved me," a ranch, a barn, and plenty of children.[12] But Velma kept her fantasies to herself. The Bronn family and their friends were certain of a different fate: For a girl who looked like Velma there would be no job working for an important man, no ranch, and certainly no Prince Charming to carry her away.

# TWO

# Charlie

VELMA BRONN SPENT her teenage years learning to live with polio's scars, daily confronting each imperfection. She called it "whipping my gremlins."[1] Reconciling her intelligent and passionate inner self with a distorted outer appearance was the first step in persuading others that the contents counted for more than the package.

"Gradually I learned that certain hair-dos created an illusion of features more in alignment than they really were; that such a small thing as an eyebrow re-shaped helped to even up the face. By concentrating on it very hard, I learned to hold my shoulders level, and if I was careful and did not stand squarely before a person but rather slightly sideways, the difference in me was not so noticeable. Or so I have told myself. Good grooming and stylish wardrobes had a tendency to draw attention from that about which I was so shy."[2]

Most women sewed in the 1930s, but Velma made herself into a professional-quality seamstress. She copied the latest styles from magazines and studied the fashions on display at Reno's better stores. From her sketches of dresses, coats, blouses, and skirts, she created patterns on sheets of newsprint. While the original might have been made of satin, shot silk, or wool crepe with mother-of-pearl, stag horn, or glass buttons, Velma substituted readily available cotton, rayon, sturdy gabardine, or less expensive wool she could buy locally or order from the Sears Roebuck catalogue, and she used buttons salvaged from older garments. She matched the fine finishing work that distinguished couture garments with precise top stitching, flat felled seams, bound buttonholes, and long darts slit and pressed open to produce a smooth curve on the body.

But no amount of attention to wardrobe, or hair, or artful body positioning could entirely deflect the startled double takes of people seeing her for the first time. An encouraging smile did little to help. The right side of her mouth drooped slightly as her lips stretched wide, while the left side hitched up on an angle toward her left eye, accentuating the flattened cheekbone. If she smiled too broadly, one eye bulged and her upper gums were exposed, revealing teeth made crooked by the cast and emphasizing her sunken chin. Nonetheless, Velma grinned easily and often, convinced her smile was one of her best features.

Velma enumerated her assets and faults with almost actuarial precision. Right below the smile in the asset column, she listed her voice, a genuine plus. In contrast to a frame that suggested frailty, Velma spoke with the rich vibrancy of a stage singer or classically trained actor. By her thirties, a fierce cigarette habit had thickened her vocal cords, imbuing her voice with a smoker's husky undertone. Velma also had a comic's sense of timing and the ability to slide humor, irony, and occasional sarcasm into her conversation.

Pain was another gremlin Velma had to whip. Sometimes the misery of her muscles and joints could be relieved only at Saint Mary's Hospital, where she joined the war injured in submitting to the new regimes of experimental physical therapy. Her spine was manipulated and massaged, and if that didn't work, traction pulled her joints apart in an attempt to relieve the pressure on damaged nerves. When Velma was ill, she couldn't bear to stay in bed, because no position was comfortable for long. Family and friends marveled at her energy, but the truth was she didn't dare stop "the eternal keeping moving, no matter how uncomfortable it might be, for the doctor says that is the only way to keep from being immobilized."[3]

In 1930 Velma graduated from high school with top marks in the required courses for girls—English, domestic arts, typing, dictation, and shorthand—and went right to work as a stenographer at the Farmer's and Merchant's Bank in Reno. Later renamed First National Bank of Nevada, it had survived the wave of bank failures after the 1929 stock market crash and by the time Velma was hired, it ranked as the dominant banking institution in the state. There she achieved the first of her childhood dreams, eventually becoming the secretary to an "important man," Gordon Harris, an executive expected to go far within Reno's business community.

Velma thrived in the atmosphere of the bank, which valued accuracy and efficiency above all. Organized and painstaking by nature, her skills were honed to a fine edge. Typographical errors weren't tolerated, and it wasn't unusual for managers to hold letters up to a light to see if corrections had been made. Though only 23 percent of Nevadans had telephones in their homes, the instrument was quickly becoming essential to business, especially after dial phones replaced operator-assisted systems. Velma discovered that the telephone leveled the playing field; because callers had no idea what she looked like she could establish a friendly relationship before meeting face-to-face. It didn't eliminate shock on first sight, but it tempered reactions considerably.

Velma may have dreamed of a large circle of friends, but the reality was quite different. She had few friends and no beaus during her teenage and young adult years. When she was sixteen, she suffered through one summer of unrequited love. She never actually spoke to the young man, but somehow discovered that he was a reader, and she spent considerable time hanging around the library hoping to catch sight of him.

Velma wanted a husband and children as much as any woman, but she was pragmatic. No man had ever courted her and there were no prospective suitors on the horizon. Her job might be an inferior substitute for a family of her own, but she was intensely proud of it—if for no other reason than that she had proved her parents' friends wrong. A personal secretarial position in a bank was a high-status job for a woman, and those lucky enough to secure such jobs were typically well-bred and well-educated spinsters with excellent deportment. Young women like Velma, without the means to attend secretarial school, usually had to be satisfied with a desk in the steno pool until marriage. Furthermore, although disability was common in the 1930s, with hundreds of thousands of war wounded and survivors of disfiguring diseases like polio, the afflicted did not often work in banks where every employee was expected to present an unblemished face to the world.

Velma's job also gave her the satisfaction of influence, even power. A personal secretary's sphere was akin to a spouse's, without the physical relationship. In concert with Harris's wife, Velma organized the life of the man she called "my executive" to ensure that his work schedule ticked along smoothly, that his personal chores were dealt with, and that even his nonworking hours were arranged to best advantage. From preparing fresh coffee in the morning, filing, dictation, and typing, to coordinating meetings, travel, and social engagements, Velma deftly engineered Gordon Harris's life. She was masterful at subtly directing him, but careful to stay on her side of the line; she never referred to him in either personal or business correspondence as anything other than "sir," her "executive," or "Mr. Harris."

Early on, Velma joined the Reno chapter of Executive Secretaries Incorporated, an elite association of women dedicated to advancing the careers of their bosses. Membership was paid for by the employers, who understood its benefits. At association meetings their secretaries learned of advances in business-related technology and passed on to each other efficiencies in office systems and organization. Membership also offered companionship and travel for those who served on committees and, even though women had taken over most lower-level secretarial work from men by 1935, the association helped many navigate a particularly difficult time for working women.

Reno's Executive Secretaries chapter was also an invaluable source of unofficial information about what was going on in the city's business circles, be it individual company fortunes or the details of their managers' personal lives. Velma became adept at using the pipeline, at first for Gordon Harris's benefit and later for her own. One of the "girls," as they referred to themselves, worked for the man who booked most of the entertainment into Reno's hotels and casinos. Scarce tickets to a visiting celebrity's show were nice perks to pass on to Harris's clients.

From the moment she joined the association, Velma made herself indispensable, stepping forward whenever there was a job to be done. For years she edited and largely wrote the chapter's monthly newsletter. At monthly meetings and during the annual conventions, she mingled with national and international members, women who worked for some of the most prominent figures in corporate America. Inevitably she compared herself to the top secretaries in the nation and concluded she was every bit as skilled and competent. This assessment allowed Velma's ego to blossom into true self-confidence, at least in her professional abilities.

Velma's early twenties, though more active socially than her teens, remained relatively bleak. Like most unmarried women, she lived at home. She socialized with other secretaries—a favorite outing was to the elegant Mapes Hotel for cocktails after work—but there were no young men coming to call. Then one day in 1936, Velma accompanied her mother to Saint Mary's Hospital to visit her father, who had injured himself repairing a truck. Walking down the corridor, she heard a booming voice and a loud laugh from her father's room. Velma was astonished to find her normally withdrawn father carrying on a lively exchange with the man in the next bed.

Charles C. Johnston had been working on a construction site in downtown Reno when a heavy ceramic water jug fell on his head from the third floor. He gave the impression that a fractured skull was of no more consequence than a splinter in his finger. Velma made a covert but thorough appraisal. She estimated he had at least a decade on her twenty-four years and judging by the roughness of the hand that smothered hers in greeting, he was an outdoorsman. Charlie, as he insisted she call him, was six feet four inches, and he more than filled the narrow hospital bed. Gauze swaddling couldn't quite hide the burnished top of his mostly bald head, nor did the smoke spiraling up from the cigarette clenched between his teeth obscure the intense blue of his eyes.

Charlie's conversation was laced with profanity, yet one of the stern-faced nursing sisters stood at his bedside, laughing along with him. And her father, who didn't hold with cussing, especially in front of ladies, seemed oblivious to the cheerful invective issuing from Charlie's mouth. Everyone seemed to like him no matter what he said or how he said it. Velma felt the same; in fact, she felt considerably more. Always sensitive to the reactions of others, Velma was thrilled that this man looked at her with frank interest, that he included her in the conversation and listened to her responses intently. He also appeared completely unaware that she was anything less than a perfect physical specimen. Still, she sat carefully with her better side facing him while they chatted. After that first meeting Velma found herself paying daily visits to her father.

A few weeks after Charlie left the hospital, he and Velma met by chance at a Commercial Row bar in Reno. Velma felt all the awkwardness of her inexperience as she stammered an invitation to Charlie to join her and her companions for a nickel beer. From there they intended to move on to a nearby hamburger joint. "Charlie denied being hungry and I insisted that I wasn't hungry either."[4] Instead they sat in Charlie's car in the parking lot and to Velma's surprise, talked for hours about poetry. Only months later did she learn that Charlie had been famished that night, but feared he didn't have enough money to pick up the check.

Charlie had come to Reno from West Virginia for a fast divorce. He and his wife, Anna Myrtle, had been living in Akron, Ohio, where Charlie worked in the rubber plant during the early 1930s. He said little about the marriage, only that it was childless and loveless. Fragments of Charlie's life came out in his stories. Over the years, he'd done a bit of everything: a tour in the trenches of France as an eighteen-year-old, a few years with the Mexican border patrol, a stint as a motorcycle cop, and a lot of wrangling. He told riveting tales about panning for gold and chasing cattle rustlers. Once he'd cornered a rustler only to be thrown to the ground when a rattlesnake spooked his horse and then bit him. He fractured several ribs but managed to get to a doctor on foot.

Family members recall Charlie's stories as enthralling adventures full of vivid detail; whether the accounts were true or not they had no idea, though his body was seamed with enough scars to lend credence to the tales. They also remember his reticence. He spoke of the war but never about the killing, nor would he elaborate on his adventures along the Mexican border. Some family members suspected there was more to the Mexico episode, perhaps a woman, possibly some kind of trouble or illegal activity. There were also hints of his involvement in gun running during the final years of the Mexican Revolution. But it was a part of his life he kept to himself, and if he revealed anything to Velma, she shared none of it with family or friends.

Aside from his height, Charlie Johnston seemed typical of most other Nevadan men who had little formal education and had worked most of their lives at some form of physical labor. An excellent horseman, good enough to impress Joe Bronn, Charlie was equally skilled with a rifle and pistol. At some time in his past he had become an accomplished tracker with enough knowledge to live off the land, a talent he didn't mind showing off or bragging about when given the opportunity. He habitually greeted people with a boisterous, "It's a hell of a good day!" no matter the weather or the circumstances. Charlie enjoyed an argument, even if it turned into a fracas. He didn't hesitate to use his fists when it was necessary and occasionally when it wasn't. A black-and-white photograph of Charlie in his fifties, cigarette cocked in one side of his mouth as he rides along stony ground, shows a man with warmth in his eyes. But a closer look at his expression suggests a man who shouldn't be crossed.

Tilting against type, Charlie was an avid reader, and not just of horse literature. He had a fondness for poetry and recited favorite passages at the slightest provocation. On the face of it this made Charlie Johnston an anomaly, but such a poetic bent actually put him squarely in the tradition of philosophically inclined cowboys of the old West, a breed that was fast disappearing by the Depression. Artist Charles Russell and Will Rogers, the lasso-twirling pundit, were among the most famous of the literary cowpokes.

Born in 1899, Charlie was thirteen years older than Velma and considerably more worldly. It would be easy to peg him as a father figure to a woman with no sexual and little social experience beyond family and work, especially someone like Velma who still idolized her father and suffered from his withdrawal. But there was far more of the lover, mentor, and friend in Charlie than there was father. His steadiness and equanimity provided ballast to Velma's emotional volatility and he buoyed her confidence by supporting her as an equal, not as a child.

When he proposed, Velma had to choose between her career and her man. Like many banks, First National had an inviolate policy against the employment of married women. Many single women worked as nurses, secretaries, and shop assistants, but it was understood that once a wedding ring was secured, their jobs were left behind.

Velma was the first career woman in the Bronn family, much to her father's disapproval; he didn't believe any woman should work, married or single. Large segments of American society felt the same. As the

Depression deepened, resentment toward women in the workplace intensified. In 1932, when the Dow Jones Industrial Average sat at just over forty-one points, down 91 percent since 1929, and "Brother, Can You Spare a Dime" was one of the year's top songs, *Good Housekeeping* magazine ran an article encouraging women, married or single, to give up their jobs if the reason for working was merely to fill time or earn money for frivolities. By the mid-1930s there was a rising tide of criticism against those "thieving parasites of the business world . . . married women whose husbands have permanent positions."[5]

Federal law prohibited members of the same family working in the civil service, ostensibly to prevent nepotism. But such legislation also effectively kept many women out of this well-paying sector while placating those who claimed the government wasn't doing enough to help men—the traditional breadwinners—find employment. Virtually every state legislature passed similar bills restricting and sometimes

*Velma and Charlie in Reno, 1942*

forbidding married women to work outside the home. Though it was acceptable for a single woman to work, especially in clerical fields, senior secretarial positions in business and government were still dominated by men. The career woman, especially married, was neither welcomed nor celebrated.

Charlie suggested they marry secretly since he couldn't yet support her; he was still recuperating from his head injury. They would need her income, but Velma knew that even though Charlie was unemployed the bank would not allow her to continue. No one could be told, not even her mother. Reno was a small town and even the tightest lips might let the information slip. There would be time enough later to make their marriage public.

The pair eloped, after a fashion, on a hot Sunday in early July 1937. That morning Velma dressed and dressed again, deflecting questions from her mother and nosy younger sisters, Loreene and Betty Jo, about why she was taking so long and changing so many times. But Velma brushed them off. When she finally left the house, her shoes, elbow-length gloves, and handbag in a soft lavender hue complemented a sundress and matching jacket. Her hat was stylish, a touch jaunty but sober enough to befit an about-to-be married woman. Lipstick, rouge, and a dab of eyeliner completed the look. Velma could barely control her tremors of joy and anxiety when she thought about what they were doing.

As they waited for Reno's justice of the peace to call them in for the brief ceremony, Charlie spontaneously burst into song, his gravelly voice crooning "I'm in Love with Blue Eyed Sally."

*She's my queen and my heart's delight*
*The flower of Magherally*
*I hope the day will surely come*

*When we'll join hands together*
*'Tis then I'll bring my darling home*
*In spite of wind or weather*

*And let them all say what they will*
*And let them reel and rally*

*For I shall wed the girl I love*
*The flower of Magherally.*

Charlie's unexpected serenade made Velma even more fearful of discovery, but the groom was completely sanguine. They celebrated with martinis at the nearest bar and Charlie gave Velma a leather-bound copy of his favorite book, *The Rubaiyat of Omar Khayyam*. Inside he inscribed his own version of the author's most famous lines:

*A loaf of bread, a jug of wine, and thou,*
*Was old Omar's desire.*
*Mine . . . a cabin in the pines, and thou,*
*A dog and an open fire.*[6]

Afterward, they didn't dare invite a scandal by taking a hotel room together, so Velma returned to the family home on Washington Street and Charlie to a downtown boardinghouse. For the next year, Charlie and Velma kept up a courtship charade, holding hands in the parlor of her parents' house and trying hard not to behave with the affectionate license of husband and wife.

———

POLITICAL STRIFE CAN be wonderful for economies. As tension mounted in Europe, the long Depression began to lift, especially in ore-rich Nevada. American industries geared up to produce mountains of raw materials, munitions, and supplies to sell to both sides in the approaching conflict.

Towns long abandoned revived as metals and minerals of all kinds were once more in demand. In 1938, Charlie landed the deputy sheriff's job in Gabbs, a town about seventy miles southeast of Reno. Velma quickly found secretarial work in the office of the local mine company, which had no reservations about hiring married women. Husband and wife were ecstatic; Velma could finally declare herself Mrs. Charles C. Johnston.

Trudy was stunned; she couldn't believe Velma had kept such a secret from her for so long. Joe was quietly delighted. Charlie was exactly the kind of man he would have wanted Jack to become and he never expected anyone to seek Velma's hand. Trudy was not about to let the marriage to go uncelebrated and she hastily convened a ceremony at their home. "Coming as a surprise to their friends was the marriage of Miss Velma Bronn and Mr. Charles Clyde Johnston," the Reno *Evening Gazette* reported of the August 14, 1938, event. Velma dressed in a dove gray day dress she sewed herself, adorned with a gardenia corsage to remarry Charlie. In her picture her hair is drawn back demurely in a bun and only the good side of her face can be seen. But her smile is broad.

Stuck out in the middle of the central Nevada desert, Gabbs owed its existence to brucite, a magnesia-bearing mineral. The town, initially christened Brucite with the 1920s discovery, had been deserted since the early days of the Depression, but in 1938, the town, renamed Gabbs, boomed again. Hundreds of miners and their families stampeded into Gabbs, swelling the population to over one thousand. People arrived in such numbers that even tents were at a premium. Charlie and Velma counted themselves lucky when they found a two-room shack without electricity, running water, indoor toilet facilities, or adequate heat. These were privations Velma had never endured, but she hardly noticed. She'd finally married the tall, handsome man of her dreams and there was plenty of socializing and partying in this raw town full of young people.

Periodically, Charlie and Velma drove to Reno where they visited family and Velma scouted the latest fashions. Their route took them along a section of the Truckee River, which flowed from its source at Lake Tahoe, through Reno, past the tiny community of Sparks and on to Painted Rock and a handful of little communities and ghost towns until its terminus at Pyramid Lake on the Paiute reservation. Painted Rock, about twenty-seven miles southeast of Reno, was a favorite vantage point. They usually stopped to take in the view of fields of hay and alfalfa hugging the river, a delightful contrast to the gray peaks and shoulders of the nearby hills. Closer to the road, mineral deposits, called desert varnish, gave the rocks a dozen subtle shades of color.

One day Charlie spotted a small band of wild horses drinking from the Truckee. "They were posed, looking toward us, on a sort of a rock outcropping, almost like sentinels. They were quite close—just across the river and higher than us. Something startled them, for they wheeled and were off in flight, their movement almost as though they were equipped with wings, and their feet seemed hardly to touch the earth."[7]

As the war wound down, demand for magnesium collapsed and Gabbs caved in on itself like hundreds of mining towns before it. After the war, working married women were no longer the pariahs they had been in the thirties. Velma found a stenographer's position with Washoe County Title Guaranty in Reno and she and Charlie bought a small house on East Seventh Street, not far from where Velma grew up. Charlie found work with one of Velma's cousins repairing motorcycles and with the regular parties they threw it seemed as if Mr. and Mrs. Johnston were happily settled into town life. But neither could shake a longing for land. Velma, now connected to the real estate industry, was perfectly placed to know what was coming on the market.

The land in the area they both loved near Painted Rock along the river was mostly owned by wealthy landowners with large holdings. Miraculously there was one sixteen-acre parcel for sale, precisely where they'd seen the wild horses during one of their trips. Velma and Charlie quickly made an offer and put their house up for sale. At the same time, Gordon Harris had opened his own insurance business and he wasted no time hiring Velma.

Charlie and Velma never expected the ranch to be a paying proposition—no one in Nevada could make a living with sixteen acres—but they could take enough hay off the fields to feed some livestock and grow their own vegetables and Charlie could hunt for game. Money, he assured Velma, would take care of itself.

Before there was a single building on the acreage or animals of any kind, Charlie and Velma christened their new home the Double Lazy Heart Ranch.

# THREE

# The Double Lazy
# Heart Ranch

A SIDE FROM A handful of large ranches along the Truckee River, the arid, rolling country surrounding the Double Lazy Heart was sparsely settled. Old Joe the Hermit, as the locals called him, squatted in a small shack half a mile from where the bumpy lane to Velma and Charlie's property met Route 50, the road to Reno.

In the Truckee River basin itself, grass was more abundant than almost anywhere else in Nevada. The river, one of the few sources of plentiful water in the state, was controlled by two dams and supplemented by a canal running south of Velma and Charlie's ranch. The system had been constructed in 1913 between Reno and Fallon to improve irrigation and attract ranchers and farmers. It was a highly desirable location for ranchers, enhanced by nearby rail yards in Sparks and the Reno slaughterhouses. Those who located along the Truckee enjoyed a bountiful year-round water supply, but they also suffered occasional flooding in spring when melt water swelled the river beyond its banks, cutting off access to Route 50 and, to Velma and Charlie's great delight, isolating the Double Lazy Heart.

They were so broke after they bought the land, Velma wondered how they could afford both a barn and a house. Charlie was confident they'd find a way. While he and Joe worked on the barn, a one-room cinder-block cabin on a windblown plot near Wadsworth served as Charlie and Velma's temporary home. "The Palace" had a rusting, corrugated tin roof and linoleum floors so worn, the subfloor showed through in splintered patches. A fringe of cottonwood trees offered welcome shade just north of the house, but the stand wasn't big enough to shield it from Nevada's scorching summer heat. Late into the night the walls still seemed to throb with waves of heat. The "facilities" were situated behind the house, ten long strides for Charlie, a couple of dozen for Velma.

Velma doubted there was a windier place anywhere. If gales weren't howling down the slopes of the Virginia and Sahwave ranges to the north, gusts whirled up from every other direction. Sand penetrated the walls, coating everything. Velma's city clothes had to be shaken before she put them on, and if she left her dresser too long without a thorough cleaning, a fine layer accumulated in the bottom of the drawers. At night the sheets were often gritty and after a particularly fierce blow, the bar of soap at the washstand felt like a pumice stone. Charlie laughed as she swept and dusted and cursed. "Don't work so hard!" he'd chide, oblivious to the infestations of sand.

Velma loved color. The classic English cottage garden palate appealed to her most, but she was a daughter of Nevada, the monochrome state. Grays, taupes, and tans on virtually every horizon, save for a few lush valleys and the thickly forested mountains on the east side of Lake Tahoe, were unexciting to the eye. You had to dress it up a bit. Velma sewed cheerful bark cloth pillows to disguise a dull sofa and made bedspreads with matching shams and skirts. Colorful needlepoint samplers with amusing sayings adorned the walls and hand-knit cozies sheltered the coffee- and teapots from the sand. She hooked a rug in a rainbow of shades to hide the worn linoleum. Wherever there was a mournful corner or dark nook in the tiny house, Velma transformed it. She also designed the Double Lazy Heart emblem, two side-by-side hearts touching at the top, with "The Johnstons" above and "Ranch" below. To the right was a large J cradling Velma's maiden initials, VB, and on the left a mirror image J sheltering Charlie's, CC. She couldn't wait to hang it on the wall of their own place.

As soon as an area was fenced Charlie brought in horses. Hoodoo, a pretty iron-mouth gray who treated any bit as a trifling nuisance, and Foxy were the first two. Charlie rode Foxy, a big-bodied chestnut, draft cross stallion with massive feet. No one knew where Foxy came from, but by the time Charlie got him he'd been running wild for some time and had the manners to prove it. Charlie, according to observers, worked magic on the hardheaded stud, turning him into a fine riding horse with one fault. He hated snakes. The only time Charlie got bucked off was on their annual ride to Reno to participate in the Fourth of July parade. When a snake crossed Foxy's path he lit up like a rodeo bronc and dumped Charlie in a ditch.

On Mondays Charlie drove Velma into work from Wadsworth, then picked up Joe to bring him out to the ranch. The two men had developed a deep friendship, the kind that solidifies in sharing a satisfying task. Together they erected a hip-roof barn below the house site, which was close to the road. The men worked steadily, though Joe had to take frequent breaks to rest. It was one of the happiest times in Joe Bonn's life. Lumber was in short supply after the war but Charlie found a load somewhere; he was rather vague about the details. From Monday night to Friday morning, Velma stayed in town with Trudy, returning to the Palace on Fridays when Charlie brought Joe home. Saturdays and Sundays were spent working on the barn, clearing rocks where the house would eventually sit, and erecting fences. It was the beginning of fifteen years of weekend marriage.

*(Left to right) Velma on Hobo, Betty Jo on Hoodoo, and Charlie on Ranger*

When he wasn't at work on the barn, Charlie was preparing a surprise for Velma. He wasn't satisfied with either Hoodoo or Foxy for Velma. He wanted her to have a reliable horse that was an especially comfortable ride. He settled on Hobo, neither mustang, draft, nor quarter horse but a breed harkening back to the plantation and mountain horses of Tennessee, Kentucky, and Missouri. Hobo carried Will Rogers's brand, though no one recalls where Charlie either bought or found him. Unlike his trotting cousins, Hobo had a gait called the single-foot, which produces a smooth ride even at high speeds. His buckskin coat, so dark it appeared almost bay, shone in the Nevada sun while his rather plain head was improved by a kind eye and well-placed ears. Hobo had worked on the rodeo circuit and was exactly the kind of sensible, seen-it-all horse Charlie had been searching for.

When Charlie presented Hobo to Velma, she was uncharacteristically speechless. Happily, her allergy to horses, which had appeared suddenly after the polio attack, disappeared as quickly when Hobo came into her life. Though Charlie worked hard to turn Hobo into a rock-solid trail horse to spare Velma unnecessary jolting, he never completely cured him of a tendency to spook sideways when startled. Fortunately, Velma was a competent enough rider to cope.

Charlie's chestnut mustang, Ranger, had the head of an Arabian, with an elegant, slightly dished nose, tapering muzzle, and wide, finely carved nostrils. It was a type of head common among the Nevada wild herds, a result of mustangs crossed with those Arabians imported from Spain or from Arabia itself. Because Ranger had a tendency to buck, Charlie trained him to stop if the reins were dropped. At first only Charlie could ride him, but eventually he became gentle enough for children.

On the bitter afternoon of New Year's Day, 1946, Velma and Charlie moved their furniture from the Wadsworth Palace to the Double Lazy Heart Ranch. They partitioned off a small room inside the barn, just spacious enough for a couple of single beds, a woodstove, and their two cocker spaniels. It wasn't much but it was all their own and not a grain of sand blew through the walls. Charlie promised they'd have a real home before she knew it.

Though he'd somehow conjured up lumber for the barn, Velma had no idea where the house would come from. Charlie received a small disability pension from his accident with the falling jug and Velma earned only a little more than enough to support a single woman living with her parents. The battle for minimum wages generally and for fair wages for women specifically was just beginning in the United States. Even when it was acknowledged that women should earn a "provider" wage, since many were raising children alone or caring for parents, few employers were willing to ante up. Certainly a woman with a husband, even one on a disability pension, was not regarded as needy enough.

Nevada's postwar mining slump was a boon for a resourceful man like Charlie. He found two abandoned buildings in Gabbs, free for the taking. They were long, narrow, and almost flat-roofed, utilitarian but solid. He jacked them up off their foundations and eased them onto a large trailer he'd borrowed for the 120-mile journey.

Charlie set the two buildings in an L-formation on a stone foundation, then framed the two sections together. Every weekend Velma joined him to work on the house. She looked too fragile to lift a hammer, but she found pleasure in the physical labor, at least most of it. "Charlie and I built every inch of the Double Lazy Heart, except that I chickened out when it came to helping him shingle the roof. I literally froze to the darn thing, flat on my stomach, and he had to pry me loose to get me back down the ladder. Other than that, though, I had my hand in all of it, including the plowing, planting, irrigating, hauling hay, and on one occasion milking the cow."[1]

Charlie created a living room where the buildings joined and built a large stone fireplace "for the dogs." Across from the fireplace they eventually placed an old piano; though she wasn't particularly skilled, Velma loved to play and belt out show tunes at their parties. They put the kitchen at the end of one cabin and Velma's bedroom at the end of the other. A small bathroom with a tub that could accommodate only half of Charlie was next to Velma's room. In the living room a picture window overlooked the fields and the river beyond.

Initially, the house betrayed its origins: two rectangles stuck together, offering all the charm of an industrial outbuilding. There was no proper entrance, just a step up from the dirt and a narrow door leading into what had once been a mine site foreman's office. When Charlie put in a front door and veranda, he fashioned a Double Lazy Heart door knocker with a movable spur providing the percussion.

Velma couldn't wait to decorate a fresh canvas. Her room faced the road and the irrigation canal; she made it into a sanctuary where a woman could feel like a girl. Elsewhere in the house everything matched. She embroidered the Double Lazy Heart brand on the table linens and sheets and found dishes decorated with cowboys and cowgirls. She painted the same design on the kitchen cupboards. Out on the new front porch, Velma positioned matching metal rockers with heart motifs.

Velma was more skilled with needle, fabric, canvas, and paint than she was with pots and pans. Pain often took the edge off her appetite and food didn't matter to her in the same way that decor and clothes did. Still, a kitchen was at the heart of a wife's role. Velma didn't have the culinary flair of her mother so she stuck to the basics—steaks, roasts, and chicken—which satisfied Charlie, who liked his food simple and plentiful.

*(Right to left) Velma, Betty Jo, Charlie, Jack McElwee,*
*and an unidentified man*

Adjacent to the kitchen was Charlie's bed. They slept separately for most of their married life. He was too big to share a bed comfortably with Velma, who hadn't slept easily since the polio. And Charlie had his own complaints, chiefly severe headaches caused by the construction mishap. Velma left him alone when the attacks came. Nothing relieved them, not pills, drink, or cold compresses, only quiet, darkness, and rest.

On December 11, 1946, Joe Bronn died after months of illness. Velma rarely mentioned her father in her correspondence except for occasional references to her respect for him and the infrequent comment about his aloofness toward her. The change in his attitude after polio struck had made a lasting impact.

On their first wedding anniversary after moving to the Double Lazy Heart, Charlie produced a finely tooled leather bridle with sterling silver conchos on the cheek pieces and a Spanish-inspired sterling plate on the brow band. "This'll look good on Hobo," he told her casually, as if he'd picked up a cheap saddle pad at a local auction. The beautiful but obviously expensive bridle prompted one of their rare fights, with Velma demanding that Charlie take it back.

Charlie seldom refused Velma, but this time he was adamant. "Just give it a try," he insisted. "You'll see it's perfect. The money doesn't matter." Velma retorted he'd soon see it mattered when he had only potatoes on his dinner plate. But when Velma slipped the loops over Hobo's ears, his plain head was transformed. A few months later Charlie added matching silver spurs; Velma accepted them without protest.

When they wanted a break, Charlie tied on a couple of bedrolls and they rode into the hills taking little with them except a fifth of bourbon. Charlie seemed able to find food anywhere: wild onions, edible mushrooms, birds' eggs, the fleshy roots of the sagebush, and fat nuts from piñon pines, which didn't begin to produce the oil-rich seeds until they were over a hundred years old. There were also rabbits, woodchucks, and birds to shoot. They frequently talked about a riding trip they'd take one day, following the gold trail of ghost towns from Nevada across the Sierra Nevadas and into California.

On every excursion Velma and Charlie scavenged. The area was littered with abandoned shallow mines as well as the castoffs of homesteaders and travelers heading to California. Once they came across a wagon wheel partially buried in the sand, which they hauled back for decoration. Another time they unearthed a rusted tin cup, and still another they uncovered a weathered saddle and a silver-boom era tin cookware set.

The highlight of any trip into the backcountry was catching occasional glimpses of mustang bands. Charlie estimated there were a couple of hundred wild horses in the area in herds ranging from seven or eight to twenty or more. The mustangs' only predators, other than man, were mountain cats, variously called cougars or mountain lions, which preferred more cover than the Painted Rock area offered. The horses occasionally came down to drink from the Truckee River but only when their water holes in the hills dried up.

Charlie's prowess as a tracker became known and neighbors often called on him to find stray cattle or horses. Once a wealthy rancher lost a fancy mare; the rumor was he'd paid the unheard-of sum of five hundred dollars for her as a gift to his daughter. The man asked Charlie to retrieve the mare from the band of a notorious red roan mustang stallion, well known for his forays to local ranches to enlarge his harem. It was said no fence existed that the stallion couldn't jump, or a mare he couldn't cajole. The ranchers hated him.

The western frontiers were alive with stories of legendary stallions using sophisticated tactics to penetrate the defenses of human encampments in their quest for mares. "They always attacked the domestic herds coming at them at the gallop," observed Spanish naturalist Félix de Azara in 1809, "and passing them or stopping nearby, calling to them and wooing them with low neighs of affection, exciting them and incorporating them into their bands without difficulty, wherat they would all go away together forever. . . .

"The way of attacking is not as in a line of battle, but rather some go in front and the rest all follow in a column that is never cut or interrupted but which at the most might be twisted out of line if [the defenders] succeed in frightening them. Sometimes, they circle back many times before being sent away; others pass by only once and do not circle back; yet other *baguales* [wild stallions] come on so blindly that they shatter themselves against the wagons."[2]

Charlie spent a week trailing the herd before successfully cutting out the mare. When he returned her, the rancher offered a reward, but Charlie wouldn't accept it. Though he and Velma certainly could have used the money, he didn't believe in getting paid for simply being neighborly.

Velma wasn't often alone at the Double Lazy Heart, but Charlie had a "just in case" attitude to life. He insisted she learn to shoot. "Out here you never know what you're going to come up against," he told her. "Animals you can usually handle, but people are a different story. Best be ready." Velma loved the sensuous feel of Charlie's .38 Special in her slender fingers; its weight alone made her feel safe. (Charlie had won it back in Gabbs in an all-night poker game.) She turned out to be an excellent marksman; more than once she shot the head off a rattlesnake, not an easy target, when there was no other recourse. Her wrists were tiny—Charlie could encircle both of them in one hand—but her hands were strong. "Typing is hard work," she said after he made some teasing comment. "If any man tried it for an hour he'd be flat out pooped."[3]

Charlie and Velma referred to the Double Lazy Heart as their cathedral because "we felt very close to the Almighty there." They were not churchgoers, but the expression captured the idyllic contentment they felt, despite their separation during the week. Only one element was missing—children. They consulted a doctor, who, well before the era of fertility tests and reproductive technologies, simply advised them to try harder. When the years passed and nothing came of their efforts, they chalked it up to fate and except for a couple of brief comments later in life, Velma never discussed the subject with anyone.

But there were plenty of children at the Double Lazy Heart. Few weekends passed without at least one youngster in the house and often many more. Jack, the son of Velma's sister Loreene and her husband, Robert McElwee, spent as much of his summer with Velma and Charlie as he could. The children of friends and even casual acquaintances were also frequent visitors. Tom McCord, the young son of Ruthie McCord, a single mother hired by Gordon Harris to help Velma, was a frequent visitor. When Tom was around, Charlie was never alone. Whether Charlie was walking to the barn, ambling down to the river, marching off to check the fences or catch one of the horses, Tom trotted at his heels. One day Charlie stopped short and Tom's face comically connected with his backside. "I'm going to the john," Charlie barked. "You gonna join me or something?" Tom stepped back and grinned sheepishly. "Good!" declared Charlie. "A man needs some peace."[4] In July and August, the boys often stayed with Charlie during the week, but the girls went back to Reno with Velma. Charlie was uncomfortable with the ways of girls and he was terrified one of them would ask him for help with a "female" matter.

In contrast to her immaculate workday ensembles, Velma's favorite ranch attire was an old fringed buckskin jacket. "It's a terribly disreputable looking garment, but even the pockets are full of fun memories and I love to wear it. Sometimes when a little kid would be at the ranch, and get a little bit cold, I could put that jacket on him or her, roll up the soft buckskin sleeves, and there would be a miniature Davy Crockett or a Daniel Boone or a Sacagawea. And there was always a lump of sugar in a pocket for a velvet muzzle to find. I even gathered a litter of puppies in the pockets [after they] had been dropped one at a time from one end of the ranch to the other by their casual mother."[5]

The children learned the rudiments of tracking and at night they sat around a fire as Charlie explained celestial navigation. Velma took every new arrival to view the deep wagon ruts in an old trail near the ranch and told the story of her grandparents' trek to California and, of course, how mustang milk had saved her father's life. Charlie and Velma also taught them how to approach the horses, how to brush them, pick out their feet, and clean tack. Some of the children returned many times; the girls idolized Velma and the boys hero-worshipped Charlie. One young boy was so tickled at being allowed to wear his stockman's hat, he included "God Bless Charlie Johnston's hat" in his prayers for years afterward.

Velma tried not to organize the weekends because her busy workweeks were scheduled down to the last detail. As much as possible, she wanted the weekends to unfold without direction or timetables. On Sundays, if there were no children around, she and Charlie rode out into the hills beyond the dam, letting the horses explode in a full-out run. Despite her size and twisted frame, Velma rode Hobo with author-

*(Left to right) Rob McElwee (Loreene's son), Velma, and
Charlie at Double Lazy Heart*

ity. A casual observer would not notice she wasn't seated quite straight
in the saddle.

In the absence of their own children, Charlie and Velma made a
family with their dogs, a passel of cocker spaniels. "I shall never forget
the incredible receptions that always were given to me when I returned
to the ranch in the evening particularly when our canine family numbered five."[6]

In 1942, during the Gabbs years, Charlie bought Velma a golden-
blond cocker puppy she christened Daiquiri. "As with an eldest child,
Daq was the most adult of any of our dogs, for he spent his formative
years with the two of us, and no younger attractions to affect his growing up. . . . He was too aloof to learn any tricks, and when we would
try to encourage them, he told us with his eyes that it was beneath his
dignity."[7]

At night Charlie carefully banked the coal in the heating stove to
stave off the desert chill, but one evening the fire smoldered, filling the
cabin with carbon monoxide. Daq, sleeping on the floor, was unaffected

but Charlie and Velma slipped toward unconsciousness. The little dog tugged at the covers of their bed, yapping and licking their faces, until Charlie woke up and groggily pulled Velma into the fresh air. Eventually, Velma and Charlie moved to an apartment above a club and casino. While they were asleep one night the wiring of a night-light shorted and fire tore through the papery walls. Barking furiously, Daq roused them mere moments before they would have been trapped in a frame building with oiled floors and a bar full of highly flammable liquor.

When Velma and Charlie went on short rides, the dogs always accompanied them. If nothing else, they provided an excellent early warning of the abundant rattlesnakes in the area; a rising chorus of shrill barks was the dogs' rattler alarm. Velma and Charlie had to call them off quickly before they encircled the snake, risking a bite and a costly trip to the vet. Yet, when a pet sickened beyond hope, no matter how short of cash they were, Velma and Charlie always took it to a veterinarian. They didn't have the heart to put an animal down themselves by drowning or with a bullet, as most ranchers would have done. It had to be a painless needle, a trip home wrapped in a blanket, and a small grave in the cottonwood grove cemetery. Nor could they bring themselves to brand their livestock in the traditional way until freeze branding—using wood alcohol or methyl hydrate chilled in dry ice— was introduced.

Daiquiri was followed by Martini then Dubonnet. Velma and Charlie joked that they had drinkers' dogs. An essential ingredient at their parties and a staple of their everyday lives, alcohol was viewed as a cure-all in their household. "Charles and I always subscribed to the theory that whether or not the spirituous liquids actually helped a cold, it always gave one a devil-may-care, what-the-heck outlook on the world which had a tendency to minimize the discomfort. Like the time the pot-roast blew up in my face at the ranch, and we didn't have burn medicine and Charles gave me a water glass of wine to drink instead, with the comment that it wouldn't do the burns any good, but it would make me feel better. It did."[8]

Velma looked forward to a drink after a long day; the alcohol eased her constant pain. Friday evenings, when they shared the highlights of their separate weeks, were lubricated by Charlie's concoctions, which varied with the season, the available stock, and his whims. In the heat of the summer, it might be tall gin and tonics (long on the gin) or icy daiquiris. Hot toddies in front of the fire were their favorite when the winter wind whistled. And when he felt especially festive, Charlie would mix up margaritas.

Today Charlie and Velma would be considered excessive drinkers, possibly alcoholics. But within their family and social circle, drinking and socializing were inseparable. Nevada has always been considered the home of two-fisted drinkers and present-day inhabitants still have the second-highest per-capita consumption in the United States, though many point out that tourists to Las Vegas, Lake Tahoe, and Reno skew the statistics. In the late 1940s and 1950s, there was little concern about how much people drank, as long as they didn't make nuisances of themselves.

During the week, while Velma was away in Reno, Charlie sometimes saddled up one of the horses and rode, or unhitched the harrow from the tractor and drove, the three miles to the Wadsworth Hotel and its murky bar. After drinking himself into "a fine state of irritation," conversation might dissolve into argument and Charlie would start swinging. There was boredom in his solitude on the ranch and, in time, frustration, too. Charlie, like Velma, smoked heavily. He was rarely without a Duke, a roll-your-own cigarette, hanging from his lips. In his late forties persistent bronchitis plagued him. "Wouldn't you know," he joked, "it would have something to do with broncs!" Though Charlie looked as robust as ever, shortness of breath made routine farm work more tiring. Velma didn't really mind Charlie's bar fights; men were expected to blow off steam, and she did notice that he would be in a lighter mood for days following one of his dust-ups. She also observed that though his hands were bruised and nicked after such "outings," there was rarely a mark on his face. "I suppose it was like me periodically taking the Standard Typing Test to prove I can still type over 100 words a minute," she once remarked to a friend.

However, it did annoy Velma if she arrived back at the ranch on Friday night and found Charlie had gone to the hotel. She always picked him up, but reluctant to make a scene in public, she held her tongue until they got home. Aside from the occasional fiery episode after one of Charlie's episodes at the bar, they seldom argued; when they did it was, in her words, "a doozey." Even though Velma loved her job and Charlie and the ranch, a life divided between two very different worlds brought its own special tension. And there was never much money. Velma was more emotional and quicker to flare up; even-tempered Charlie typically simmered until he blew. "I'm going home to mother!" she snapped at him one weekend after an irritated exchange. "No, you aren't," he boomed back. "*I'm* going home to your mother!"[9] Velma knew that Trudy would be just as happy to see her son-in-law as her daughter.

Aside from normal matrimonial squabbles and the lack of her own children, Velma had fashioned the perfect life she'd fantasized about while recovering from polio. She had her job as executive secretary to an important man. She had her tall, handsome husband who loved horses almost as much as he loved her. And she had her ranch and her animals. Life was almost exactly the way she'd envisioned it.

— FOUR —

# The Road to Reno

E XCEPT FOR TWO weeks of holidays in the summer and a week
at Christmas, Velma rose before the sun every Monday, the day
she left for her other life in Reno. Getting up was always a chore; she
uncoiled herself one limb at a time, waiting a minute or two to allow
the ache to subside. She took care not to exert too much pressure on
any single joint. Once she was up, she felt some relief.

It was a matter of pride to Velma that no one, not even Charlie, realized the full extent of her discomfort. If anyone noticed a wince or gasp
she couldn't stifle, she'd retort dismissively, "I'm middle-aged and still
kicking! A little twinge here and there isn't going to do me in yet. All I
need is a tight girdle and a case of hair spray to keep me going."

Most Mondays Charlie was still asleep and snoring heavily in his
bed near the fireplace when Velma brewed a pot of strong coffee and
smoked her first cigarette of the day. Then she'd slip into her tattered,
fringed leather jacket, check the pocket for carrots, and stroll across
the fields and down toward the river to caress Hobo's nose and say
good-bye for the week. Horses are simple animals, all stomach and fear,
food and flight, but in times of calm the gut rules. The old admonition
about "give 'em an inch" must have been written with a horse in mind.
Charlie didn't like her hand-feeding the horses, knowing they could
become nippy and aggressive. But Hobo was a gentleman who waited
patiently until the treats were offered.

Each Monday Velma left herself enough time to stop for coffee and
a chat with her mother before she was due at the office. From the ranch
it was only twenty-six miles to Reno, but it took close to an hour on the
twisting gravel road, an interlude that allowed her to make the transition from the Double Lazy Heart to the busiest insurance company in

the region. Velma drove confidently, even a bit aggressively, a cigarette spiraling smoke from the dashboard ashtray.

One spring morning in 1950 the trip passed uneventfully until she caught up with a livestock truck. Despite a postwar population boom, there were fewer than sixteen hundred licensed vehicles in the state, three-quarters of them in the Las Vegas area, so any traffic this early in the morning on a lightly traveled road in west central Nevada was unusual. The old truck with wooden slat sides and a canvas roof was obviously heavily loaded; it moved slowly, kicking up puffs of dust in its wake. As Velma pulled closer looking for an opportunity to pass, she noticed a dark fluid glistening on the bumper and dripping onto the road. Blood. She suspected it came from an injured steer or sheep.

Though accidents happened when transporting livestock, especially along rough roads in the spring with potholes formed in the frost-heaved ground, ranchers were usually careful hauling cattle or sheep because they were paid by the pound on the hoof. On long trips, stressed livestock lost weight, which meant money gone from the rancher's pocket. It was worse if there were serious injuries, since the slaughterhouse would refuse animals that couldn't walk off the truck. The law required livestock haulers to stop regularly to feed and water the animals at a secure facility where they could be unloaded and reloaded safely. However, it was different for animals not intended for human consumption. The Killer Rate Exemption spared truckers the time spent watering or feeding the animals en route.

The livestock in the truck might also have come from one of the so-called tax-dodge ranches, operations with absentee owners notorious for their neglect of their animals. All they were interested in was the tax write-off for ranching. Nevada had more than its share of such ranchers because the state offered generous incentives to attract and keep people on the land. After mining activity dropped off in the postwar years, ranching became the state's lifeblood, and the Nevada tax structure was aimed at providing the best possible environment for ranchers. Free of state income taxes, ranchers could put every penny they made back into their operations. And when they died, there were no worries about crippling inheritance taxes, forcing children to sell the land their parents had worked for decades.

There were also federal government concessions and healthy subsidies for those who would grow food on the hoof or in the ground. No one wanted a repeat of the exodus that had occurred during the dust bowl years, a flight from farm and ranching communities that had never been completely reversed, despite innumerable government programs aimed at repopulating rural land. While incentives breathed some life back into ranching, they also attracted those who saw an opportunity for an easy tax credit, a hobby, or a get-rich-quick scheme. Native Nevadans dismissed the tax-write-off ranchers as carpetbagging easterners. But many of the well-to-do in Las Vegas and Reno owned ranches for the tax benefits.

As Velma followed the listing truck, the dribble of blood increased until it was a steady flow, too much for a single hurt animal. She hated the idea of animals suffering but no one, especially ranchers, liked busybodies. Still, Velma decided it was her duty to alert the driver in case he didn't know. She followed the truck into the Sparks stockyards, four miles east of Reno's downtown.

Velma walked over and peered through a gap in the slats, expecting to find cattle or sheep. Instead she saw a horrifying tableau of mutilated horses, some barely alive. Her eyes caught sight of a colt, or what was left of him, lying trampled, his bones crushed and coat blood-soaked. A number of horses had bloody stumps instead of legs. Others had sections of their hooves torn off and hides shredded by buckshot. A stallion stood with his head bowed, blood seeping from empty eye sockets. He had been blinded to subdue him. It was only the tight quarters that kept many of the horses upright. A penetrating stench, the combination of blood, urine, and feces, rose from the truck while flies swarmed over the brutalized animals, jammed so tightly they couldn't flick the insects away with their tails.

"Where did these horses come from and why are they in such terrible condition?" Velma gasped.

"Oh, they were run in by plane out there," the driver replied, indicating the hills of the Comstock Lode.

Velma was sensitive when it came to animals, but she wasn't squeamish. She'd stood by Charlie when he'd been forced to put a calf out of its misery after a birth gone wrong, and then there were all those puppy litters. She'd hardly shed tears since her days in the polio cast. But what she saw on that truck was beyond anything she'd ever experienced.

"No point in crying your eyes out over a bunch of useless mustangs," the driver told her. "They'll all be dead soon anyway."

———

VELMA WAS DETERMINED to do something about the atrocity she'd witnessed at the Sparks stockyards—but what? There was no wildlife protection agency to call, no advocacy group to alert. She didn't even know if the capture and brutalization of wild horses was illegal. Velma was a right-of-center Republican who followed politics in the newspaper, but she had neither government connections nor any direct experience of the political process. Though she had a passing acquaintance with the wealthy, politically active James Slattery, who owned property near the Double Lazy Heart, she didn't know him well enough to call on him for advice.

After a sleepless night, Velma resolved to learn as much as she could about wild horses. For the next week she arrived at work an hour ahead of schedule and left an hour early in order to spend time at the library before it closed. She found a few files of relevant newspaper clippings and a handful of magazine articles. Most were romantic pieces extolling the chase of mustangs for sport or stories of legendary wild horses like the Pacing White Mustang of the Cimarron, who eluded his frustrated pursuers for decades. There were plenty of local news stories about marauding stallions stealing mares from ranchers and later being captured or shot. She found dozens of place names throughout the West that commemorated mustangs—Wild Horse Mountain, Red Horse Creek, Red Roan River, Wild Horse Plains, Broomtail Flat, Pony Hills, Mustang Bayou, Wild Horse Gap, and Mestano Mesa—but very little information about the horses that inspired those names.

There were books by admirers and students of the wild horse, authors such as the famous Texas folklorist and mustanger Frank Dobie, who opined that there were plenty of dumb men in the world but he had never come across a dumb mustang. "No one who conceives him as only a potential servant to man can apprehend the mustang," he observed. "The true conceiver must be a true lover of freedom—a person who yearns to extend freedom to all life. Halted in animated expectancy or running in abandoned freedom, the mustang was the most beautiful, most spirited, and most inspiring creature ever to print foot on the grasses of America."[1]

Other mustangers wrote fulsome, self-aggrandizing accounts of their escapades; a few offered poignant descriptions of an era and a vocation that were receding into history by 1950. Wild horses had been pursued from Mexico to Canada for over three centuries. Most old-time mustangers had at least a grudging respect for their prey. Many were professionals whose livelihoods depended on capturing as many horses as possible, but the animals had to be in good condition or they couldn't be sold.

A few mustangers became celebrities, their exploits and record numbers of captures admiringly reported in the popular press. Former buffalo hunter Buffalo Jones reinvented himself as a flamboyant mustang showman in the tradition of Buffalo Bill Cody, and in 1912 he staged a mustang chase through the streets of New York City.

To be a successful mustanger, a man had to know the habits and understand the instincts of wild horse herds. "We had to use our heads because the fuzztail sure used his," wrote cowboy and novelist Will James in one of his 1930s bestsellers.[2] Part of the wild horse's canniness, according to professional horse runners, was a sort of *moccasin* telegraph that alerted the herds to danger. "[Horses] will gossip about these things," wrote author Walter Goldsmith in 1944.[3]

There were grave consequences to underestimating mustangs. "You never knew for sure about the stud," advised Herman Smoot, who chased wild horses in the hills outside Carson City in the 1920s. "Sometimes when he saw you coming he would lay his ears back and charge up to you, maybe fifty feet or so just to bluff you while his mares took off. . . . He then usually turned right around and flowed after them. That was one type. I've seen others: they're rare, leave their herd and trot up to you like some friendly horse wanting to have its nose rubbed. Then, when they were close enough, they'd explode in a lunge that stopped your heart. My god! You don't know fright until you have a stud towering over you with hooves and a gaping mouth almost big enough to swallow you."[4]

The most intriguing mustanger of any era was Charles "Pete" Barnum, dubbed "King of the Wild Horse Catchers" by *Life* magazine. Little is known of his early life other than that he grew up in the Dakotas, the son of a federal Indian agent, and attended college at some point. Barnum was in his late twenties when he arrived in Reno around 1904. He knew horses but he didn't know mustangs, so he threw in with other horse runners to learn the craft.

Early in Barnum's career in what he called "the truest sport and finest business in the world," he earned a reputation as a maverick while attempting to capture a particularly elusive palomino stallion nicknamed El Rio Rey, also called the Yellow King. The stallion and his herd were chased for eighteen miles by relays of riders. First the foals dropped off, followed by the lactating mares, and finally the weaker males. Only El Rio Rey and four other horses were left by the time the final rider, Hank Connors, took up the chase.

Connors managed to rope the exhausted stallion, but the Yellow King slipped the loop and lunged away. Furious, Connors pulled out his .44 and brought the mustang down. At that moment his hard-running horse stepped in a badger hole and the two somersaulted to the ground. Barnum and the rest of his crew rode up to the two horses and Connors, all dead.

"What had we better do first?" asked the foreman.

"The first thing you will do," answered Barnum regarding the field of triple tragedy, "is to bury that grand old horse. I wouldn't care very much if you left that coward of a man to the coyotes."[5]

Barnum concluded that even the most experienced horse runners' methods were inefficient; 25 to 30 percent of mustangs were killed in the pursuit and capture. The chases also took a toll on the saddle horses. "To capture them [wild horses], the riders must actually outrun them, generally on the roughest mountains where loose or jagged rocks, huge boulders, dead or scrub timbers are constantly in one's way. In making the long runs, which are necessary to exhaust a frightened bunch of wild horses, the saddle horses are generally forced to run up hill and down from five to ten miles; frequently runs of twenty miles and even more are made. . . . Doubtless, this constitutes as hard a task as horses are called upon to perform in any part of the world;

*Charles "Pete" Barnum*

for a band once started is pursued by one man at a time, and if the run is to be successful the rider must travel at a speed equal to that of the band."[6]

Barnum reasoned that if he was going to make horse running a paying proposition he had to deal in larger numbers with fewer casualties. Typically mustangers used pradas or corrals made of wood reinforced with wire to contain captured horses, but these materials were too heavy to transport into remote areas the herds frequented. And prados couldn't be constructed on the spot because the country was virtually treeless. Moreover, corrals could agitate rather than subdue a wild animal. During one roundup, twelve of sixteen horses died when they threw themselves against the corral wire in an attempt to escape.

Barnum had noticed at rodeos that even the fiercest broncos, usually mustangs, rarely tried to jump or smash into walls they couldn't see through or over. Such enclosures actually seemed to calm the animals. But that still left the problem of transportation. Barnum built a prototype corral out of canvas, seven feet tall and one hundred feet in diameter, strung around seventeen flexible cottonwood poles. When the poles were erect and anchored to the ground by ropes, the canvas walls would give if a horse ran into them but the structure wouldn't collapse. Barnum also fashioned long "wings" of canvas to funnel the horses into the corral. "It was late November when all was ready," he wrote of the first test.

We were anxious to try the corrals, so prepared for a short trip to the mountains. . . . Saddle horses, forty-six in number, and already nearly worn out with work, were again gathered. . . . We successfully packed corrals, poles and camp outfit on the chosen six pack horses [but] every animal lay down. Although I asked them politely, and later used persuasion of a more decided character, they refused absolutely to get up so we had to remove the packs, divide the loads among four more horses and found that they all had enough even then.

There were four men beside myself: Dicey, a full-blooded Shoshone Indian, Miguel Quiroz, Chico and Bascus, three Mexican vaqueros possessed of good judgment and plenty of experience. Before starting out the next morning I explained to them that much depended on the success of the undertaking, that I expected every man to ride through blazes if necessary to corral these horses and hinted that any lukewarm performance would be noticed by me and dealt with accordingly.

Miguel and Chico understood . . . both rode at breakneck speed directly down the side of the mountain, knowing that about a half a mile below was a pass that the leader was striving to use in his effort to get his band to the flat country to the east. To get there first would cause the mustangs to turn south, which would eventually lead them back to the mouth of our corrals. The movement called for quick work and hard riding but we knew that the time to outrun a wild horse is to do it down hill—for if you cannot beat him down hill, you surely cannot do it going up! Quirt and spur were not spared and we gained our point!

Miguel, Chico and myself were below these wild horses and running as fast as the leaders, and they gradually turned from us toward the mountains above. The horses carrying the Mexicans were badly distressed, having been running as fast and a little farther than the wild ones and carrying about two hundred and thirty pounds of man and rigging, so believing that I would be able to handle the band until relieved, they returned to camp for fresh horses.

The sagebrush was very thick and high, my horse jumped much of it instead of going around. This together with the fact that we had to cross many washes and ditches and were constantly climbing the mountains drew heavily on his reserve strength. Inwardly I was losing hope. The wild horses were running very strong, all staying close to the leader and only a few suckling colts being very far behind.

Just then out from behind a rocky ridge rode Dicey, the Indian, with a yell and a dash that was a credit to his race, straight for the leader. Over rocks and badger holes down the side of a mountain that would cause a man to exercise care afoot, this daredevil Indian rode at race horse speed until he was just ahead of the big bay stallion in the lead. The stud saw and heard him and turned away from him. I knew now that we had a chance to win, so closed in behind and to the right of the band.[7]

After Barnum's team drove the herd into the corral, two of the men flung themselves off their horses and dragged the high canvas gate across the entrance. Just as Barnum hoped, the mustangs milled uneasily but didn't attempt to breach the high sides of their enclosure. He later refined the canvas system to allow for easier transport and assembly.

During his fifteen years in Nevada, Barnum caught over fourteen thousand mustangs, making himself a considerable fortune by using effective and relatively humane techniques. In 1914 he left the business in disgust over the continuing mechanization of the chase.[8]

---

THE ONLY ACADEMIC work Velma found was *The Wild Horse of the West,* published in 1945 by Walker D. Wyman, a professor of history at Wisconsin State College in River Falls, Wisconsin. She plowed through its 348 pages of dry social and economic history, soaking up details of the mustang's origins and its pivotal role in settling the West. Some of this she had already absorbed as a child, hearing her father speak of the quality and characteristics of the horses he trained.

Though diluted through the centuries, a Nevada mustang's conformation revealed the history of the horse in the Americas, from the first landing on the mainland of New Spain in 1534 with the invading force of Hernán Cortés, to the trek north in the herds of Francisco Vásquez de Coronado as he advanced across the Rio Grande into present-day New Mexico in a quest for gold and silver riches beyond any man's imaginings.

The conquistadores soon learned harsh lessons about their mounts—the true source of their military superiority—and the danger of allowing them to fall into native hands. The Indians of the West Indies proved exceptionally adept at stealing horses and then adapting the techniques of the Spanish horsemen. Neither death nor mutilation discouraged the thieves, so the Spanish confiscated saddles, bridles, halters, even riatas or ropes, whenever they found them in native hands and forbade the trade of anything equine to the tribes of the islands. Forced to improvise, the Indians learned to ride bareback with bitless bridles fashioned from hide. In short order they became better horsemen than the conquistadores themselves.

The first wild horses likely carried the bloodlines of those used by Juan de Oñate y Salazar, the ruthless governor of New Spain known as "the Last Conquistador." Starting in 1598, he swept across northern Mexico toward the Rio Grande, trailed by a colonizing expedition of 400 settlers, a clutch of Franciscan priests, his army, and 7,000 head of cattle, donkeys, sheep, and goats. With them came horses: 1,007 stallions, 237 mares, and 137 colts. They were muscular and low-slung with wedge-shaped heads, smallish ears, arching necks, and a low tail set.

De Oñate's horses were descendants of the Barb war mounts brought across the mountains of Spain by the Moors in their conquest of Iberia centuries earlier. Called jennets—a type rather than a breed— the sturdy animals were favored by the soldier class who rode *à la jineta,* using stirrups and a slightly bent leg in the saddle. Most of the horses then in the Spanish colony of New Spain could be traced to the breeding farms of Andalusia where the jennet body type was popular.

Less than a century after de Oñate crossed the Rio Grande, the wild horse herds had spread north through the mesquite grasslands of Texas and New Mexico and into the Great Plains, as one Spanish expedition followed another looking for gold and attempting to settle the northern lands. Most failed from ineptitude, Indian attack, or both, and all left horses behind. Desperate Spanish settlers traded some to the Indian tribes for food, others were stolen, and thousands more were lost to stampede or simply abandoned when the would-be conquerors fled their attackers. No other animal has ever occupied so much territory in such a short period of time.

The horse was pushed west and north by the Gila Apaches of western New Mexico and Arizona where they were traded to the Navajo, then to the Ute and Shoshone, then west to the Paiute and east to the Cheyenne and the Pawnee. The tribes of the Taos and Pecos regions also nudged the horse east. The Comanche and the Apache of the southern Great Plains took to the horse as if the animal were their destiny. Not content to wait for animals to be lost or traded, the newly mounted tribes aggressively raided Spanish settlements to increase their herds and in the process transformed themselves from subsistence hunter-gatherers to formidable warriors.

The Shoshone, trade-masters of the western tribes, acquired not only horses but also saddles, bridles, spurs, and blankets and took them across the Rocky Mountains as barter with the Flathead, Yakima, and Walla Walla of Idaho, Washington, and Oregon. It is likely that the Shoshone also introduced the horse to the Nez Percé in Washington and Oregon. The Nez Percé would become some of the most skilled horse handlers on the continent and the only Indian nation with a highly selective breeding program designed to produce colorful paints and Appaloosas.

As the wild herds spread, the Barb and jennet bloodlines were diluted by infusions of genes from the Hobby horses of the English, the Friesians of the Dutch, and the so-called Iron Horse of the French colonies in Canada. The Canadian horse strongly influenced the early wild Spanish horse of the West, giving it a distinction of size and type, particularly among the northern herds, that endured for hundreds of years. The long, thick, and sometimes curly manes, heavy necks, and thick legs found from Colorado to California strongly resemble the original Canadian brought to New France in the 1600s.

There's also evidence that the famed Appaloosa of the Nez Percé may have originated with a spotted stallion given to New France, now Quebec, by King Louis XIV in the late 1600s. The king sent three shipments of horses to the colony, including a magnificent stallion whose coat was a riotous leopard pattern from nose to tail and all the way down his legs, set off by a black mane and tail. He was Breton bred, with a strong dose of Andalusian and traces of the heavier-bodied Dutch Friesian that showed up in the feathering on his legs. The stallion, along with nearly forty others, both stallions and mares, became the foundation stock of the Canadian horse. Oddly, the Iron Horse that evolved from those Breton and Normandy horses came to be exclusively black or darkest bay, but the spotted gene, a cipher for geneticists even today, laid color on the western mustangs as the far-ranging French fur traders took horses from New France across the continent to barter with the Nez Percé and others. Like the Spanish a century before, the *voyageurs* also lost horses to theft, stampede, and to a new adversary—the marauding stallions of thriving wild herds.

———

VELMA'S READING OF Walker Wyman's tome also revealed why those brutalized horses came to be in the back of the truck at the Sparks stockyards. In the early 1920s the concept of a "balanced daily ration" was introduced as the preferred diet for dogs, rather than table scraps. P. M. Chappel of Rockford, Illinois, and his two brothers canned the first pet food under the Ken-L Ration brand, using the meat of aged horses destined for slaughter. When they couldn't get enough old horses, the brothers raised their own pet food herds. Dogs gobbled up just under one hundred fifty thousand pounds of tinned meat from a variety of sources in 1923; in 1930, the amount consumed rose to nearly 23 million pounds. Increasingly, the primary ingredient was horsemeat. There was no expense involved in raising horses on the range, only in their capture, slaughter, and shipping. The early years of the Depression didn't diminish Americans' demand for canned pet food; the industry processed 50 million pounds in 1933–34. If only half of that meat came from wild horses—and some government reports indicate that is an accurate estimate—then thirty thousand to thirty-five thousand horses in those two years alone were killed to feed dogs in the United States.

The relentless pursuit of wild horses pushed the surviving herds, most of them in Wyoming, Colorado, Montana, Nevada, California, New Mexico, Arizona, Texas, and Oregon, deeper into mountainous areas and inaccessible valleys, making their capture difficult and expensive. But as airplanes became more common after World War I and again after World War II, air-assisted roundups made pursuit in even the most remote locations economically feasible. Though Wyman acknowledged the contribution of the mustang to western colonization, he had little sympathy for their imminent extinction. "After 1900 [the wild horse] no longer deserved the reputation his mustang ancestors made for him. Today he is headed for the cauldron."9

It wasn't only pampered pets that were eating the mustang into extinction. Long before the Chappel brothers sold that first can of horsemeat pet food in 1922, competition for forage played a role. Grass had been currency in the West since the early 1800s when the first large cattle ranches had been established. After the Civil War most of the land west of the Mississippi River belonged to the federal government, but those who dared to claim it, and could hold on to it, essentially owned it. In a territory where virtually every man carried a gun and what law that existed could be ignored by those who wielded the most firepower, disputes over grassland inevitably escalated into shooting wars.

The first of the western rangeland battles was sparked by the arrival of sheep herds in the 1860s. Cattlemen blamed sheep for polluting water holes, killing grass by nibbling it down to nothing and then trampling its roots with their sharp hooves. Some claimed sheep left a scent on the grass and in water holes that was repugnant to cattle. At first the cattlemen tried to get their own ranch hands to do the dirty work but they refused. "The men working for the cattle barons," complained one Wyoming foreman at the time, "seemed to have an understanding among themselves that they were being paid so much a month for working, not fighting, and it is up to the owner or manager to do his own fighting."[10] The cattlemen turned to professional gunfighters, euphemistically called "cattle detectives" or "stock inspectors." The most effective ones collected fees of $100 to $250 a month, about three times a U.S. marshal's salary.

Ostensibly, the cattle detective's job was to find cattle rustlers and gun them down. But as competition for grass intensified with settlement, the definition of "rustler" was often expanded to include not only those who stole cattle but also those who took food and water from cattle—namely sheep ranchers. "Killing men is my specialty," explained former Colorado deputy sheriff Tom Horn, the most famous cattle detective. "I look at it as a business proposition, and I think I've got a corner on the market."[11] Horn, rumored to have dispatched seventeen rustlers during his four years with the Pinkerton Detective Agency, charged as much as five hundred dollars for each one he shot. The law looked the other way, and in any event witnesses to rangeland killings were rare. Horn was eventually hanged in 1901, condemned only after he drunkenly confessed to a marshal that he had mistakenly shot a fourteen-year-old boy instead of his sheep-ranching father.

Between 1869 and 1906 cattlemen attacked sheep ranchers and their herds all across the western states, slaughtering tens of thousands of sheep and murdering countless herders. One of the first recorded incidents occurred in 1869 when Charles Hanna, who introduced sheep to Brown County, Texas, went out to his corral one morning to find his 300 sheep dead, their throats cut. In 1900 Wyoming raiders slaughtered nearly 12,000 sheep in a single night and in another incident, set fire to a herd of 2,600, killing most of them. The secretary of the Crook County Sheep Shooters Association in central Oregon boasted that his organization had killed between 8,000 and 10,000 sheep in 1904 and intended to redouble its efforts the year after.

The enmity against sheep began to soften after 1910 as cattlemen, forced to diversify, started raising sheep themselves as a hedge against volatile beef prices. In the process they learned that sheep could happily coexist with cattle, actually improving the soil by aerating it with their smaller hooves and fertilizing the grass with their droppings. Moreover, sheep ate some grasses and weeds that cattle spurned.

The competition for grass wasn't just between sheep and cattle ranchers; cattlemen had a long history of battling among themselves for supremacy over rangeland. In most of the western states, huge allotments of land were necessary to feed cattle. The fabled King Ranch in Texas, for example, encompassed six hundred thousand acres when its founder, Richard King, died in 1885. Containing cattle on such immense holdings was problematic, especially with wood in short supply in arid regions. Barbed wire, sometimes called devil's rope, was invented in the 1860s and solved the problem for those who could afford it. The Frying Pan Ranch in the Texas Panhandle spent thirty-nine thousand dollars in 1882 on a four-wire fence to contain 250,000 acres of grazing land. Other large operators followed suit, with a propensity to annex public land, especially if it held water holes. Sometimes the fences ran across public roads, preventing neighbors from getting into town or attending church, but anyone who cut a fence was liable to be shot.

At the same time, the grass itself was becoming badly overgrazed by waves of newcomers. Many of the first homesteaders intended to farm, but when they found that the land was unsuitable for agriculture they turned to livestock. Government land grants were later doubled when it became clear that in many areas of the West, far more land was necessary to raise a herd large enough to provide a man and his family with a living. Even a section, 640 acres or a square mile, couldn't begin to support moderate-sized herds, so land grant settlers began pasturing their herds on public land. There they ran up against the cattlemen who felt they owned the same range because they had arrived first. Hostilities—including lynchings and targeted murders by hired gunslingers—escalated between the cattle barons and the smaller operators, finally culminating in the infamous 1892 Johnson County cattle war in Wyoming, between a squad of twenty-two professional gunmen hired by the cattle barons and three hundred ranchers with smaller holdings. The U.S. Cavalry finally brought the standoff to an end.

But it was not the end of the struggle. As long as grass was the life-blood of the ranching economy and while huge tracts of it remained, at least on paper, in public hands, there would be competition to control it and attacks against whoever or whatever trespassed over it—sheep, cattle, rustlers, or wild horses.

The first systematic elimination of wild horses occurred in California. The abundant grasslands of the California central valley, the foothills of the Sierra Nevadas, and even the sparser desert ranges of the interior offered ideal terrain to mustang herds. The palomino coloring, common in many Spanish breeds, had become well established in the far West. The "yella" horse of the later western cowboy derived from the Ysabellas brought to the Californias by the Spanish. They were named for Queen Isabella, who favored golden horses, and the color had found its way into the jennet and other regional breeds of Iberia and then to the New World. Called California Sorrels, Dorados, Claybanks, and Tarrows, the creamy pale or deepest gold palomino, together with the Paint and Appaloosa, epitomized the wild horse of the far western frontier.

During the mission era, between 1769 and 1833, the Californios had little interest in the mustang herds. In 1790 there were only nineteen private rancheros in all of California; the rest were owned by the church and attached to the twenty-one Franciscan missions strung along the Pacific coastline from Sonoma to San Diego. But after the secularization of mission lands, the number of ranches quickly increased as the Spanish government handed out large land grants and cattle took over from agriculture. With cattle came conflict. Some of the largest wild horse herds in America were in California, and the new Spanish and Mexican ranchers wasted little time slaughtering wild horses at will. In the 1850s after nearly two years of drought in southern California, rancheros killed seven thousand horses by driving them off the cliffs at Santa Barbara. Thousands more were penned and left to starve or driven into chutes and stabbed with a vaquero's lance.

Once American stockmen took control of California from the Mexicans in the late 1850s, after the state joined the Union, they killed as many of the Spanish-blooded horses as they could, but not only because they competed with cattle for grass. The stockmen considered the *mestaños* to be inferior to the larger American horses they brought with them from east of the Mississippi and they didn't want wild horses breeding with their own stock. By 1875, most of the California wild herds had retreated into arroyos and remote deserts or up into impenetrable mountains and high plateaus where they were left alone because ranchers didn't want that land.

In other ranching states mustang herds were eliminated wherever they interfered with cattle. Long after they were hunted out in the Dakotas, Missouri, the flatlands of Colorado, and much of Arizona, Texas, and California, mustangs still thrived in rugged, thinly populated Nevada. The eastern Sierra Nevada counties of Washoe, Douglas, Lyon, and Storey were ideal for the hardy wild horse. Mustangs also proliferated farther east, especially in Eureka, Elko, and Lander counties. These badlands of Nevada's interior were home to as many as a hundred thousand wild horses in the early 1900s, but not for long.

After lobbying by the Nevada Live Stock Association, the state passed a law in 1900 allowing wild horses to be shot wherever they were found. Within two years ranchers and guns-for-hire killed fifteen thousand of them. Then as mechanization transformed one industry after another in the early twentieth century demand grew for horse-hides — the raw material of superior conveyer belts. Most of the hides were processed in Chicago, where prices were high enough to make the hunt and the transport worthwhile. As Nevada's herds also withdrew into more inaccessible terrain, the mustang hunters became less particular about whether a horse in their sights was branded or not. "The farmers came to be afraid to turn out old Dobbin for a Sunday run on the plains about their ranches, lest some skulking hide-hunter pot him," noted cowboy poet and novelist Will C. Barnes.[12]

Within a couple of years, the same stockmen who'd pushed for the original law grew tired of having their own horses killed by hide hunters and lobbied to rescind it. Instead they paid their wranglers, who could be trusted to recognize the cattlemen's brands, a bounty on each pair of mustang ears they turned in. But the wranglers weren't as motivated as the hide hunters, and by the time America entered World War I, the Nevada mustang proliferated once again.

After the war, competition for control of rangeland intensified when cattle and sheep herds grew larger in response to a buoyant economy. But as the livestock ranches expanded, forage from the Mississippi to the Pacific and from the Missouri to the Rio Grande started to disappear. In 1880, estimates placed the carrying capacity of western public land at 22.5 million head of cattle; by 1930 that number had dropped to 10 million. In just fifty years, the land had degraded, irreparably in some areas. Livestock grazed such quick-regenerating and edible native grasses as oat grass, dropseed, giant wild rye, ricegrass, and bluebunch wheatgrass virtually out of existence. In their place grew the relatively unpalatable greasewood, zucca, sand sage, and winter fat. And the new grasses didn't bind the soil together as effectively. Dust and sand replaced topsoil over vast areas.

There was no incentive for conservation on the public land: Everybody owned it and nobody owned it. It was the classic dilemma of the commons, where no one takes responsibility for a resource that is free to all, and therefore it is ruined by all. And ruin was exactly the state of the grazing lands in the early 1930s when drought struck.

By 1934, the abuse of public rangeland had become so serious that Congress called for hearings. Underscoring the urgency, dust from a massive prairie storm made its way east and coated Washington right at the height of the debate. On June 28, 1934, Congress passed the Taylor Grazing Act, named after its sponsoring congressman, Edward Taylor of Colorado. Historian Walker Wyman called it the Magna Carta of the western range.

The Taylor Grazing Act gave the United States Grazing Service— later renamed the Bureau of Land Management—responsibility for controlling and regulating 143 million acres of public lands located primarily in the ten western states of Arizona, California, Colorado, Idaho, Montana, New Mexico, Oregon, Utah, Wyoming, and Nevada. The Grazing Service created a permit system for use of the land, charged nominal fees for those permits, and pursued a mandate to protect and improve grazing land.

The Grazing Service's main customers were the roughly sixteen thousand cattle and sheep ranchers who were the principal users of public land. From the beginning, the stockmen were a powerful influence on the Service and later on the Bureau of Land Management, thanks to the introduction of eight-man advisory boards for each of the fifty-two western districts. Ranchers, elected by secret ballot by other stockmen who held permits in the area, sat on the advisory boards and appointed state representatives to lobby for their interests in Washington.

Undermanned and underfunded from its inception, the Grazing Service relied heavily on the advisory boards, which functioned more like a private company's board of directors than advisors to a government agency. In many ways, the creation of the Grazing Service finally gave the big cattlemen their victory over the smaller operators, who didn't have the time, resources, or connections to secure seats on the powerful advisory boards.

The Grazing Service was in an unenviable position. Charged with divvying up land that was losing its ability to feed livestock, it had no mandate to purchase more and insufficient funds to rehabilitate the range. At the same time its officials were heavily influenced by a powerful cattle lobby that essentially ran the various advisory boards. The Grazing Service did what many organizations do under pressure and cast about for a scapegoat. "A wild horse consumes forage needed by domestic livestock, brings in no return, and serves no useful purpose," declared Archie D. Ryan, acting director, Division of Grazing, in 1939.[13] Over the next eleven years, the Grazing Service and then the BLM facilitated the "range clearance" of tens of thousands of wild horses by allowing permit holders to poison water holes, shoot the horses without limit, and otherwise slaughter them. Nevada, with by far the largest population of wild horses, attracted their concerted efforts.

Aided by the airplane, a new breed of mustanger came into being. They were essentially bounty hunters who took horses off BLM-managed rangeland in return for six cents a pound, on the hoof, paid by the rendering plants. "Within a period of four years [1946 to 1950] we removed over 100,000 abandoned and unclaimed horses from Nevada ranges," boasted a BLM officer. "Branded horses were turned over to the owners for disposition by sale. Unclaimed horses were taken by the people operating the airplanes under title from the state and sold as compensation for their work. This program was carried out without cost to the government except some assistance in building holding corrals and truck trails where needed."[14] The BLM's campaign had been stunningly effective: Officials estimated that fewer than four thousand mustangs were left in all of Nevada by 1950.

————

FIVE DAYS AFTER encountering the bloodied stock truck, Velma stood nervously in front of the Bureau of Land Management's regional district offices in downtown Reno. She concluded that all trails led to the BLM; most of the remaining wild horse herds were living on land managed by the Bureau. But she had no idea whom to ask for or what to say about her concern for the captured horses.

As Velma entered the dreary county building and made her way to the BLM's offices she remembered one of her father's sayings. "Act like a lady, think like a man. That way you'll get respect *and* you'll get what you want." She introduced herself as Mrs. Charles Johnston of the Double Lazy Heart Ranch to Dante Solari, a stocky, prematurely balding young man in his late twenties. Solari was the local range manager, responsible for the area that encompassed the Double Lazy Heart, all the way up to and including Virginia City. A recent graduate of the University of Nevada in Reno, Solari spoke enthusiastically and with an assurance beyond his years. Velma needn't have worried about confrontation. No sooner had she uttered the words "rancher's wife" and "wild horses," than Solari assumed she'd come to complain about her ranch being pestered by a marauding stallion or a local herd that was damaging water holes in the area.

Solari assured her that the BLM was doing everything it could to rid the range of mustangs by issuing round-up permits to private interests, most of whom used airplanes to capture as many horses as possible. He told her the horses were useless except for chicken feed and pet food and they would proliferate like vermin if they weren't removed. He emphasized that the herds presented a threat to forage on public lands and to the livelihoods of sheep and cattle ranchers. The stallions in particular were a terrible nuisance, knocking down fences, fouling water holes, and stealing domestic mares.

Until the development of specialized western breed registries in the 1930s and 1940s, primarily for the American Quarter Horse, Paint, and Appaloosa, most ranch horses carried some degree of mustang blood. Broodmares were routinely released to winter over on the range and be bred by a wild stallion because the offspring were usually superior in vitality and endurance. In Nevada, where hay was an especially precious commodity, the ranchers also turned loose their remudas, or remounts, for the winter. Often a mare with a large cowbell belted around her neck was used to keep the domestic herd together. The clanging bell mesmerized horse, mule, and burro alike and none would stray far from the belled horse. In the spring ranchers simply had to catch the bell mare to recover their herd. But belling had one major drawback. If a wild stallion stole the belled mare, for he, too, was attracted by the sound, the rest of the rancher's horses would follow. Retrieving them from the stallion was a far more difficult task.

Solari gave no credence to old-fashioned notions about improving bloodlines by breeding with wild stallions. He explained to Velma that the mustang of 1950 was nothing more than a mongrel, not a wild animal at all but merely feral. Ignoring the fact that many Nevada ranchers still worked livestock mounted on horses with mustang blood, Solari assured Velma that even a captured and gentled wild horse could never be fully trusted. And in any case, the BLM had determined that most of those remaining in the wild were stunted and inbred and that disease was rife among the herds. He touted the Bureau's policy of allowing ranchers, or anyone else for that matter, to apply for a permit to take wild horses off government land, a process he referred to as culling and range clearance.

In his eagerness to demonstrate the BLM's efficiency, Solari mentioned that there was a distribution center very close to the Double Lazy Heart where wild horses were held pending shipment to Sparks, Reno, California, and even north to Canada. Calgary, Alberta, was home to one of the largest rendering plants in the West. In fact, he added, there was a load of horses waiting for shipment as they spoke.

On Friday night of the same week, Velma rushed home to bring her news to Charlie. In short order they were on the porch, drinks in hand. Normally Charlie reported on his week first—the cow's blocked teat or

*Velma and Charlie, 1952*

half a day of back-busting jockeying to get the mower blades out of the hay cutter—but that evening Velma blurted out the story of the truck, her hours in the library, and her conversation with the BLM man.

Charlie was appalled at the gratuitous violence suffered by the horses and sorry that Velma had to see it. But he marveled at how much information she'd pulled together. As they stirred more cocktails, their talk turned to the contrary opinions Velma had read about the quality of wild horses, a debate that dated from the earliest European explorers and military men in the West. They concluded that an appreciation of the wild horse's beauty and utility was a function of how much contact the observer had with them and how much he needed them. They knew from their own experience that mustangs weren't the stunted beasts Dante Solari described, and they certainly weren't useless. And though they both felt the amount of Spanish blood was a red herring, they could see with their own eyes that Ranger had clear Iberian and Arabian signatures in his conformation, as did many mustangs in the Comstock and Virginia ranges.

As they talked and drank, Velma and Charlie became increasingly incensed at the treatment of the mustangs and at the BLM's complicity. When she reflected on Solari's enthusiasm for culling, Velma could not help but think that after polio struck she might have been regarded as less than useful, and certainly not very pretty; perhaps some might believe that she should have been "culled," too.

The more emotional of the two, Velma suggested they string up or geld those responsible. "I'd like to chase them through the mountains with a plane and a shotgun, and see how they like it," she announced. Charlie nodded in agreement, knowing that she'd calm down after she got it off her chest. Then they'd get down to business.

Finally, a well-lubricated Charlie put his arm around Velma's slender shoulders and asked, "So what are we going to do now?" Velma smiled at his words, especially the "we."[15]

# FIVE

# A Law of Our Own

FIRST THING SATURDAY morning Velma and Charlie readied themselves for a reconnaissance of the wild horse holding center described by Dante Solari. Charlie, who knew the country around the Double Lazy Heart intimately, had a good idea where it might be. He tacked up Hobo and Ranger while Velma shooed the dogs into the barn. Their route would traverse steep and rocky terrain, far too taxing for the dogs. Besides, the idea was to approach stealthily, impossible with a retinue of five cockers.

They didn't expect to be gone more than half a day, but Charlie brought along a rifle, a handgun, and his "just-in-case" saddlebags filled with food, water, ammunition, and bedrolls. They could survive a week with what he had packed.

In the early hours the Nevada air was cool and tangy, though the day promised temperatures of ninety degrees or higher. Velma, as usual, dressed carefully. She wore pale, doeskin riding pants and tied a bright scarf around her neck, the knot sitting jauntily to one side. Like Charlie, she rode in a long-sleeved shirt to protect the arms, but hers sported pearly buttons and contrasting top stitching. Anyone might have assumed she was off to make a splash at a rodeo rather than take a dusty ride in search of captive mustangs.

The impressive-sounding "distribution center" turned out to be a decrepit one-room cabin of the sort prospectors knocked together. The surrounding yard was littered with the remains of campfires and the detritus of human habitation, including empty whiskey bottles. A corral of rusty pipe fencing contained some sixty horses. A cable held the gate closed, but there was no lock. On the east side, a tire-worn turnaround, big enough to accommodate a livestock transport, was evidence of shipments in and out. There wasn't a soul in sight.

The horses milled anxiously as Charlie and Velma approached. They were in better condition than the maimed mustangs Velma had seen in the truck, but one stallion, hamstrung by a knife or bullet, limped badly.

The technique of hamstringing had been used by North American natives since the earliest days of the mounted buffalo hunt. Young braves risked their lives by galloping into a stampeding buffalo herd and slicing the hamstrings of the leaders with twelve-foot lances. Immobilizing the animals instead of killing them kept vultures at bay. Once the hunters had brought down sufficient game, they returned to finish off the injured and strip the hides in preparation for carving, drying, and salting the meat, which could then be rolled into large balls and coated with tallow for storage. Indians rarely hamstrung horses, even those of their enemies. The animals were too valuable to mutilate, and possessing the horses of their foes ranked as counting coup against them.

Mustang hunters knew that disabling the lead stallion would throw the rest of the herd into disarray, making it easier to drive them toward capture. But hamstringing on the move required considerable skill, so the mustangers often waited until the animals were penned before shooting the stallion's tendon to disable him.

Velma and Charlie surveyed the nervous herd for several minutes. A handful of foals looked on the verge of collapse. There wasn't a scrap of grass in the stony paddock, and neither hay nor water. Judging by the piles of manure, the horses had been trapped there for a couple of days.

"What would happen if that cable fell off?" Velma asked finally.

"You mean like this?" Charlie strode purposefully to the gate and removed the cable.[1]

At Charlie's advance, agitation rippled through the herd; it reacted as one, pressing into the far end of the small corral where the horses jostled with one another to get as far away from the human as possible. After he swung the gate open, Charlie stepped aside, a wide smile on his face. For an instant sixty pairs of eyes focused on him. Then they were gone in a surge of horseflesh, brown, black, pinto, palomino, and gray pounding past. In scant seconds the horses crested the hill and flew toward the Lahontan dam to the south, the crippled stallion laboring in their wake. The smell of the mustangs' sweat mixed with plumes of dust thrown up by the herd's dash for liberty and Velma's joyous shrieks joined Charlie's booming laugh.

Velma and Charlie's impromptu act of mercy was soon followed by others that were equally exhilarating. Many of the horses they set free had been legally captured by mustangers with BLM permits; others were confined on private land. They let them loose anyway, having discovered that some operators didn't bother with permits but simply chased the horses onto private holdings where the mustangs became trespassers and therefore fair game. "We had to be our own law," Velma explained later, justifying their actions as an answer to the brutality of the roundups, the days without food or water, and the terrible transport conditions.[2]

Inevitably news spread that some crazies were letting horses loose in the rangeland around Reno. In 1950 the city had a population of only ten thousand, and despite the gambling tourists and temporary, divorce-seeking residents, it was still very much a small town. Everybody knew everyone else's business. Velma didn't advertise what she and Charlie were doing, and only once did she admit in writing to releasing horses. But she made no secret of her anger with the traffic in mustangs.

By early 1951 Velma had become acquainted with a few like-minded individuals. After work she occasionally had a drink with Lura Tularski, a journalist and author who had written a young adult horse novel called *Star of Stonyridge,* and was closely connected to Nevada's horse community. Velma expected that all it would take to save the mustangs was exposure of the facts of the hunt; surely ordinary citizens would rise up in protest if they knew. Like many people, however, she had an exaggerated notion of the power of the press. Tularski was as appalled as Velma about the mustang roundups, but she emphasized she couldn't write about them unless she had some evidence, preferably photographic.

Charlie was affronted that a wild horse distribution center had operated right under his nose, so he frequently checked the corral where they had set free that first group of horses. The mustangers had become more vigilant; one day he discovered several armed men guarding a small herd of battered mustangs. He galloped back to the ranch and alerted Velma, who grabbed her camera, mindful of Lura Tularski's advice. They returned by car to the corral, where Velma scrambled onto the hood for a better vantage. At the sight of the camera, the mustangers jumped into their pickup truck and hurtled toward Charlie and Velma, aiming to graze the bumper and knock Velma to the ground. They veered off sharply when Charlie leaned out and took a bead with his .38. "He would have killed them, had I been hurt," Velma later said. They left rather than risk harm, and her snapshots did not turn out.

Tularski was astute in emphasizing the need for photographs, not just of captured horses but of the brutal nature of the hunt itself. Evidence would protect the newspaper and its reporters from potential legal action and reinforce the point that mustang hunts were not just sport. Chasing wild horses had long fascinated journalists and with the advent of the camera, photographers as well. But virtually all the articles documenting mustang hunts, whether on horseback or by airplane, depicted them as adventures steeped in Old West traditions. Popular magazines like *Harpers, Life, Reader's Digest,* and *Sunset* portrayed the mustangers as dashing daredevils who came to the aid of beleaguered cattle and sheep ranchers by ridding their rangelands and water holes of the marauding herds.

In 1948, freelancer Clifton Abbott wrote a lengthy article in the widely read *True* (subtitled *The Man's Magazine*) about mustang hunter Frank Robbins, "a combination Buffalo Bill, Paul Bunyan and Will Rogers."[3] Abbott's often hilarious recitation of an airplane-assisted roundup reads like a grand escapade. "If they should turn and run out of the trap, Frank is directly behind on Buck, riding close upon their heels and yelling like a Comanche full of canned heat." Robbins claimed to have captured tens of thousands of mustangs, but admitted he couldn't have done it without an airborne partner.

"When a bunch is sighted he dives directly down upon it and pulls out at an eight- or ten-foot altitude behind an already running and mighty scared bunch of horses," Abbott wrote of Robbins's pilot, Roy Lamoureaux. "With wheels actually touching the sagebrush, he leans out of the window and fires a pistol-gripped sawed-off shotgun at their heels. He sometimes chases the band forty or fifty miles from the pickup point to the trap."[4] The white-knuckle flying was so hard on his nerves Lamoureaux had to take the winters off to recover. Spectacular photos, giving no hint of the impact of the airplane on the mustangs, accompanied the story.

By midcentury, mustang hunting seemed the epitome of western manliness in an increasingly urban and white-collar world. It was man against beast, intrepid hunter against wily prey—never mind that rounding up horses with an airplane was a sporting proposition akin to hunting big game with a machine gun. "As I approach the sunset of life, I no longer follow them down the trails. But when something new comes up, it must be seen," former mustanger Charles Keas wrote in 1952.[5] That new thing was the helicopter. While costly to hire, with six dollars a head going to the pilot, helicopters improved the odds and the profits for the mustangers. "It has the horse so badly outclassed, that it took all the excitement and thrills out of the sport," wrote Keas. The helicopter, with its superior agility, allowed the horse runners to cor-

*Frank Robbins's roundup, 1948*

ral two or even three herds at a time, something they could never have done with horseback relays or the less maneuverable airplane.

This latest efficiency created mayhem when stallions and mares from different herds were mixed together for shipping. "How vicious those old stallions fought in the trucks. As they stand on their hind legs, biting and striking each other with their front feet, they make a noise somewhat between a roar and a groan, which is their way of bluffing and calling each other dirty names. Sometimes there were two or three fights going on in one trailer or truck at the same time," Keas marveled.

Very occasionally the press's coverage aroused a short-lived public protest. In 1938, after *Life* published a photo spread of a mustang hunt, one reader wrote: "Sirs: With indignation and sorrow I viewed your pictures of the aerial cowboy who rounds up wild horses by airplane. I wonder if this man does not know that without man's best friend, the horse, this great West of ours could never have been pioneered as it was. In time to come mayhap some man will take his small son up to a glass case and say 'Son, that is what was once known as the Western pony.' Our Government should take shame for allowing an insensible machine to so terribly frighten beautiful, innocent colts."[6]

The letter to *Life* prompted the Department of the Interior to send an investigator to Nevada the following year. The resulting report by the Grazing Service defended the airplane-assisted roundup as a more humane practice, especially for the mustangers' horses, than the old method of relays of riders chasing herds to exhaustion over rough ground, injuring many. One of the protesters had charged that the young colts were left behind to die when they could no longer keep up with the herd, but the report's author, a Grazing Service official, claimed to be satisfied that every care was taken to ensure the young ones were captured with the mares.

———

INITIALLY, VELMA AND Charlie spent many weekends navigating the bumpy back roads of Washoe and Storey counties looking for distribution centers and taking note of remote corrals. They had no plan. They simply believed that the mustang hunt was an abomination and they were doing the only thing they could think of to stop it. They didn't consider the bigger picture of distribution, transportation, and slaughter, nor did they think much about what was going on beyond the immediate area of the ranch.

Their perspective broadened the day a stranger dropped by Gordon Harris's office, asking for Velma. He had heard of her opposition to wild horse roundups and had come to volunteer his services. But this man wasn't any casual well-wisher; he worked in an integrated livestock operation run by a wealthy rancher with investments in trucking, rendering plants, slaughterhouses, and meat processing. He told her that the rancher also owned an airplane and quietly ran his mustang capture and slaughter business behind the cover of front men.

Velma called him Zeke, "even to myself for fear of accidentally saying his name." He was disenchanted with the brutality of the wild horse roundup and regretted his complicity in hauling the mutilated horses to the rendering plants. Still, he had to feed his family, he said. But he assuaged his conscience by giving Velma specific details about how and when the roundups were conducted and who was profiting from them. In essence his information provided Velma with a primer on an industry built upon the wild horse.

Zeke prefaced every revelation with the same plea: "God, Mrs. Johnston, don't ever tell them how you find out these things. I don't know what they'd do to me if you did."[7] He would telephone at all hours, once ringing Velma at midnight at her mother's house with a tip about a roundup taking place the next day. Sometimes he'd drop a note through the mail slot at the office, revealing the location of penned horses or the names of individuals involved in a chase. His intelligence was always accurate and timely and as Velma came to trust him, she probed for more details. If Zeke didn't have the answers he'd find out. The only thing he asked of Velma was to never call him at work.

Velma guarded Zeke's identity faithfully during their twenty-five-year association and left nothing in the thousands of pages of her letters and notes that might betray him. Nonetheless, when it came to protecting her "wild ones," Velma respected few boundaries. She assumed the righteousness of her cause was justification enough to ensure forgiveness when she stepped over the line.

Velma caught wind of a consignment of four hundred horses being gathered for shipment to a pet food processing plant, but she didn't know where or when. The chance to save that many animals was so tempting she risked telephoning Zeke at work. After recovering from his initial consternation, Zeke promised to look into it. When he called back, he confirmed that the four hundred horses were being held in a facility 150 miles northwest of Reno, just across the state line in California. Zeke figured they'd be there for a few days because the poor roads in that remote location meant small trucks would have to be used and the removal would take some time.

Velma immediately called the Washoe County sheriff, who, she had heard, disapproved of airplane-assisted roundups. The sheriff alerted his counterpart on the California side of the border and the official located the horses, guarded by hired hands. The California sheriff had no evidence of a crime, but he asserted his authority to bluff the men into releasing the horses since none of them could produce a BLM permit.

It was Velma's first success in liberating horses with outside assistance, and the help of a lawman at that. The four hundred mustangs represented a payday of almost $19,000 at the processing plant's doors—over $275,000 in 2008 dollars.[8] That scale of lost revenue heightened Charlie's concern about Velma's safety. It was one thing to let loose a few horses near their ranch, quite another to deny a sizable fortune to men with money and power. Charlie had no illusions about the type of people they were up against, and he insisted Velma carry a gun in the glove compartment of the car. He was particularly concerned about the twenty-six-mile drive to and from Reno. Few people traveled that road, and Velma would have been an easy target for anyone who intended her harm.

With the help of Zeke's clandestine information-gathering, Charlie and Velma extended their liberation forays across as much of Nevada and the adjacent northern counties of California as they could reach in a day of driving. Velma never recorded how many horses they freed, but it appears she and Charlie spent many weekends throughout 1951 and into the spring of 1952 riding or driving to the rescue of penned mustangs.

Gordon Harris's insurance business prospered in the 1950s and he became a prominent figure in Reno, serving as a director of a local utility company and of the Union Federal Savings and Loan Association. He was also involved in real estate, buying and selling properties at a time when the city was attracting an influx of new citizens from San Francisco, Sacramento, Merced, and Fresno. The city's population increased by 75 percent between 1950 and 1960 as new businesses followed on the heels of two casinos built in the shadow of the famous "Biggest Little City in the World" arch over Virginia Street.

Velma's workload also grew, but there is no indication that she was anything but proud of the additional responsibility. While she referred to the office as "the salt mine," there was always affection in her tone, and she indulged Harris the way a doting sister might a younger brother. Though privy to the personal and professional details of his life, Velma was circumspect with Harris about her own.

Harris knew about Velma's interest in the plight of wild horses, since she'd received calls and visitors at the office, but he had no idea what she was really up to. From the beginning Velma worried that her activities would draw the attention and ire of Harris's clients, among them some of the most prominent ranchers in the area. There was also the issue of decorum. Harris had firm ideas about how a lady should comport herself, especially if that lady was his secretary. A gun-toting, mustang-saving vigilante hardly fit the image he wanted an employee to project.

On June 6, 1952, Velma was working at the office when Lura Tularski telephoned. She told Velma about a BLM permit hearing scheduled for Virginia City that night. Because the proposed roundup would take place near the Double Lazy Heart, Tularski assumed Velma and Charlie would be interested. She added a surprising bit of information: A petition *against* the roundup would be presented at the hearing. Velma stepped into Harris's office to request the rest of the day off—a rare event. She had just enough time to stop at her mother's home for clothes, make a quick visit to the BLM office to see what she could find out about the permit application, and then drive out to the ranch to pick up Charlie.

Assuming she was a supporter, the garrulous BLM range manager, Dante Solari, and his supervisor, Edward Greenslet, were happy to provide Velma with details of the application. Velma went along with the pretense, concurring that the whole business was commendable and necessary. "He was a really leaky bucket," she observed.[9] Then she and Charlie set out to cover the fifty-five miles to Virginia City.

Set high in the hills of the Virginia Range, the town's only access from Reno or Carson City was via two steep, twisting roads, both frequently blocked by snow in winter and flash floods in spring. Its main street seemed frozen in time, dominated by buildings that dated from the original silver boom. Newspapers, milk, and eggs were still delivered on horseback, and in the winter mustang herds, normally wary of human contact, sometimes loped through the town.

Virginia City's citizens had a reputation for being a bit eccentric, a trait attributed by outsiders to their isolation, and the community was home to colonies of writers and artists. Its historic newspaper, the *Territorial Enterprise,* had recently been purchased and relaunched by a new proprietor, Lucius Beebe, a journalist who had risen to fame in New York and San Francisco. Gourmand, history buff, and bon vivant, Beebe was a flamboyant figure, outspoken and controversial, but nationally influential. Under the guidance of Beebe and his companion and lover, Charles Clegg, the *Enterprise* published some of the preeminent writers of the day, continuing a tradition at the paper that dated back to the 1860s when Samuel Clemens, writing under the pen name Mark Twain, was a regular contributor.

---

VELMA AND CHARLIE pulled up across the street from Virginia City's Storey County courthouse just before 8:00 P.M. High above the courthouse doors, set into an alcove and perched near the base of the American flag, a zinc statue of Justice gazed down on them. In one hand the statue clasped a sword, scabbard forward, tip pointing back to the courthouse, while the other hand held aloft the scales of justice. Hundreds of similar statues graced courthouses across America, but this Justice was one of the few without a blindfold. Her installation had unleashed a torrent of complaint from unhappy traditionalists and much witticism from skeptics. "When one considers that this representative dispenser of awards and punishments will be compelled to stand out and take all the sand thrown in her eyes by the Washoe zephyrs, it will be readily conceded that her eyesight would not last long enough for her to get so much as a glimpse of the great wealth to be obtained by wickedly swaying the scales of Right and Wrong," Alfred Doten noted in the *Gold Hill Daily News*. "It makes but little difference whether the blind is on or off."[10]

Velma expected they would sign the petition opposing the roundup and provide moral support for whoever spoke on the petitioners' behalf. The idea of making any sort of speech in public still terrified her. Even when required to report to her chapter of Executive Secretaries, before women she'd known for years, she described herself as a "cat on a hot frying pan." Walking up the wide wooden steps to the double oak doors, Charlie crooned a few lines to distract her, just as he had before their secret wedding. "He was just a lonely cowboy / With his heart so brave and true. . . ."

The high-ceilinged courthouse, an imposing structure among Virginia City's false-fronted shops and saloons, was designed to impress and intimidate. Everything was oversized, including the towering interior doors topped by deep transoms. Running along the right side of the courtroom was a raised platform where the jury normally sat. In their place that night were the three Storey County commissioners and behind them the two sheep farmers who were applying for the roundup permit. Beside the ranchers sat four Bureau of Land Management officials, including Dante Solari and Edward Greenslet.

On the other side of the room a crowd filled the sixty available seats alongside the petitioner, forty-two-year-old Edward "Tex" Gladding, Virginia City's postmaster since 1933; his wife, Marion, sat beside him. Gladding had started the petition after witnessing an aerial roundup. "Fliers were driving some horses down a canyon, running them out on the flats and then shooting them from the air for sport," he later told a reporter. "The mustang deserves better than that. It stands for the Old West, just like the Indian and the buffalo. There used to be a thousand broomtails here in Storey County; I doubt if there are sixty now. We must preserve them."[11]

At 8:10 P.M., County Commissioner Bill Marks, who had a reputation for fairness, called the meeting to order, commenting dryly that normally permit hearings didn't draw flies, so he was glad to see such a turnout. Marks owned Virginia City's Crystal Bar, a popular local hangout where most of the town's business was carried out informally over beer, whiskey, and coffee. He looked shorter than his five-foot-ten height, with a plump, cherubic face lit by a permanent beam. In the bar, he habitually wore an old-style wraparound apron, but this night Marks was all business in a suit and tie.

The permit hearings were typically rubber-stamp affairs attended only by those directly involved. If the BLM officials were dismayed by the packed public gallery, they gave no sign. Greenslet provided the details of the permit and the sheep farmers waded in with their reasons for the application. They hit all the notes Velma had heard before: the "overabundance" of wild horses, "the lack of feed for them," "better to be rounded up than starve slowly," and her favorite, "roundups offer a quicker and easier death with the product of their bodies providing much needed food for other animals."[12] The two pilots who worked for the sheep ranchers nodded vigorously from the audience.

Solari added his assessment that the herds were multiplying uncontrollably, trampling precious water holes and denuding entire ranges by pulling out the grass by its roots. The horses represented "a danger to Nevada's public lands" and the depredation they caused was such that "granting of the permit was the only recourse to keep [the farmers'] sheep from starving."[13]

Their presentation complete, the BLM officials and sheep farmers sat back while Marks opened the floor for discussion. For a long moment the crowd sat in silence, as if what they'd heard was so compelling it couldn't be challenged. Then Tex Gladding broke the spell by formally registering the petition signed by 147 opponents of the roundup. He and a friend, Jack Murray, also of Virginia City, had gathered the signatures. "These roundups are completely against the spirit and tradition of the West," he declared, "they must be stopped!"[14] Then Gladding abruptly sat down. Velma was taken by surprise; she assumed Gladding would have more to say. But he remained seated and no one else seemed prepared to speak. Velma felt she must do something but the only thing she could think of was what she feared most.

Charlie felt Velma quivering beside him, trying to summon her courage. He stood and introduced himself as a rancher. He looked much taller than six foot four inches in his cowboy boots and he spoke solemnly and sincerely. "I was most impressed by the Bureau of Land Management's statistics and I'd sure as hell like to have the secret to making stock multiply the way they said the mustangs did: one hundred this year, two hundred the next, four hundred the next, and so on. Yes, sir, I'd sure like to know that secret."

Mr. Frick, a retired cattleman, hollered from his seat, "Yeah! I'd sure enough like to know how to get a 100 percent increase in my livestock, too!" Unlike Charlie's, Frick's remark dripped sarcasm.

There were snickers and several loud guffaws. The BLM officials smiled, too; no damage done, just a small-time rancher having his joke. Emboldened by Charlie's overture, Velma drew a deep breath and stood up, angling her body slightly as she always did to make her head and neck appear straighter to those directly ahead. She identified herself in a quavering voice as Mrs. Charles Johnston and explained that their ranch was three miles west of Wadsworth. Velma consulted a spiral-bound notebook in her hands.

"Mr. Chairman, if I may, I'd like to address a few questions to Mr. Greenslet."

Bill Marks waved his permission.

"Now, sir, I'm sure you recognize me. I was in your office earlier today. I'd like to discuss some of the things you told me."

"That was a private conversation, Madam!" Greenslet protested. "It was not intended for public dissemination!"

"Mr. Chairman," Velma's voice gathered strength. "I'm just a simple secretary but I spoke with this gentleman in the BLM offices at 1:00 P.M. today. My understanding is that Mr. Greenslet is a public employee and I'm a member of the public. What's more, our conversation was in full view and full earshot of other employees, notably Mr. Solari, who is sitting beside you. I don't call that a private conversation."

"Neither do I," Marks agreed, turning to Greenslet. "Answer Mrs. Johnston's questions."

"You told me how proud you were of your department's glorious—

that's the word you used, glorious—record of saving taxpayers a great deal of money. Now, the way you are saving the taxpayers so much money is by allowing gentlemen such as these," she pointed toward the pilots, "private capture. I believe that was your term. Isn't that correct?"

"This is a very complicated issue," Greenslet said. "This woman is simplifying beyond all common sense—"

"These aren't hard questions, Mr. Greenslet," cut in the chairman, "a simple yes or no will do just fine." This brought more chuckles from the crowd.

"Well, yes then," Greenslet grouched.

"Thank you, Mr. Greenslet. I'm sure everyone applauds your glorious efforts to save the taxpayers money," said Velma, gaining confidence. Outright laughs escaped the audience. Not everyone agreed with Velma's position but Nevadans enjoy their blood sports.

"Today you kindly informed me that the going rate at the rendering plants for horse on the hoof was six and a half cents a pound."

"That's right, give or take," Greenslet said cautiously.

"And this permit that you're supporting," Velma continued, "allows these gentlemen to take, or harvest, as you call it, fifty to sixty horses. Isn't that correct?"

This time Greenslet only nodded.

"So if we take the halfway point on this, say fifty-five horses, and let's say conservatively the average weight of the horses was 850 pounds. That would make these horses worth $3,038. That's what you make it, give or take?"

Greenslet sat stone-faced.

"Three thousand dollars," Velma mused. "That's a lot of money." There were mutterings of agreement in the crowd. Attaching a dollar value to the roundup put a different slant on things.

"Now, this land where the roundup is proposed is not private land, correct? It is public land administered by the BLM, isn't that so?"

Greenslet made no move to answer, but when Marks ostentatiously cleared his throat, he offered the briefest of nods.

"That would make these horses public property unless my thinking is completely off-kilter."

"This isn't fair, Mr. Chairman," Greenslet said plaintively, starting to see where Velma was heading. "This woman is distorting everything I said."[15]

"Mr. Chairman, I'm just a simple secretary and all I'm doing is reading Mr. Greenslet's words back to him as I recorded verbatim using Pitman shorthand."[16]

"I'm sure that there's nothing at all simple about you, Ma'am," smiled Marks, "and from what I've seen here tonight anyone who thought that would be making a serious mistake."

"Why, thank you, Mr. Chairman," responded Velma, now almost enjoying the spotlight.

"So where were we, Mr. Greenslet?" Velma continued. "First you're doing a glorious job ridding the country of these terrible wild horses, at no cost to the taxpayers. We've established that these horses are on public land which makes them public property. We've also established that these horses are worth at least $3,000 at the rendering plant."

Velma took a breath and snatched a look at the audience. They were rapt, waiting for her to continue. Dante Solari sat glowering and red-faced.

"Now, it looks as though this glorious cost savings is actually a giveaway of public property to the tune of $3,000. What's more, I jotted down a few numbers and it looks like the folks Mr. Greenslet is giving this public property to are making $1,500 each, cold hard cash. And that's if there are only fifty-five horses. This permit seems pretty wide open as to horse numbers so we could easily be talking $5,000 or more."

Velma waited for an answer. When none was forthcoming, she forged on.

"I don't know about anyone else but I call that very generous of you, Mr. Greenslet. Are these folks you're giving all this money away to friends of yours or family?" Velma's barb brought the house down.[17]

The rest was mere formality. The Storey County commissioners unanimously voted to refuse the permit application.

Soon afterward, the jubilant "agin'" group gathered in the dark interior of Bill Marks's Crystal Bar. Marks shed his suit in favor of a bartender's apron and he stood the first round. Lucius Beebe strolled in, accompanied by Charles Clegg. Beebe had attended the hearing but wanted to pick up a few extra nuggets for a fire-and-brimstone editorial in the *Territorial Enterprise*. "Every so often there is put in motion agitation for the destruction of one means or another of the bands of wild horses which still roam the Washoe Hills. The current pressure is being applied solely for the benefit of two sheep ranchers who claim their grazing lands are being impaired by the horses. In view of the practically unlimited grazing lands in Western Nevada and the absurdly small number of the horses, such claims are purely fictional," scoffed Beebe. "The wild horses, harmless and picturesque as they are, are a pleasant reminder of a time when all the West was wilder and more free and any suggestion of their elimination or the abatement of the protection they now enjoy deserves a flat and instant rejection from the authorities from within whose province the matter now lies."[18]

Ten days later, another delegation led by Gladding asked the same commissioners to ban the airborne pursuit of wild horses.

"Whereas, after due consideration, this Board believes that the use of any airborne equipment, including airplanes, helicopters, etc., as a means of chasing, rounding up, spotting, during a roundup, of Wild Horses or Burros, in the County of Storey, be prohibited."[19]

The resolution passed unanimously. It was a small victory and the first-ever attempt to protect wild horses legally, but it applied only to state-owned land in Storey County and not to any of the range overseen by the BLM. Furthermore, there was no enforcement agency to police the resolution. Still, Velma, Charlie, and Tex Gladding were elated.

The morning after the Virginia City meeting, Velma floated into the office where she found a grim-faced Gordon Harris at his desk. After a few stilted pleasantries he came to the point—his displeasure with her role in the goings-on in Virginia City. "What I cannot understand, Velma, is why you don't write charming little books for children or something along that line, instead of plunging into this rough and probably hopeless fight."[20]

After Charlie and her father, Gordon Harris was the man whose approval meant the most to her. "I was somewhat taken aback at the question," she admitted, "for the reason seemed such a simple one to me. . . . There are many, many people who are writing charming little books for children," she told him stiffly, "and no one is doing a thing to stop the exploitation and annihilation of the wild horses."[21] Velma didn't expect Gordon Harris to endorse her out-of-office activities, but it had never occurred to her that he would dismiss them so condescendingly.

For the first and probably only time in their long relationship, Velma set her boss straight. She described the horrors of the hunt in unsparing detail, though she didn't reveal anything about her and Charlie's rescue missions. She explained that the roundups took place secretly because the operators knew full well their activities would be stopped if the public became aware of them. Harris may have been surprised by Velma's passion, but he wasn't persuaded.

Despite the success in Virginia City, Velma's crusade remained largely reactive. When she was told about captured horses, she and Charlie did their best to free them or arrange to have them freed. There were kindred souls like the Gladdings, but she had no plan of action or any goal larger than liberating as many horses as possible.

Then, early in 1953, Velma met Charles L. Richards, a seventy-six-year-old Reno lawyer and former congressman who had served a single term between 1923 and 1925. For the past few years, he had been doggedly pursuing a personal but largely futile campaign to ban the airborne chase of wild horses in Nevada and the use of any motor-driven vehicles in their capture.

Richards was long accustomed to tilting at windmills. A Democrat in an overwhelmingly Republican state, he had taken an unsuccessful run at a popular sitting governor, Frederick B. Balzar, in 1930 and then ran for governor again in 1934 when Balzar died in office. Richards finished last behind six Democratic and Republican candidates. Now he'd set himself against ranching interests in an attempt to protect wild horses. He got as far as having a bill tabled in the Nevada legislature in 1953, but it quickly died in committee. He told Velma he intended to reintroduce the bill in 1955.

Velma was taken with Richards's courtly manners, though she observed that he seemed discouraged and weary. Slightly stooped, he still walked with the loose-limbed grace of an athlete and his weathered outdoor skin spoke of years under the Nevada sun. His stockman's hat, worn as if it was part of his body, was the same style that Charlie favored, the flat brim sides narrower than those of a Stetson but wider than those of a fedora, with the front brim tipped down. Velma also felt there was an undercurrent of sadness in Richards. She knew that his wife had died the year before, but he didn't mention it and she didn't ask.

He impressed her with his willingness to champion a cause that could only rile ranchers. The practice of law depended on goodwill and a favorable reputation; most lawyers did not go out of their way to be unpopular in their communities. But Richards shared Velma's outrage at the plight of the mustangs. Velma volunteered to help; she had no political experience but she could type, compile mailing lists, and stuff envelopes. Richards emphasized that success depended on careful planning and thorough research, skills Velma believed she already possessed. But he'd assembled a wealth of material she'd never seen before.

Most striking was a remarkable sequence of black-and-white photographs taken by Nevada photographer Gus Bundy at a 1951 mustang hunt. One image showed a pickup truck chasing a mustang across the desert, its front bumper closing on the horse. A man anchored to the bed of the truck was unfurling a lasso attached to two truck tires. After the horse was roped, the tires were flipped out of the truck bed. Another picture showed the same horse near collapse after dragging the heavy tires across the desert until it could run no longer. The next featured the horse bound and trussed as a group of men winched it up a rough wooden ramp onto the deck of a larger truck. The terror in the animal's eyes had been replaced by dull submission.

Richards emphasized that the published word would lend credibility to their position. Press coverage would demonstrate unequivocally that there were others who were likewise concerned. His strategy dovetailed in Velma's mind with what Lura Tularski had told her: She needed proof, preferably photographic, to sway public opinion.

Richards's research files also confirmed something that Velma had figured out before the Virginia City hearing: Airborne roundups were not just about grazing issues, sport, or even the livelihood of ranchers. They were about money. The details of a 1938 roundup published in *Life* magazine reported that aerial cowboy Floyd Hanson had captured two thousand horses in the previous two years and netted $5 a head. In the final years of the Depression, $10,000 was a considerable sum. A new Ford Deluxe four-door sedan carried a base price of $770, a year's

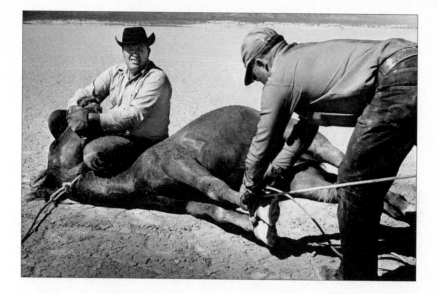

*Opposite: Preparing to lasso wild horses (top); a wild horse dragging a tire necklace (center); a wild horse fighting against ropes (bottom). A wild horse hogtied (above); a horse being dragged into a truck (below).*

wage for the average working man. The article noted that some of the mustangs were broken for saddle use while others were consigned to dog-food packers or glue factories. Velma suspected that for every mustang put under saddle in 1938, thousands more went to slaughter. The number would be even higher in 1953.

Supportive newspaper and magazine accounts were invaluable but difficult to initiate. Skepticism about do-good missions and worthy causes was a basic job requirement for editors of independent publications. Charles Richards had been promoting his mustang legislation for years, but his efforts hadn't resulted in a single column, article, or editorial in any Nevada newspaper. This time, he hoped to bring his bill to public attention through a mass-mailing campaign, an unorthodox approach in the early 1950s.

Direct mail was in its infancy, with retailers still relying heavily on newspaper and magazine advertising and door-to-door sales. In 1952 the U.S. postal system began offering bulk third-class rates to encourage more advertisers to use the mail, but most mass mailings were labor-intensive distributions of mail-order catalogues, flyers containing coupons for specific products, or solicitations from the larger charities.

Richards had already compiled lists of state and federal public officials who might be in some way involved with wild horses, ranching, or range management, as well as every state senator and assemblyman. Velma searched out membership rolls for riding clubs and 4-H Club chapters, the editors of even the smallest newspapers in the state, and any animal welfare organization to which she could attach an address. They composed a general information bulletin emphasizing the brutality of the hunt and how close the mustangs were to extinction; copies would be sent to every name on file. Editors, columnists, and legislators would receive an individualized cover letter signed by Richards.

Velma took care of the letters and copying the bulletin. Her partner was a bulky, noisy, smelly, and often temperamental Gestetner machine. Velma first typed the bulletin on a thin stencil, taking care not to smear the ink or wrinkle the stencil. She then placed it on the roller mechanism and cranked the Gestetner by hand to produce copies. A smooth-functioning machine with a firmly typed stencil could produce up to two hundred good-quality copies before the stencil degraded and a new one had to be typed. After three or four sets of stencils, the single-color ink cartridges needed refilling, a messy job involving a small funnel, which frequently tipped or wobbled. She couldn't rush the collating either, since the ink smudged easily if it wasn't completely dry.

They planned to send out the mailing just before the holidays, reasoning that people's hearts were more inclined to be open around Christmas. It also tended to be a slow news period and editors might be looking for seasonal stories about wrongs that needed righting.

Then on the morning of December 22, 1953, one of Richards's neighbors heard a shot and went outside to discover the lawyer in his driveway, dead from a self-inflicted gunshot wound to the head. Richards had written a suicide note apologizing, as a faithful Catholic, for his actions but explaining that he could no longer bear the pain and loneliness of life without his wife.

"The first batch of letters were barely off my typewriter, not as yet signed even when Mr. Richards took his life . . . I had the material, and knew what he planned. There just wasn't anyone else into whose hands to place it."[22] Velma retyped the letters over her own signature and blitzed the mailing list. The pony clubs and humane societies responded with gratifying speed, offering help. Velma wrote back, often within hours, urging them to write individually and as groups to public officials and their political representatives.

But elsewhere the campaign fell flat. She could barely contain her frustration at the lack of interest from legislators and officials, who, in the main, replied with a line or two of boilerplate acknowledgment and dismissive thanks. As for the media, there were no outraged editorials or curious reporters sent to sniff out a heart-tugging story. Even Lucius Beebe, after his first blistering editorial in the *Territorial Enterprise*, fell silent. But Velma couldn't rest. During the week Trudy often woke in the night to find her daughter in the kitchen, hunched over her Underwood typewriter banging out more letters.

One day in 1954, newly elected state senator James Slattery, representing Storey County, dropped in to Gordon Harris's office. Apart from knowing Velma and Charlie as near neighbors, Slattery had lived in Gabbs when they worked there before the war. He credited them with saving him from ignominious injury during one of the many windstorms that ripped through the mining town. A particularly vicious blow had toppled the outhouse shared by the occupants of a number of house trailers and had rolled it some distance away. Slattery happened to be suffering one of his periodic bouts of disabling joint pain, probably arthritis, when Nature called, and he laboriously made his way to the "Chick Sale," as outhouses were dubbed after the humorist of that name who wrote about an outhouse builder. But in his pain and with the windstorm raging, he didn't notice it was gone. From their window Charlie and Velma spotted him heading straight for the exposed pit. They yelled and waved madly, managing to catch his attention just in time.

Though they were friendly back in their Gabbs days, the Johnstons didn't travel in the same set as Slattery, and Velma had no idea where the senator stood on the subject of wild horses. He was a rancher, after all, and a sportsman who loved to brag of his hunting prowess—hardly the sort who would fight for wild horses.

Slattery's face was set in a scowl when he addressed Velma.

"Mrs. Johnston," he said portentously. "I've had a complaint about you from my colleagues in Washington."

Velma's heart took a lurch.

"'Who the hell is this Mrs. Johnston?' they are asking me. 'She must know everybody in the state, and everybody must know her!'" Slattery, now laughing, added that Nevada governor Charles Russell told him he was getting more correspondence on the hunting of wild horses than any other subject. Then, to Velma's astonishment, Slattery offered to sponsor a bill in the Nevada legislature banning the mechanized hunt of wild horses.

Slattery was a far right Republican who opposed any kind of gun control. He had spoken against legislated civil rights and he had compiled lists of alleged communists at the University of Nevada, Reno. Later he would be labeled "the paid senator of the gaming industry." But it has never been easy to pigeonhole Nevada politicians. Slattery was an astute monitor of the political winds, and he sensed that the wild horse issue could resonate with his nonranching voters—a constituency that was growing as Reno expanded. He was likely also influenced by his animal-loving wife. Visitors to their ranch were frequently shocked to find a large sow in their bathroom; Shovelnose took up residence there every year to give birth and wean her piglets. Mrs. Slattery hovered close for weeks, afraid that Shovelnose would roll over and squish her brood.

Slattery's participation added legitimacy to the campaign. Almost overnight the media began picking up on the material Velma had been firing at them. Lucius Beebe took notice again and in an editorial thundered that the "extermination of the horses for the benefit of greedy and brutal interests would be a reproach to all citizens of good will who are coming to realize that recognition of the rights of animals is, in itself, intimately bound up with the civilized conduct of human beings."[23]

But no major newspaper endorsed the campaign until the influential *Nevada State Journal* published one of its trademark mocking editorials, striking just the tone to arouse its readers. The bill, the editorial explained, drawing from the popular "Saddle Chatter" column that day, "makes it unlawful to poison waterholes where wild horses drink. Don't know anybody could be low enough to do just that, but they have— and more than just once. Let's for once not let these wild animals die in agony and torment because we let the bill to protect them die in committee without even getting it out of the Senate or Assembly floor as in past seasons. If down-to-earthism removes us from the realm of decent, charitable thoughts, if 'viva la commercialism' is the order of the day, we're losing a real part of our human dignity. The United States has laws, enacted by the will of a majority of the people, protecting the bald eagle, a bird of not much practical use to anyone, but the symbol of the history and strength of the United States. By the same token, why cannot we in Nevada afford some protection to an animal which, more than any other, symbolizes the history, the strength, the progress of Nevada and the west—the wild horse."[24]

On February 16, 1955, a month before the scheduled legislative hearings in Carson City, Velma issued a four-page press release. "The cruelties attendant in the capturing and transporting of the animals to their slaughter, at distant processing centers, is an effrontery to the decency of most," she wrote. "Nowhere are the wild creatures safe from pursuit, for from the highest mountain tops, or the most rugged canyons, these airborne cowboys bring them in to the level area where the job is taken over by other handlers. Often the bedeviled animals in their flight break their legs, or have to be clubbed in loading, and small colts who cannot keep up with their mothers are left behind, for they wouldn't weigh enough to bring sufficient return [to] warrant any extra effort in their capture."[25]

Slattery invited Velma and Charlie to the Senate chamber in Carson City for the public hearing phase of the debate. The first face Velma recognized when she entered the chamber was the puffy, balding visage of her old BLM foe, Dante Solari.

"Well, here comes Wild Horse Annie herself!" he sneered.[26]

Charlie turned abruptly toward him and whatever Solari saw caused him to clamp his mouth shut.

By then Velma was aware of disparaging references to her as "a crazy woman," and "that little old lady in running shoes," though at forty-three she was hardly elderly and she certainly wouldn't have been caught dead in running shoes. Still, one of the surest means to discredit a woman was to dismiss her as an old kook. Solari's "Wild Horse Annie" put-down, though, was a new one.

A Senate clerk read out the proposed bill. "It shall be unlawful for any person, under the provisions of NRS569.360 to 569.430 inclusive (a) to hunt horses, mares, colts or burros by means of airborne vehicles of any kind, or motor-driven vehicles of any kind. (b) to pollute watering holes in order to trap, kill, wound or maim such animals."[27]

Velma was delighted when the bill was quickly referred to committee for further study, but a few days later Slattery informed her that ranching interests on the committee refused to release the bill with a "do-pass" recommendation to the legislature without a specific amendment: "But the provisions of NRS569.360 to 569.430, inclusive, shall not be construed to conflict with the provisions of any Federal law or regulation governing the hunting or driving of horses, mares, colts or burros by means of airborne or motor driven vehicles."

Since the BLM controlled 88 percent of the land in Nevada, the amendment effectively castrated the bill. Velma was devastated, but Charlie urged her to accept the deal as a step, albeit small, in the right direction. "It killed my soul to have to agree, but I had to indulge in this type of horse trading to get it out of committee."[28]

# SIX

# Moccasin Walking

ORKING WITH CHARLES Richards and then James Slattery to pass the Nevada bill taught Velma the essence of effective political action: organization, meticulous research, and the patient laying of one brick upon another until the legislative castle was built. She also came to understand that being in the right or on the side of justice mattered little. In the year following passage of the bill, Velma didn't uncover a single instance of the state legislation being enforced. The Bureau of Land Management was still rubber-stamping permits for roundups on federally owned land, even as the mustangers bypassed the permit process entirely and simply drove the horses onto private property before corralling them.

Nevada's new law actually created a fresh threat to the survival of its wild horses and to those in the other western states—Texas, Wyoming, Montana, Colorado, and parts of California—where sizable numbers remained. As a harbinger of future legislation, it encouraged mustang hunters to scoop up as many horses as possible, before the hunts were ended altogether. Though the legislation was largely impotent, it signaled the first stirrings of the embryonic movement to protect the wild horse. As soon as the bill passed out of the public limelight, its opponents regrouped to nullify it.

"Tex, guess you heard the news broadcast," Velma wrote to Gladding on March 11, 1957. "We're in the grease again, thanks to Roy Young from Elko County, sponsor of AB 404."[1] The previous day Young, a Nevada state senator, had introduced legislation to allow airplane roundups on state land, once permits from the BLM and from the relevant county commissioners had been obtained.

"In talking with Jim [Slattery] this morning, he said he had visited with one of the Washoe County assemblymen who told him he intended to vote for the passage of AB 404, 'because four or five men in my district make their living that way,'" Velma reported to Gladding. "He made the statement as though he were referring to the horse-meat merchants, because his area is not noted for cattle production. That makes me believe more than ever that it is the intention of this bill to exploit the horses to the fullest extent." Velma told Gladding that the *Sacramento Bee,* northern California's leading daily newspaper, was "going all out for us," but indignation from that quarter wouldn't likely have much influence across the state line. "Best of luck," she closed, "and do everything you can. We haven't much time."[2] With the help of Slattery and Gladding, Velma successfully beat back the proposed bill, but Young's challenge demonstrated the tenacity of the opposition.

Velma concluded that only a federal law, superseding state law, would truly protect the wild horse, but that realization merely magnified the scale of her problem. Her core wild horse supporters were Charlie, Tex, her mother, and the few individuals she had temporarily co-opted. Lobbying for federally legislated protection would be a far more daunting task, and they would be breaking new ground the whole way. While there was steady growth in the number of animal protection groups through the 1950s, none considered the wild horse part of their mandate. The Humane Society of the United States, incorporated in 1954 and headquartered in Washington, D.C., focused largely on the treatment of domestic animals while also lobbying for more humane cattle-slaughtering procedures. In 1958 the organization was instrumental in the passage of the Humane Methods of Slaughter Act, legislation primarily designed for cattle.

The Society for the Prevention of Cruelty to Animals was founded in 1824 as a movement to protect London's carriage horses from abuse. An American version started up in 1866, similarly devoted to horses, but domestic ones only. By mid-twentieth century, the SPCA had broadened its mission to embrace the treatment of domestic pets and livestock, neither of which included wild horses. Special-interest groups advocating for any kind of wildlife, let alone an animal many considered merely feral, were largely nonexistent.

Influencing public opinion at the national level and challenging powerful and entrenched interests would require considerable resources. Velma's salary and Charlie's disability checks barely covered their own living expenses. Occasionally a sympathizer made a small donation, but the contributions came in dribs and drabs. In later years Velma hinted at the financial strain of the early campaigns, but she never approached friends for help or appealed to her family, even though sisters Betty Jo and Loreene were considerably better off financially. As newlyweds, Betty Jo and her tall, genial husband, Roy Larson, lived briefly in her parents' Washington Street house, where Velma and Charlie taught Roy how to drink and party. Loreene wed Robert McElwee, a navy captain, and lived the life of a military wife at bases across the country.

Trudy might have dipped into her pocket to help with mailing costs and long-distance telephone bills, but it wasn't because her daughter asked. Velma, the queen of cheap and cheerful, was masterful at making do, and she never spoke about her own financial concerns except in a very general way. Furthermore, Velma compartmentalized her life; her sisters and nieces and nephews, whom she doted on, weren't involved in the wild horse fight nor were they invited to lend a hand. Trudy stuffed and addressed envelopes, but she was not in on any planning or execution. Charlie was the only one who knew about every facet of Velma's life, though even he wasn't fully aware of the extent of her physical difficulties. As for money, Velma tried not to worry about it and Charlie had an even more blasé attitude. Both were far too proud to take handouts.

Before mounting a national campaign to stop aerial roundups, Velma knew she needed ammunition in the form of facts and eyewitness testimony to counter the BLM's propaganda. But aside from James Slattery, she knew no one from the political, ranching, or business communities who might be willing to speak out. When she cursed people for their lack of courage, Charlie chided her. "We should walk in another's moccasins before judging him." He urged her to seek out support, instead of waiting for it to come to her. "If you go and meet them you'll get to know them better and you'll force them to get to know you better. Maybe they'll try to walk in your moccasins."[3] He also pointed out that if people came to know her, they'd realize she wasn't the unstable harridan portrayed by Dante Solari and the BLM.

Common sense told Velma that not all ranchers thought alike, but she still felt she was on one side of a line and they were on the other. To win the fight at home and on the national front, that line had to be erased. Men who knew the rangelands could refute the BLM's routine pronouncements about the numbers of wild horses and their preferred habitat. They could testify with real authority about the horses' forage and water consumption, about herd behavior and movement patterns.

Making contact with ranchers was more easily said than done. They were spread widely around the state, many in remote areas, and besides, it was just not acceptable to go knocking on doors uninvited. Velma hit upon the idea of approaching sheep and cattlemen at the Washoe Market, a Reno retail fixture owned by the Games brothers. Situated between First and Second streets on the city's main thoroughfare, the store stood across from Colonel Brant's speakeasy, quiet during the day as people went about their errands. It was said that if you spent enough time at the Washoe Market, you'd eventually meet just about everyone living in the city and a good proportion of those from the outskirts.

Velma stayed over with her mother one Friday night, and the next morning, with Trudy along for support, she went to the Market, where she buttonholed ranchers out with their wives on Saturday shopping errands. She was still naturally reticent, and her nervousness came across as aggression. That, coupled with her odd appearance, sent several couples scurrying. After a number of embarrassing fiascos, Velma abandoned the scheme.

For months she pressed her contacts to connect her with anyone who might be willing to offer expertise about wild horses and rangeland. She thought she might find a measure of support among ranchers with small holdings, who were predisposed to condemn anything the larger landowners did or the BLM promoted. But many of them lived far from any town, along poor roads and without phone service. Even if they had a telephone, it would be awkward, especially for a woman, to call a complete stranger.

Velma kept reminding herself that the preservation of wild horses in America would not be accomplished by playing the "sad heart card," as she called it. "I have given a great deal of thought to the matter in order not to appear hysterically oversympathetic and just another "do-gooder," she explained to a magazine writer in 1957. Even though she thought of herself as a "womanly woman" and a "feminine female," she knew she must do exactly what her father once advised her and Charlie reinforced: Act like a lady, think like a man, and arm herself with reason, logic, and facts, expressed with a minimum of sentimentality. At the office Velma presented such an unflappable, cool-headed demeanor, few realized how emotional she could be, especially about the welfare of animals. Even among close family and friends, she masked or made light of hurts and disappointments.

The other side of Velma was a fun-loving party girl who delighted in entertaining guests, enjoyed clever conversation and risqué jokes, and cheerfully pounded out show tunes on the old piano while singing along at full volume. But her deepest emotions she kept to herself and Charlie. Very occasionally she allowed her outrage at the "filthy business" to seep into letters, condemning the mustangers and their financial backers as "ruthless, brutal, greedy and completely without compassion . . . an ugly force to oppose." When things weren't going well, Velma sometimes fantasized about catching the mustang hunters in the act, preferably with a gun in her hand. By 1957 Velma always had a gun close by, a pistol in her car and a shotgun handy by the front door of her mother's home.

Finally Velma received a promising referral from Tex Gladding, who offered an introduction to a Reno man by the name of James Stoddard. At first glance Stoddard, a semiretired furniture and upholstery repairman in his seventies, seemed an unlikely ally. But like many Nevadans, he had another life. "Mr. Stoddard has ridden the ranges of Nevada for the past fifty-five years and has handled stock all his life," Velma noted in her summary of their first conversation. "Until a short time ago, he owned extensive grazing lands in the Sutro Range. He sold his holdings to Curtis-Wright Corporation, but has a grazing lease on the land."[4]

Stoddard was known and respected in the ranching community

for his extensive knowledge of rangeland, not only its existing condition but its ever-changing nature. Land transforms under the hands of those who work it—sometimes for the better, sometimes not. Stoddard could tell exactly where the squirrel grass gave out to Indian ricegrass, how many piñons grew in a certain stand, and whether a water hole had dropped an inch or two in the past thirty years.

Stoddard agreed to meet Velma at his Reno home. After introductory pleasantries, Velma got down to business. Her goals were to determine the number of horses on particular ranges, the condition of the ranges as well as the condition of the horses, and, of course, the details of any airplane roundups—all crucial to undermining the BLM's assertion that wild horses were destroying forage and water holes. She was also anxious to have an educated estimate of the number of wild horses left in Nevada. She pulled out her notebook and asked first about populations.

"In this locality there were about 380 head of horses," Stoddard said slowly, speaking of the Virginia Range where the horses Velma saw in the truck had been caught years ago. "Today I doubt if you would find 150."[5]

Velma inquired about the condition of the land where the horses grazed, noting her own question as well as Stoddard's answer in shorthand.

"The sheep come through the hills and trample out the feed. Feed horses eat, a sheep won't touch. Sheep have ruined our ranges. No question about it. If they could be kept off the ranges for a few years it would be entirely different. There would be lots of feed."

"But the ranchers keep saying the horses are making a terrible mess of water holes and digging up roots to eat during the winter. And the BLM backs them up," Velma countered.

"Horses will keep springs open and paw out water holes," Stoddard explained. "When I was a kid there was lots of bunch grass, lots of feed. Horses re-seed the ranges. They feed here today, and tomorrow five to ten miles away. Grass seed goes through a horse and is not destroyed. Any old-time stock man will tell you the same thing."

Not for the first time did Velma wonder why, if men like Stoddard had this information, knew it because they'd seen it with their own eyes and heard it from their fathers and grandfathers, the BLM and so many range lessees maintained the opposite. Velma concluded that the attitude toward the wild horse was proof that if bureaucrats and those pushing a certain agenda said something often enough and with sufficient conviction, it would come to be accepted as fact, regardless of evidence to the contrary.

If Velma could get a dozen James Stoddards to testify she might have a chance. But arguing with the cattlemen over whose experience was more valid simply reduced the debate to school-yard bickering. The only way to counter ingrained prejudice was with numbers—hard facts about how many horses there were and how it was impossible for them to ruin the grazing lands because their numbers were too few. She asked Stoddard about survival rates in the wild horse bands, without the interference of airborne roundups.

"The mortality rate is high," Stoddard told her. "In a band of seven or eight, maybe there will be four or five colts in spring—only one left by the fall. Cougars are bad on the colts and hunters will take a shot at them. There's also a disease that gets among horses; encephalitis almost wiped out all of them. Very rare to have it happen on the range but it did one year."

Velma gently eased the information she needed out of the stockman. She knew most ranchers couldn't abide senseless cruelty toward animals or heedless degradation of the land. The trick was to find those who had thought about the issues and coax them to express themselves. With Stoddard, she had no difficulty when she asked how captured mustangs were shipped.

"In trucking them, some fall down and are stepped on by the others. At the rendering works their condition is poor. They are always scratched and cut up from being roughly handled. . . . I'll tell you that. There is no doubt that most of the horses have no feed or water for several days while a sufficient load is being gathered. The worst part is running them by plane which scares them to death."[6]

"At the rendering works three years ago, I saw one little brown mare in foal, fairly well along. Her right front leg was swollen to immense size, from hoof to withers. Ordinarily you can't walk up to a mustang. But this little horse was so sore that I could walk right up to her.

Another, a roan, had her whole neck and withers cut where it had been shot by a shotgun."

Velma assumed he was talking about creasing, the technique of firing a bullet across a horse's neck, injuring but not killing it. Pulling it off required superior marksmanship. Stoddard set her right: Those wounds were inflicted by airborne shooters with no particular talent.

"Horses learn to get into sheltering growth. Planes fly over trees and shoot them to get them out. About six years ago, I saw a roan horse that had been trapped up in the rimrock. Evidently it had been trapped for a number of days for it had jumped and fallen so many times over the rocks and crags that its ribs were nearly all broken, as shown by the lumps in the hide where the ends were sticking out.

"The horse was still alive," Stoddard recalled. "I shot it."[7]

Stoddard was precisely the sort of witness Velma was looking for, a no-nonsense, straight-talking rancher who couldn't be intimidated. But she needed more than one retired stockman. Stoddard himself delivered up Arne Bailey to her. Ten years younger than Velma, Bailey worked for the Southern Pacific Railroad but spent a lot of his time around cowboys and horses. Best of all, he had ridden extensively in the western Nevada ranges and knew the terrain, flora, and fauna intimately.

In a rare departure from form, Velma allowed her "hobby," as Harris called it, to intrude on her workday when Stoddard brought Bailey to the office one scorching hot afternoon in August. Velma extended a hand in greeting to Bailey, her grip firm and her "squished" side angled away from him.

She was careful not to let her eagerness show or to press too hard for information, even from someone who had taken the trouble to come to her. Oftentimes with ranchers it was like peeling a rock to elicit even a tiny fragment of new material. But with her first question about roundups, Bailey leaned forward eagerly in his chair.

"There are two men staged on horseback in a flat area where the men on horseback will have easy running. The airplane pilot has got a shotgun in his plane and he goes out and locates the horses and starts them running toward the horsemen. They rope them and tie them down until they can haul them away by truck."

As he spoke Velma scribbled quickly in shorthand so as not to lose a word.

"Have you ever seen the pilots use their shotguns?" she asked.

"The wild horses are smart. They hide in the juniper trees. In order to make them run the pilot flies over them and shoots them. When they are running he leaves them alone. He shoots to turn them or keep them running, else they would stop in the juniper."

Velma opened her mouth to ask if Arne had ever seen one hit but he needed no prompting.

"Any time they're hit, it penetrates. I have seen many bloodied at the rendering works from bullets. But it's not just that. Legs are burned with ropes until there is no hide left on them."

Velma recorded his words, adding exclamation points.

"To tie them, they do what is called side-lining. It's to tie the front leg to the hind with rope. The horses are left where they are tied until they've got sufficient [number of horses] to bring in. I've seen 'em side-lined for over twenty-four hours." More exclamation points, and beside her note Velma scribbled, "Food?! Water?!"

"Do they quiet when they're roped?" she asked, thinking of how quickly even the most difficult ranch horse submitted as soon as it was haltered or roped.

"Not hardly!" Bailey scoffed, as if reading her mind. "Velma, these horses aren't like anything on a ranch. A wild horse has no judgment in how to keep from hurting itself in trying to get away. It will do anything! When it's tied down it will fight tremendously and if the ground is rocky it beats itself half to death on the rocks. I've seen 'em with heads so swollen they can't even see."

"How do they get them loaded, then?"

"To load the horses, a rope is tied around its neck, then run up through the truck ramp. One or two saddle horses do the dragging, however they can, in any position the wild horse drags best."

Velma asked about weanlings and yearlings.

"The colt can't keep up. The mother will desert it when chased by a plane."

Velma needed numbers, and men like Bailey could supply them.

"The most I have counted in one full day's riding is fourteen," he said. "I would really be crowding if I said there were 300 in all of Storey County. And that is the heaviest area in Nevada."

"Do you know any of these men who are doing the running?"

"Lazy cowboys that won't do anything else. For about three years after the war the rendering plants were just bulging. When fliers got out of the service, they went out and started to annihilate the horses."

"It's all wrong-headed, Velma," Bailey added urgently, as if he needed to convince her. "Cattlemen had cattle for years and there was room for both horses and cattle. Horses range high and stock doesn't range high. If it wasn't for our water problems, you would never see wild horses in the lowlands."

Like Stoddard, he told her that the horses helped reseed the range, and he lamented the degradation of the forage that resulted from their absence.

"You have to stop this pretty soon as there's hardly any feed any more. All this fighting between horses and cattle. The only purpose in chasing the horses is to profiteer."[8]

Velma showed Bailey out into the punishing heat and watched him walk to his truck along East First Street. The sidewalk seemed to shimmer under his feet. Finally she was getting to the truth.

Arne Bailey's interview with Velma was graphic and specific, but the information she omitted in the typed transcript of her notes was even more interesting. In later confidential correspondence she revealed, "He has volunteered to get information for me, and pictures, for he is on terms with the men who are running the horses." Bailey offered details of roundups, legal and illegal, even providing specifics about permit applications, including names, dates, and locations.

Arne Bailey was mesmerized by Velma just as Zeke, her first spy, or "outlander," had been. Those drawn into her web convinced themselves that what they were doing was their idea, not hers. "As Mr. Bailey and I both feel that he can be of more help to me if it is not known by the fly-boys that he is working with me, it is important that his name be withheld as much as possible. However, he assured me he is prepared to swear to his statements and his convictions."[9]

Tom McCord, a frequent visitor to the Double Lazy Heart as a boy, had taken a job at a local airport. He phoned Velma whenever a mustanger's plane was being readied for takeoff. She code-named the hulking young man Penelope.

Eventually Velma interviewed quite a number of ranchers but only after the proper introductions were made. One name led to another, to personal interviews or long evenings on the phone. Beside each name she noted the date of contact and whether the person was "pro," "con," or "on the fence" with regard to saving the wild horses. And if the person was a "pro," she indicated whether he would be a "stand up" supporter or a "background" supporter. It was easy to determine which ranchers were against Velma. Harder to read were the seemingly neutral parties or those who might agree with her but remained close-mouthed. They were legion in a rural community where people made a virtue of minding their own business.

Shortly after meeting Bailey, Velma made another valuable contact in Mark Shipley, who had been involved in range management projects in the northeastern portion of Nevada for the BLM itself. He offered to provide information from his research, giving Velma access to authoritative data for the first time. She felt that if a federal bill were to succeed, it must answer the needs of all range users, but first she had to know who was using the range and for what purpose.

The proposed amendment of the Nevada bill had given Velma some desperately needed publicity in California. *Sacramento Bee* columnist Alvin Trivelpiece, in a story headlined "Desert Wild Horses Face Extinction by Hunters for Pet Food Canneries," wrote the first substantive article about the plight of wild horses that featured Velma as their champion. The story, illustrated with three of Gus Bundy's evocative photographs, supplied by Velma, described a mustang chase and laid out the economics of turning the horses into pet food.

But the tipping point in media attention ultimately came with a brief mention in the *New York Times,* which piqued the interest of a *Denver Post* editor, who commissioned freelancer Robert O'Brien to write a story. O'Brien was the first writer from a large American daily to give exposure to the wild horse cause. He also came with a little "frosting on the cake," in Velma's words; *Reader's Digest* intended to reprint his article.

"We talked at great length," Velma wrote after O'Brien had stayed several days at the Double Lazy Heart, "and he contacted many people in this area, including the representatives of the Bureau of Land Management, and men engaged in the rounding up of the horses. Time did not permit him to interview everyone whom he wished to see, and he returned to New York on Wednesday. I have his assurance that he will not hurt us in any article he writes, and I know that the national publicity will help a lot toward national legislation."[10]

Forty-eight-year-old O'Brien had been a newspaperman for more than two decades and from the outset he looked for verifiable, quotable, first-person accounts of roundup brutality. Velma was eager to oblige. She called on her Executive Secretaries contacts, begging women to step forward if they knew anything about mustang roundups or could direct her to witnesses. A secretary in Reno, Enid Johnson, referred her to Zelda R. Smith, a secretary with the Nevada Southern Gas Company in Las Vegas, who was sympathetic to mustangs. Velma immediately fired off a letter.

"I understand that you planned to go to Pioche, in Lincoln Co. 180 miles NE of Las Vegas, to take pictures [of a roundup]. . . . Will you write to me and tell me all you can about the situation? Also, can you get eye-witness stories from others in your area? . . . If you can tell me specific incidents, and give descriptions, the approximate dates and locations should be included." Then, two sentences later, "Be assured, I shall appreciate all you and your associates can do to help. May I hear from you real soon?" And finally in a postscript, "Pictures would be of tremendous value, as the most recent ones I have are those taken by Gus Bundy that appeared in the *Sacramento Bee*."[11]

Eventually Velma sent a six-page letter to O'Brien with every eye-witness account she could muster. "Mrs. Zelda Smith reported seeing small wild horses brought in with their hooves nothing but bleeding stumps from having been run over the rocks by well mounted cowboys," Velma summarized.[12] Another member of Smith's group of observers offered a horrific account of what he had seen: "a corral of wild mustangs and burros rounded up and waiting for shipment. The eager bounty hunters, who received $5 for a pair of ears, had already cut their ears off," he said. "Bleeding and exhausted, covered with flies and vermin, without food or water for almost a week, they were a sad commentary on our humanity."[13]

The flurry of activity surrounding O'Brien's visit and Velma's subsequent pursuit of witnesses was exhilarating. Still, when Velma returned to the Double Lazy Heart on Friday nights she could hardly wait to kick off her pumps, peel off her stockings, and pull on her riding slacks, a crisp white shirt, and a neckerchief in a happy red, white, and blue design. Then she would flop into one of the porch chairs and let the dogs fuss over her while Charlie shook up a big pitcher of cocktails. The evenings passed quickly as she reported on her week.

One of Charlie's strengths was his ability to distinguish between the ideal and the possible. Velma wanted to save each and every mustang right now; Charlie made her see that the best she could hope for was to save some of the herds, in some of the rangelands, so that wild horses would still be around when their nieces and nephews grew up. He frequently reminded her that when they first began fighting for the mustang's survival, many people had predicted the herds would be gone in just a few years. But here it was 1957 and the horses were still hanging on.

Some Fridays when Velma pulled into the narrow driveway, she'd find Charlie standing out front, cigarette clenched between his teeth, Hobo's reins in one hand, Ranger's in the other. "It's a hell of a good day!" he'd bark, puffing hard and smiling at the same time. The saddlebags would be bulging with victuals and libation and the week forgotten as Velma changed and they rode off together. Nothing could rejuvenate her like Charlie and the horses.

But as Velma pushed the wild herds toward the national spotlight, she had less and less time to spend with her own horses. She stayed late at the office during the week to catch up on her personal correspondence; by 1957 the volume was such that she was forced to take it home with her on the weekends, something she hated to do. After March of that year, there is no further mention in her letters of riding into the hills with Charlie.

It wasn't just the wild horse campaign that kept her out of the saddle. The persistent bronchitis that had plagued Charlie since the late 1940s was replaced by early-stage emphysema. Though he was still physically strong and able, his endurance deteriorated alarmingly. Taking in the hay, changing the oil in the tractor, all the innumerable tasks of maintaining the Double Lazy Heart demanded more effort and twice the time. Charlie would work for twenty minutes, take a cigarette break, then work for another twenty minutes. He also started drinking more during the week while Velma was away.

After one evening at the Wadsworth Hotel bar, Charlie got on Ranger for the ride home, only to tumble off almost immediately. Charles C. Johnston had been inebriated many times; he'd stumble, slur, swear, and sometimes fight. But he never fell off his horse. Tom McCord recalled a night when "he was passed out in a chair outside the bar when I went in and he was still there when I came out hours later. I loaded him crosswise on his horse, and walked him home."[14]

Whether it was alcohol, the advancing emphysema, or both, height-

*Charlie on Foxy, circa 1955*

ened by the brutal Nevada summer heat, Charlie took a serious turn in August 1957. He literally couldn't get out of bed, and Velma had to ask neighbors for help with the ranch chores. Charlie was humiliated but he had no choice. During that period Velma drove home from Reno every night to care for him.

"It is very pleasant at the ranch this Sunday afternoon. Charles is sleeping, the cockers are in various positions on the floor near him, lost in canine slumbers, and the steady hum of our tractor sounds real good as a kindly neighbor mows our hay so that our three horses may fare well this winter," she wrote to Robert O'Brien. "Charles has been very ill, and I thought last week he wouldn't make it. He's better now, a little, and I hope he will be well again. A week of commuting, plus all the worry, and keeping things going on an even keel here has proved what I've always known—that this special Utopia of ours would be a real nightmare without him."[15]

Velma was forty-five years old in 1957, well into middle age by the reckoning of the times. But her body felt older thanks to the polio. The aches never left her and the hours of driving and sitting only made her discomfort worse. She kept herself together with painkillers, generous cocktails, and periodic spinal traction—she called it getting strapped to the rack. And there were many visits to her dentist, who did all he could to keep Velma's teeth, set in a jaw twisted by polio, from falling right out of her head. Though there was no name for it in 1957, Velma was experiencing the initial stages of postpolio syndrome, which cruelly strikes some polio survivors as they age. She had all the symptoms, including fatigue, chronic musculoskeletal and joint pain, and a distressing weakness in previously affected muscles. She also found that routine illnesses like colds came more frequently and lasted longer.

Fortunately, in the fall of 1957 Charlie bounced back. Velma was relieved by his return to good health and they planned a big wingding at the ranch. In the past there were often parties at the Double Lazy Heart or at the Washington Street house with Trudy, who loved an all-out bash. Velma threw herself into elaborate preparations with a Hawaiian theme. During the week she and Trudy made dozens of colorful leis out of salvaged plastic packaging and bongo rattles from cardboard toilet paper tubes. For the children she intended to make flowered headbands out of real flowers from her garden, a job she would save until the night before so the flower tiaras would be fresh. On the appointed day, she welcomed her guests with a heaping buffet of South Seas dishes, Hawaiian music at full volume, and island-inspired games for a throng of adults and a posse of children.

# SEVEN

# Mrs. Johnston Goes to Washington

I N LATE 1957, Velma waited on tenterhooks for the publication of Robert O'Brien's story in *Reader's Digest*. That his piece would appear in the *Denver Post* a few weeks in advance was not a concern; it was the *Digest*'s version that made her anxious. So much depended on this single article, the first major national story about the wild horse protection movement.

*Reader's Digest* was at the peak of its circulation and influence in the midfifties. It boasted sales of 10 million copies a month and a readership of 38 million, 22 percent of the U.S. population. It reached tens of millions more through its fifty foreign editions. No other publication of the day had its power to sway or, indeed, set public opinion. Politically the magazine was right of center, aiming its content—much of it reprinted and condensed from leading newspapers and magazines—at the average white, middle-class American family. But occasionally left-leaning readers, bohemians, and even radicals could find ideological comfort within its covers, especially in its humor segments that poked fun at both suspected communists and those determined to root out the Red Peril.

The cover of the fat, digest-sized Christmas issue featured a pretty bouquet of holly berries and pine branches drawn by Robert H. Blatt-ner, one of the magazine's favorite cover artists and a specialist in appealing compositions inspired by nature. But the cover wasn't a reflection of the content. James P. Mitchell, President Eisenhower's rags-to-riches secretary of labor and a man described as "the social conscience of the Republican Party," had written a thoughtful social commentary titled "The Negro Moves Up." Economist, journalist, and avowed liberal Henry Hazlitt contributed "No Time For Hysteria," an analysis of the Soviet Union's eclipse of the United States in the space race with the October launch of *Sputnik-1*. A complimentary profile of Edward R. Murrow—the respected broadcast journalist who had taken on Senator Joseph McCarthy—placed the issue well outside its normally conservative editorial stance.

"The Mustangs' Last Stand" fit the lineup perfectly. In a skillfully crafted story, O'Brien sketched the history of the mustang, emphasizing its importance to western settlement and celebrating in particular two "mustangs of great heart [who] remain immortalized in the mythology of the Old West."[1] O'Brien then turned to present-day conditions, revealing that one hundred thousand mustangs in Nevada alone had been captured in the eight years after World War II. "Most of them were trucked out of the mountains to West Coast chicken feed processors and dog and cat food canneries where they were sold for about six cents a pound."[2]

O'Brien judiciously presented the BLM's point of view: "One mustang eats 25 pounds of grass a day—enough to feed one cow or five sheep; moreover, the wild horses broke down fencing and ran cattle away from water holes." But his provocative portrayal of the roundup methods left no doubt about whose side he favored. O'Brien described the practice of lassoing fleeing horses with ropes tied to tires, then allowing them to run until they staggered with exhaustion. He quoted Vern Wood, a photographer from Rawlins, Wyoming, who had witnessed what happened after a roundup. "The men were roping stallions and slitting their nostrils with pocketknives then sticking baling wire through the slits and twisting it tight so the horses couldn't get enough air to make a break for freedom."

Finally O'Brien introduced the savior. "The most tireless, outspoken friend the mustang ever had is Mrs. Velma B. Johnston, of the Double Lazy Heart Ranch, Wadsworth, Nevada. She stands five foot six in her high-heeled riding boots and weighs a spunky 108 pounds. But her diminutive size has not kept her from waging a bitter battle for the country's mustangs—so bitter, in fact, that friends and opponents now refer to her as 'Wild Horse Annie.' 'I was born on a horse. I love horses, tame or wild. . . . We are trying to prevent another brutal mass extermination. Those animals that are left must be protected before it is too late.'"3

Velma couldn't have wished for a more fulsome endorsement. "But Annie and her friends have a long, rocky ride through state and federal legislatures before the mustangs are saved," O'Brien concluded. "The latest Department of Interior report estimates that there are only 20,000 wild horses roaming the ranges where once there were millions." The day the issue hit the newsstands Velma rushed out and bought twenty copies.

After the *Reader's Digest* story appeared, the flow of incoming correspondence became a torrent. Letters arrived from all over the United States, Canada, and Mexico, from Germany and even Norway. Many bore no address other than "Wild Horse Annie, Nevada." One was inscribed to "Annie Who Loves Horses, USA," and another to "Mustang Annie, somewhere in Nevada." Velma answered every correspondent, carefully storing the carbon copies.

"Dear Tex, (my fellow crusader)," she wrote to Gladding on December 9. "Greetings from me, wallowing neck-deep in letters from all over the United States. If you are getting as many as I am, you are about waist-deep, because you are taller than I am. . . . Without exception each letter contains offers of help, and Tex, I know this time we will make it. When the hearts of the American people are touched, as they have been by O'Brien's article, they respond with a will and a might that will carry our legislation along.

"I am setting up a 3 x 5 inch card file with the name, address and comments, of every person who has offered to help us. That is for use when we send the final letter instructing the people to write to their delegation in Washington and urge their support of the bill.

"Now this is what I want you to do. You probably don't have the time to answer all your letters, so will you either make a list of the names and addresses, with proper comment, such as juvenile, teenager, nature of offer (such as political connections, riding group affiliations, etc.) and send it to me, so I can make up cards; or type the information on cards for me. Either way that is easier for you. This should include the names of all the people who have offered to help prior to this article too. Tex, if you don't have the time to send me the names of the people who have written to you, would you like to loan me the letters so that I can do it? Now is the time for us to move in—or never."[4]

While Velma was basking in the sudden national and international attention, the pages of Nevada's newspapers were largely empty of any mention of the mustang issue or Wild Horse Annie, not entirely surprising since Nevada was heavily dependent on ranching and was the hub of the wild horse trade. And with most of the Silver State's land under federal control, any change in the status of that land would have a significantly greater impact there than elsewhere in America. Still, the silence of her home state press rankled. "The local newspapers are probably saving any space they might allot to me to be used for my obituary, instead of devoting a couple of columns now when I could really use it," she complained to Gladding.[5]

"I have an expert [Mark Shipley] working on drawing up the bill to present in Washington, and shall submit it to you for your approval before I send it on. It will carry provision for all future control of the animals, for as this person mentioned to me, maybe ten or fifteen years from now there will be no Tex or Velma, and the exploiters will use over-abundance of the animals as an excuse to resume their mass slaughters."[6]

It was in 1957, too, that one of Velma's few childhood friends, Walter Baring, reentered her life. Now a Democratic congressman, Baring dropped in at the office one day and offered to sponsor a bill to protect wild horses and burros from airborne roundups on federal public land. He suggested to a surprised and delighted Velma that they aim to introduce new legislation in 1959, giving them more than a year to prepare.

Baring was a quixotic Democrat in a state that consistently voted Republican. The bearlike, 250-pounder began his political career as the most liberal of Democrats, but after failing to be reelected following his first two terms in Congress he successfully reinvented himself as a Dixiecrat. Baring was a self-styled maverick, as many Nevada politicians seemed to be, trumpeting his dislike of fellow Democrats John F. Kennedy and Lyndon Johnson and disparaging ethnic minorities, foreign aid, and socialists—all views widely shared in Nevada. "I don't think he believed most of the things he said himself," said Senator Howard Cannon, who lost to Baring in the 1956 congressional primary, then went on to serve as a Democratic U.S. senator from 1958 to 1963. Baring's stock retort to criticism was, "Nobody likes Walter Baring but the voters." And he was right: They reelected him to ten nonconsecutive terms in the House of Representatives between 1948 and 1972.[7]

Childhood friendship aside, Baring was an unlikely supporter of Velma's crusade. He had no interest in nascent conservation efforts, then focused mainly on America's national parks and waterways, and he was closely tied to the ranching lobby. Supporting Velma certainly wouldn't curry favor with the local media, as they were studiously ignoring the issue. However, Baring had an enviable reputation, at least among other politicians, for getting on the right side of issues that would eventually garner publicity and public support. And was rather good at dropping out of the picture quickly when the tide of opinion turned.

Velma also drew in Baring's former opponent Howard Cannon, who later played a crucial role in the passage of the Civil Rights Act of 1964, making him and Baring odd political bedfellows. Cannon's hobby was breaking wild horses and training them to work cattle. His involvement was a godsend to Velma, who needed not only animal-loving bleeding hearts but also those who had practical experience with the utility of mustangs.

"Can you imagine my mixed-up politics?" she wrote to a friend. "I'm a registered Democrat to help Congressman Baring in the primaries, for that is always where he needs it. . . . But Jim [Slattery] is a Republican, and I can't help him until General [state] elections—so I campaign for him with my Republican friends. Out here where we are so few that we practically live in our candidate's hip pockets, politics can get quite complicated."[8]

Velma remained a staunch Republican and later an admirer of California governor Ronald Reagan, yet she made political friends of partisans from left and right. "I have quite a time with my Republican state senator and my Democratic congressman," Velma admitted in a letter to Walter Baring's administrative assistant, "but don't worry. I square it with myself by saying I take the best from both teams."[9]

Velma peppered Baring with correspondence, reporting the smallest details of her efforts to ensure that he remained attentive to the cause. "Believe me, Walter; we here are laying a foundation that will be so strong I know we will go through. As a result of the article Mr. O'Brien wrote, I am sinking in a sea of letters from all walks of life and from all over the United States, and without exception, they urge the passage of legislation for the mustangs and offer help. While I realize that legislation is not always passed just because people want it to be, nevertheless when the hearts of the American people are stirred . . . their strength is a mighty thing."[10]

As 1957 drew to a close, there seemed almost too many avenues to explore. But Velma did not want to repeat the mistake of 1955 when little discernible support resulted in weak legislation. Velma needed more grassroots reinforcement and more irrefutable facts. On December 11, she reported to Baring,

This is what I have done on this end in the past two weeks:

1. I am answering each letter as it comes in, for they all contain offers of help, and I am instructing each writer to contact his or her Senators and Representatives and urge their support of the bill when it is introduced.

2. I am setting up a card file of the names and addresses of everyone who has offered to help, and at such time as the bill is introduced, will contact them again and set forth the name and number of the bill and ask them to write Washington again.

3. I have written to Edward D. Gladding and asked him to talk with Alan Bible [a Democratic U.S. senator] in the hope that the measure would be sponsored jointly by the House and Senate.

4. I have an expert on range management working on a rough draft of what we want the bill to contain. I do not feel that any legislation should be endorsed that would work a hardship on the cattle or sheep men, and that is why I have asked someone to do the job who is familiar with range conditions.

5. I have arranged with one of the most active horsemen in the State to work with the riding groups and have them prepare resolutions as organizations, and the members write as individuals, backing this legislation.

6. I am encouraging newspaper publicity, and in my statements to the press, I say that "I am advising everyone who wishes to help to contact his Senators and Representatives in Washington. (Incidentally the local press, as usual, has maintained a discreet silence in this interesting matter.)"

‣ This is what I shall begin doing right away:

1. I shall write to the editor of the *National Humane Review* and ask him to publish an article in his magazine instructing its readers to write to their delegation in Washington. I shall also ask the National President of the Humane Society to contact the State organizations and have them get the information out.
2. I shall write to Robert O'Brien and see if he will send me the facts and figures he obtained for his article.
3. I shall begin the preparation of a folio, in which I shall include the past history of the legislation, from its inception as a resolution by the County Commissioners of Storey County outlawing the practice of planing in that County, through the State legislation, and its abuses since the law was passed.
4. I shall obtain pictures and eyewitness stories.

Will you please tell me what else I should be doing?"[11]

The international editions of *Reader's Digest* picked up "The Mustangs' Last Stand," and wire service reports spread the Wild Horse Annie story even farther. The resulting blizzard of letters filled every available shelf, drawer, and storage area at the Double Lazy Heart, invaded Trudy's Washington Street house, and overflowed Velma's desk at the office.

A sergeant of the British armed forces' Black Watch Regiment stationed in Cyprus wrote a lengthy, enthusiastic letter ending with, "More power to your elbow."[12] Another arrived from a missionary in the Belgian Congo who "had fondest memories of his younger days riding on the prairies of our Western country."[13] Velma was particularly tickled to receive a letter from a man who identified himself as a chief of the Sioux Indians. After praising her efforts to save the mustangs, he offered help of a more tangible nature. "Oh, girl, if I could have been there with a good band of Sioux warriors, armed with .30-.30 rifles we would have killed us some two-legged skunks."[14]

———

To HELP VELMA handle the deluge, Trudy learned to type and friends from Executive Secretaries, Inc., were pressed into service. She insisted that not a single note go unanswered, including a number from Spain and France that she had translated.

Federal legislation couldn't happen quickly enough for Velma. In the two years since passage of the Nevada law, the number of permits issued by the BLM for roundups on federal land in the state had actually increased and the mustangers had become more brazen. At eight o'clock on a Saturday evening in the first week of January 1958, one of Velma's outlanders called with word that a shipment of mustangs was being trucked to a distribution point less than four miles from the Double Lazy Heart.

Early the next morning, she and Charlie drove east along the canal road to the Wilson Ranch, where they found mustangs in a clearly visible corral, just off the public road near a house. There were thirty frightened horses tightly confined in the small corral with about forty more in an adjoining field. A large livestock trailer sat waiting. When they were close enough, Charlie boosted Velma up to the roof of the car and stood guard, his hand lingering near the .38 on his hip, while she snapped photos.

Three men near the corral scuttled into the house when Velma brought out her camera. Once she finished taking pictures, she and Charlie drove up to the house and banged on the door until the men emerged. When questioned, they declared they had a BLM permit and the whole thing was legitimate. Monday morning, Velma was waiting at the BLM office before it opened. She wasn't surprised to discover that no permit had been issued. But by the time Velma returned to the ranch with a couple of deputy sheriffs in tow, "the horse-meat merchants" had disappeared and the horses were gone.

Velma could hardly contain herself. "With this tossing of the ball back and forth, by the time checks can be made with the BLM, the operators have ceased to operate," she wrote to Baring. "Because there is so much wasteland in Nevada, catching the operators in the act is like looking for a needle in a haystack. There's simply nothing that can be done unless the slimy characters are caught in the act . . . there are too many loopholes, and too much time-consuming run-around, during which interval the operators can thumb their noses at us, and be on their way."[15]

All through 1958 expressions of support came in, many from organizations that had previously been aloof. Most critically, a number of humane societies stepped forward, the most important being the Los Angeles Society for the Prevention of Cruelty to Animals, one of the best organized and best funded in the country. Ernest Swift, the executive director of the National Wildlife Federation in Washington, D.C., wrote of the mustang hunts that he was "repulsed by such inhumane practices." Velma was particularly pleased when Christine Stevens, the influential secretary-treasurer of the Society for Animal Protective Legislation, offered her assistance. Dozens of special-interest magazines and women's associations, and hundreds of horsemen's associations, including the Rodeo Cowboy's Association, published helpful notices and editorials in their newsletters and bulletins. "To date, no one has offered a single discordant note to my symphony, but I'm not fooling myself that it will always be smooth sailing," she wrote to Baring.[16]

In the late 1950s Velma began to display a sense of ownership over the campaign for a federal bill, referring to it as "my bill," "my campaign," "my mustangs," "this project of mine," and "my symphony," though she was careful to characterize it as "our bill" in communications with Tex Gladding.[17] And she invariably flattered and deferred to Walter Baring, her point man in Congress.

"Please straighten me out, Walter, if I am going at this all wrong," she asked in one way or another in each of her voluminous reports. "We in Nevada should get down on our knees and thank you for holding the line there as you are doing. You have become the most immensely popular man of the day in all the circles in which I travel. On a half hour radio program over KOH each evening, where the public is allowed to call in comments and subjects for discussion over the telephone, the subject is almost completely confined to Walter Baring's merits."[18]

Velma intensified her public relations efforts with the press, bypassing writers and contacting publishers and editors directly. She bombarded them with letters, photographs, and information. When journalists came to Nevada, she spent hours indoctrinating them with her views about wild horses and public land issues. Many stayed at the Double Lazy Heart, and by the time Velma was finished with them, they left as disciples.

Early in January 1958, freelance writer Louise Huhne, accompanied by a photographer identified only as Frits, arrived from Holland to research a magazine feature that they intended to place first in the Netherlands and then all over Europe.[19] They stayed for a week at the Double Lazy Heart and Velma drove them to Virginia City to meet and interview Tex Gladding and Bill Marks. When they couldn't locate any wild horses in the vicinity of Virginia City, she arranged for a pilot and plane.

Frits insisted on a photo session with Wild Horse Annie and Hobo. "Thought it would only be a short session but it lasted two and a half hours, and although the sun was shining, it was quite chilly and I fully expected to catch pneumonia."[20] The picture is a rare one of Velma in the saddle. Hobo is rearing, with his head thrown back, his mouth open against the pressure of the bit, its silver shanks glinting in the sun. With the white of his eye and teeth showing and his winter coat thick, he looks like a recently broke mustang ready to explode. Velma, dressed in stylish western garb, sits deep in the saddle, confidently in control. Just visible are the stars on the silver spurs Charlie bought to match the bridle he gave her shortly after they moved into the Double Lazy Heart. Velma's face looks oddly narrow, with shadow concealing her bad side.

Huhne's article, titled "Scoundrels, Horses and One Woman," appeared in the Dutch magazine *Revue* in December 1958. She cast the mustang campaign as an epic Velma versus Goliath struggle and depicted the heroine just as Velma had hoped. "The horse butchers don't have any more 'Free Play.' Call the name 'Wild Horse Annie' and they run like sheep from the wolf."[21]

*Velma on Hobo for* Revue

Velma and Charlie extended themselves for their Dutch visitors, but Velma felt they'd fallen short of their usual hospitality standards. "Through the years, Charles and I have tried to establish a 'way of life' out there in the country, and it seems to have worked out, for many people have found it a happy place to be. Because of Charlie's health, we were not able to operate as smoothly as we would liked to have, but believe me, dear Louise, we were so happy to have you there with us. Being a native daughter, I am rather proud of Nevada, and am anxious to share its better points with visitors. When Charles was well, we were able to do it up real fine."[22]

Like many of the writers who met and wrote about Velma, Huhne carried on a warm correspondence with her for years afterward. Robert O'Brien fed her information from his research and provided details of the feedback received by *Reader's Digest*. After he sent her a list of names, she wrote, "Be assured, I shall treat its contents in strictest confidence . . . I have been well trained and most of my jobs have been of a confidential nature."[23]

There was gathering support for Velma's campaign to protect wild horses but there was no national, or even local, organization to assume the administrative or financial burden. Despite occasional unsolicited donations, the cost of paper, typewriter ribbons, Gestetner copies, carbon paper, postage, and telephone calls had begun to strain Velma and Charlie's limited resources. Velma was marshaling a sympathetic army, but it was one with few foot soldiers and not much cash. Fortunately, as the movement gained momentum and greater exposure, Gordon Harris's attitude softened and he offered to cover her telephone and long-distance charges. He also allowed Velma to borrow "an hour or two between 9 and 5 to meet a crisis," and refrained from commenting when his "post office box is more often than not fuller of Wild Horse Annie's mail than his own."[24]

Wielding her typewriter like a machine gun, Velma fired off round after round of correspondence. In one week in May 1958, she typed 143 pages in addition to her regular office workload, no small feat on a manual typewriter. Walter Baring sometimes received two letters a day, each as much as six single-spaced pages in length.

Baring intended to sponsor the bill, HR 2725, but he wanted Velma to make the main presentation to the congressional committee that would conduct the legislative hearings. Though she continued to claim she'd "rather take a beating than speak in public," Velma had become much more comfortable before an audience and could easily hold the attention of listeners with her distinctive voice, dramatic story, and obvious passion. Small groups like horsemen's clubs, pony clubs, women's societies, and libraries frequently asked her to talk about wild horses, and she rarely refused. "I am as bad as a politician, I guess," she admitted to Robert O'Brien.[25]

Velma began working on her presentation to the Committee on the Judiciary early in 1958. The committee members were to receive a copy of her remarks and a package of photographs in advance of her appearance. Distilling seven years of research, her interviews with ranchers, and her own experiences into a one-hour speech that would make the maximum impact on her listeners with the minimum amount of "womanly emotion" was no easy task. She wrote and revised, then rewrote and revised again. To ease the load, Velma thought of paying someone else to type up the final thirty-three-page document but was aghast at the quoted rate of $3.50 an hour. "Things have changed since I used to do typing for others, I find. So I set last weekend aside and did it myself. I am glad I did, though, for now it is just the way I wanted it."[26]

On February 28 Velma anxiously sent Baring the final draft, along with six pictures of the horse roundup taken by Gus Bundy, the photos she had first seen in Charles Richards's files. Baring distributed copies to the members of the committee.

In the background, behind the whirlwind that had become Velma's life, was Charlie. His health faltered again in early spring and he was forced to spend restless days in his chair by the fire, unable to tackle the ranch work. "We are only now having our terrible weather that should have been over with by the first of April. It has snowed almost every day for the past month, and the wind has blown very hard, causing quite a bit of minor destruction," Velma wrote to Louise Huhne. "Charles is still house-bound, and we are eagerly looking forward to when we can be outdoors in the garden. I know he will feel better then. He has such depressed feelings, and I am sorry for him. It must be difficult for an active person to have to be still."[27]

Velma no longer referred to the wild horse campaign as their joint campaign. "I think you and I can consider ourselves fortunate in having such understanding people as Marion and Charles for wife and husband," she wrote to Tex Gladding. "For surely these mustangs take up a great deal of our time. They are to be commended for being so patient."[28] Charlie slipped from the position of confidant, co-conspirator, and partner to that of understanding bystander.

Though the family could see for themselves that Charlie was ailing, they had no idea of the severity of his condition. The number of children's visits to the Double Lazy Heart dwindled and the elaborate theme parties Velma loved to organize and host were a thing of the past. But in personal letters there's no hint of regret for the loss of those simpler days. Instead, an undercurrent of exhilaration runs through her correspondence, the eager anticipation of taking her fight to the national stage.

In June 1958 a long-awaited, and several times postponed, article appeared in *True* magazine. Velma, who had been corresponding with the editor for nearly two years, had written a six-thousand-word story to be accompanied by Gus Bundy's photographs. *True,* while not as broadly influential generally as *Reader's Digest,* was popular among ranchers, cowboys, fishermen, hunters, and male Republicans who constituted the majority of its subscribers. *True* reduced Velma's six thousand words to half a dozen paragraphs but she didn't care: The magazine had embraced her cause. "One of the most outspoken members of the opposition is a hardy little ranch wife named Velma Johnston—who also gets credit for calling the story to *True*'s attention. Her efforts to protect the mustang were—and are—so intense that friends and enemies alike now refer to her as Wild Horse Annie."

The article quoted the Utah Fish and Game Department: "Large herds have been killed on the range and left lying there. Many have been made use of by shipping them to canning centers where they have been prepared as food for small animals and one plant under government supervision has canned them for human consumption in some foreign lands." *True* laid blame for the "slaughter" squarely on the federal government and specifically the Bureau of Land Management. "Strangest of all, the U.S. Government—which controls the federal lands where many of the horses are to be found—has no laws for the protection of wild horses. . . . In fact, in 1945 the Bureau of Land Management was paying trappers $3 a head to round up mavericks in Wyoming and remove them from the range. However, unless new legislation is enacted on both levels of government, there soon won't be any mustangs left in America to worry about."[29] Over the years *True* had published numerous stories glorifying wild horse roundups. To have it reverse its editorial position by endorsing protection and federal legislation was extraordinary.

Equally crucial was the active support of Christine Stevens and the Society for Animal Protective Legislation, which had been instrumental in the passage of PL 85-765, the humane slaughter law. Stevens sent out a powerfully worded call for action, buttressed by Gus Bundy's photographs, to her large and well-heeled membership. After detailing the horrors of nose threading with barbed wire and describing "pathetic colts left behind to starve to death when their mothers are carted away," she urged readers to contact Emanuel Celler, chairman of the Committee on the Judiciary. "Ask him to do all in his power to obtain favorable reports from his committee on HR 2725. Then write to as many other members of the committee as you can. Be sure to write to any in your own state. Urge them to act *now* before it is too late to save the last mustangs."[30]

———

WHEN IT CAME to protecting her "wild ones," Velma could be heedless of others' concerns and willfully high-handed in furthering her goals. This tendency sometimes showed up in her dealings with the young men who were her outlanders, but the most egregious example was her treatment of Gus Bundy.

Bundy was a painter, sculptor, writer, and photographer born in New York in 1907. He had traveled the world extensively before settling with his pregnant wife in the Washoe Valley of Nevada, just south of Reno, in 1941, because they believed Nevada would be a better place than New York to raise children.

To supplement their modest income from selling eggs and the occasional photograph, the Bundys operated a guest ranch to accommodate those waiting out Nevada's six-month residency requirement for divorce. There were dozens of so-called divorce ranches all over Nevada, many of them offering luxury accommodation, fine food, entertainment, and a Wild West experience complete with rodeos and cattle roundups. The Bundy Ranch was strictly no frills, with four basic apartments and little to do but relax or explore the spectacular desert. If guests were interested, Bundy led them on hikes to sketch, paint, or snap photos.

During his four decades in Nevada, Gus Bundy wandered all over the state taking tens of thousands of photographs. The majority were landscapes, but he was also interested in wildlife and people and on his outings with guests he would point out mustang herds if they were lucky enough to encounter them. In September 1951, *Life* magazine photojournalist Bud Gourley checked in to the Bundy Ranch to wait out his residency period. Bundy told him about the mustang herds in the area and the roundups he had observed. Gourley sensed a great photo story opportunity and soon he and Bundy, recruited to be the driver, found themselves in the middle of a hunt. The mustangers allowed them to observe the chase but confiscated Gourley's camera. They didn't notice that Bundy had his hidden in his lap. While he raced to keep up in the dusty wake of the mustangers' truck, Bundy managed to take some two hundred fifty shots capturing the most raw and vivid depictions of an airplane-assisted wild horse roundup ever recorded. They are easily among the greatest action news photographs of the twentieth century. Bundy was a skilled photographer but not much of a businessman or self-promoter. A selection of his wild horse photos appeared first in a short-lived Reno magazine called *Pace* in 1952 and then in the *National Humane Review* in 1953.

Velma coveted the photographs from the moment Charles Richards showed them to her in 1953. She realized how powerful they would be in convincing people, especially the media, of the righteousness of her cause. She had tried numerous times to take her own photos, but none turned out well enough to be useful. In 1956, Velma and Charlie visited Bundy at his ranch and viewed his negatives, but could afford to purchase only three prints that Bundy made for them. Bundy was happy to share his work for a good cause. He and his wife had recently become involved in the fledgling environmental and animal protection movements and had joined eighteen others to found the Toiyabe Sierra Club, covering Nevada and northern California. Later, he agreed to allow Velma to use his photographs in her presentation to the House Judiciary Committee.

Velma's early relationship with Bundy was friendly, though she considered him "a bit mercenary."[31] In 1957, while corresponding with *True,* she functioned almost as his agent. But she became annoyed when she found out that Bundy had been paid much more than the $250 she had received for the story, even though she admitted she was strictly an amateur writer. "In talking with him over the telephone last week, he informed me that he had just received a check from *True* for $500 for the supporting pictures. I feel that the pictures are quite important to my story, and are certainly well done, but I had hoped I would be equally reimbursed,"[32] she wrote to *True*'s associate editor, H. M. Mason, Jr.

At Velma's request, Mason sent prints of the twenty-one pictures Bundy had submitted to illustrate the story and Velma had negatives made of six from the graphic chase sequence. She then used the negatives to make dozens of prints, which she freely distributed to various magazines and newspapers as part of press kits or to accompany stories that carried her byline. For instance, the article in the February 21, 1957, edition of the *Sacramento Bee* about Wild Horse Annie was illustrated with photos of the chase sequence given to them by Velma but credited to Bee Photos, the newspaper's own photo service. Apparently Bundy was unaware of their publication, as there was no mention of it in his subsequent correspondence.

Velma sent out many more copies of Bundy's pictures over the next eighteen months, but by April 1958 she seemed to have become concerned about the possible repercussions of what she was doing. "You are aware that publicity for my project is what will carry it to a successful conclusion, and naturally I would like to help all interested outlets in any way I can," she wrote to H. M. Mason at *True*. "What arrangements should the news organizations make, either with you or Mr. Bundy, to use those particular six photographs? They are most anxious not to get into trouble with either the photographer or you people, and do not wish to violate any copyright laws, nor do I. However I would like to make the six photographs, which I consider outstandingly descriptive of the exploitation pattern, available to them for copyrights in various parts of the world, and especially Europe. I have not yet contacted Mr. Bundy, for I feel that I should first talk with you, and I am terribly ignorant of procedures in a case like this."[33]

Mason, an admirer of Velma's efforts, wrote back a few days later. "You may feel free to use Mr. Bundy's photographs in any way you wish in Europe and other parts of the world."[34] Velma had been dealing with newspapers and magazines long enough to know that Mason's blanket assurance was, at best, dubious. Photographers have always been very protective of their rights, and at the time, reproduction rights were customarily sold for one-time use only. Velma's own contract with *True* stated that while the magazine retained some reprint rights, "sixty days after publication by Fawcett Publications, Inc., it will reassign to the author upon written request all rights to the said work."[35] Even if Mason had been correct about the rights to the photos, an acknowl-edgment of Bundy's creative ownership should have been included— also something Velma must have understood.

Instead, she took Mason's words as carte blanche and sent copies of the pictures to Louise Huhne, who wrote a second story about wild horses that she expected to syndicate across Europe. Velma continued to include the photographs with the press releases she sent through-out 1958.

In October 1958, Tom McKnight, an assistant professor of geogra-phy at the University of California, Los Angeles, wrote to Velma ask-ing for her help in an article he was writing for a scholarly journal. He asked her for "photos of wild horses, of horse-catching equipments (airplanes, riders, corrals, etc.) and of caught horses."[36] Velma read-ily offered up Bundy's pictures, but didn't tell McKnight their source. Instead she used them as a bargaining chip. "I can certainly appreciate your concern as to the emphasis of my article," McKnight assured her. "I intend to write it from a dispassionate viewpoint. However, to make sure that we have a clear understanding, I suggest that we proceed as follows: when my article is completed (perhaps within two weeks), I will send it to you for reading. If it meets with your approval, you can send me the prints at that time. And, of course, I will be glad to reim-burse you. If the slant of the article is not to your liking, we can forget the whole thing. O.K.?"[37]

"The Feral Horse in North America" appeared in the October 1959 issue of the *Geographical Review*. Ironically, McKnight procured several photos directly from Gus Bundy, which he credited properly; but the other photos were credited to Velma Johnston. Bundy saw the publica-tion and fired off a letter of complaint to McKnight and Velma.

Though only peripherally at fault, McKnight gallantly took all the blame—another man brought under Velma's spell. "I would feel very badly if you requested an apology from Mrs. Johnston in this case," McKnight wrote to Bundy. "I am more at fault than she. Perhaps I should have recognized your handiwork in the photos she sent me, or at least I should have traced their source more efficiently before assigning credits."[38]

Bundy didn't let Velma off the hook. "As you can see by the copy sent to you of the letter written to me by Tom McKnight, he was most generous and thoughtful of you concerning your oversight," Bundy wrote to Velma at the end of November. "However he was very clear concerning the fact that no request was made to have credit given to the author of the negatives with which you have been entrusted. Should you have been interested in avoiding any misunderstanding over the authorship of the photos, all that was necessary was for you to include the words 'Photo Credit of Gus Bundy.' Otherwise . . . authorship will be assumed to be that of the sender of the photos.

"It will be perfectly satisfactory to me to have you discontinue using my photos and to make use of the ones you say you have taken if this procedure is simpler for you. Please remember that I am a professional photographer and that giving up the income from the photos entrusted to you was no slight matter. Please be content with this and give basic consideration to credits for photos. I trust that we will have no further misunderstanding from either of us."[39]

If Bundy had been paid for the photographs Velma gave away, he would likely have earned an additional thousand dollars in 1958, a significant sum, particularly for the cash-strapped Bundy family. Although known as a "contentious" man inclined to get into squabbles with others, Bundy was surprisingly restrained with Velma, even generous in his lack of specific accusation, though he must have been suspicious that she was intentionally cutting him out of both credit and payment.

Velma wasn't about to admit to the slightest error. "I received the carbon copy of Mr. Bundy's letter to you," she responded to McKnight. "He apparently refers to the statement (Photograph courtesy of Mrs. Velma Johnston) beneath two of the pictures. I do not interpret it as meaning that I was the photographer and am disturbed that anyone else might. There has been no desire for personal glory on my part, and certainly no desire for credit that was not earned by me. The photographs which were given to me have been furnished only to those whom I thought might assist the passage of legislation through greater circulation of their publications. . . . You are very gracious and I think too much has been made of it by Mr. Bundy."[40]

---

AT THE FIRST session of the Eighty-sixth Congress on January 19, 1959, Walter Baring introduced HR 2725, "To amend chapter 3 or title 18, United States Code, so as to prohibit the use of aircraft or motor vehicles to hunt certain wild horses or burros on land belonging to the United States, and for other purposes."[41] The act would also ban the polluting of water holes for the purpose of trapping any wild animals, horses included. Congress referred it to the House Judiciary Committee for study and hearings. It was the triumphant first step on the road to a federal bill, but Velma, exhausted by the exertions of lobbying, was in no condition to enjoy it.

"For the past three weeks, I have been on the verge of pneumonia and the most concentrated efforts of the newest antibiotics have failed to get rid of the bugs completely. I have to go Tuesday for chest x-rays, and have been feeling pretty miserable and shaky, besides looking like death. I was a sitting duck for acquiring a germ, though, because the week before I became ill, I had put in twenty-two hours of typing, outside my five days work week in the office, attended two night meetings, one until after midnight, and two business luncheons. I can't conk out now; there is too much to be done."[42]

By May 1959 the bill was attracting considerable national attention. "The volume of mail which I have received on this subject," wrote John E. Henderson, an Ohio Republican and a member of the House Judiciary Committee, to his constituents, "in comparison with the number of letters which we receive on many measures which seem to have more world shaking importance, confirms my belief that Americans are unselfish and have a soft spot in their hearts for the animal kingdom."[43]

Congressman James C. Wright, another influential member of Congress and later Speaker of the House, reported to his constituents that a group of children had brought him a petition. "Imagine making dog food out of horses. We feed the birds . . . the squirrels and the chipmunks to save them! Let's see what we can do about saving the beautiful Wild Horses!

"Am I going to be susceptible to pressure?" Wright wrote. "Am I going to be influenced by a bunch of children? Am I going to support Baring's bill because kids are sentimental about wild horses? You bet your cowboy boots I am."[44] Walter Baring gleefully informed Velma that his colleagues in Washington were astounded at the public groundswell for the wild horse bill.

When she recovered her strength, Velma went to San Francisco for a round of television, print, and radio appearances, including interviews with the major wire services. By June the prospects looked very positive for HR 2725. Senator Mike Mansfield, Democratic leader in the Senate, had agreed to sponsor the bill in that chamber with Howard Cannon. Velma made plans to fly to Washington during the week of July 22 to testify before the House Judiciary Committee.

Then, on April 14, Royale Pierson, a range officer from BLM headquarters in Washington, and Ernest J. Palmer, the supervisor of the Reno office, paid her a visit at work. It was the first time in seven years

*Velma, a studio-retouched photograph, late 1950s*

of dealing with the BLM that any official had asked for a meeting with her. They passed two hours in amiable discussion, during which the BLM officials seemed "to agree with me on many points," she reported to Baring.[45]

The duo from the BLM told Velma that they thought that "really good legislation is the legislation that comes of both sides talking the thing out, and coming up with something mutually beneficial."[46] Velma felt the same way. However, they went on to complain that the proposed bill, which outlawed the use of airplanes and helicopters in rounding up wild horses, was too strict and would hamper range maintenance, which sometimes required that wild horses be moved from one grazing area to another. But this was the whole point as far as Velma was concerned. "Since *control* and not *clearance* is now the object, mechanized and air roundups should not be necessary if an efficient supervision program is planned and carried out."[47]

Despite their collegial tone, Velma suspected that the BLM officials wanted to weaken the bill with a Trojan horse amendment, one that appeared innocuous but could be used to circumvent the main provisions. A few days later, when Ernest Palmer called to arrange a follow-up meeting, she agreed on condition that she could bring her personal lawyer, Oliver Custer, with her. "I do not intend to give up any ground, and the main reason I want Mr. Custer to be present is to avert my walking into a trap," she confided to Baring.

A meeting involving Custer never occurred, but in a subsequent conversation Palmer asked if there was any "possibility of working out something more lenient."[48] Velma suggested he put together an amendment that the BLM could live with and she would take it back to her "colleagues." A few days later the amendment arrived at the office. "Nothing in the Act shall be construed to conflict with the provisions of any Federal law or regulation which permits the Land Management agencies responsible for administration of the public lands to hunt, drive, round up and dispose of horse, mares, colts or burros by means of airborne or motor driven vehicles; but humane measures will be used and all operations will be under strict government supervision."[49]

It was obvious that the BLM's amendment would completely negate the intent of her bill, but Velma had learned some political gamesmanship. Instead of reacting immediately and emotionally, she held back, canvassing Baring, Slattery, Cannon, and Gladding for their opinions. Then she informed Palmer that HR 2725 "must remain as it is without this proposed amendment, because it weakened HR 2725 to the point where it would be of no value and gave too much leeway to the Bureau of Land Management."[50] Furthermore, "My friends who are in this with me here in the West brought out the fact that planes and trucks must be prohibited no matter who wants to use them."[51]

On June 10, she received a letter from Christine Stevens, tartly asking why she was supporting a BLM amendment to HR 2725 . The wording Stevens cited was identical to that proposed by Ernest Palmer in April. Stevens had heard rumors of Velma's capitulation, and when she dropped in on Senator Cannon discovered he'd heard the same rumblings.

Velma fired off letters to Stevens, Cannon, and Baring, hoping to nip the BLM's disinformation campaign—she called it "hogwashing"—in the bud. "I notified Mr. Palmer by letter on April 28, 1959 that HR 2725 must remain as it is, without his proposed amendment. I had hoped to work with the Bureau and that we could come up with something equitable for all, but it was so one-sided that it cannot be considered. Therefore, please be assured that I do not favor the amendment nor do any of the people with whom I am working."[52]

But Velma wasn't able to stop an avalanche of phone calls from various media sources asking for an explanation. The BLM's tactic effectively introduced confusion into the campaign just at the moment when it should have been reaching a crescendo.

As Velma tried desperately to quash the amendment rumors, she finally won the attention of a Nevada newspaper. But it wasn't the kind she was looking for. "The true picture of a wild horse is a runty, moth-eaten, mangy little scrub critter of no value anywhere outside a can," wrote Jock Taylor, editor of the *Reese River Reveille,* on June 17. "He is a curse to the stockman, a nuisance to the big-game hunter and a pain in the neck to the Bureau of Land Management whose job it is to see that the open range is properly apportioned to feed all living animals dependent on it. Getting him out of the picture as far as possible can be likened to a housewife's zeal in getting rid of cockroaches in the kitchen and moths in the clothes closet."[53]

The *Reveille,* though a small paper, was located in the heart of cattle country. It particularly annoyed Velma to be sneeringly lumped in with "easterners" when Taylor knew perfectly well that she spearheaded the movement from Reno. "Eastern humanitarians scream that the wild horses are being wiped out the same as the buffaloes were wiped out nearly a hundred years ago. They are not being wiped out, but they are being 'rationed,' and for the same reason the buffaloes were wiped out. Buffaloes and Kansas, for example, couldn't have grown up together. Neither can wild horses—in unlimited numbers—and Nevada."[54]

Velma took consolation in the wave of endorsements and articles that appeared in periodicals big and small, including the *Washington Evening Star,* the *New York Herald Tribune,* the *Western Horseman,* and *Sierra* magazine. "I understand that even the Shopping News in San Leandro contained a big spread about old Wild Horse herself," she enthused to Walter Baring. "Last week, over a radio program entitled 'Women in the World in the News,' United Press International released the interview I gave one of their reporters in San Francisco in May."[55] The topper was a favorable mention of Baring and the Wild Horse bill in Drew Pearson's "Washington Merry-Go-Round" column. Syndicated in more than five hundred papers, it was the most influential political column in the country.

Velma didn't try to contain her exuberance as her departure for Washington approached. "I am looking forward to all of it like a kid towards Christmas—except for the testimony before the committee. I definitely get heart palpitations when I think about that, but I will do a good job. I have too many people depending on me. . . . I am thrilled about the prospect of the White House tour, and will absolutely not promise to act like an excited tourist. There is so much to see and do," she wrote Baring on July 2.[56]

The same letter contained news at odds with Velma's exuberance: "Excuse the typographical errors, please. I am exhausted and will hit the sack shortly. On top of everything else, we have sold the ranch. . . . It broke our hearts to sell, but Charles is so very ill much of the time that he can't keep up the ranch, and we couldn't bear to see it not look lovely."[57]

# EIGHT

# It's a Hell of a Good Day

W HEN VELMA ARRIVED in Washington on Monday evening, July 13, she stepped off the plane wearing a lilac shirtwaist of shimmery mercerized cotton, neatly cinched with a narrow belt in the same fabric. White pumps and matching bag, a white straw pillbox hat, and wrist-length white gloves borrowed from her friend Ruthie McCord completed the ensemble. In her suitcase she'd packed "a stiff girdle, a can of hairspray and Charlie's .38."

Charlie was sick again, but they couldn't afford his airfare in any case. One of the humane societies had paid for her ticket, but Velma was responsible for all other expenses. She was grateful that Walter Baring and his assistant, Tim Seward, met her at the airport, saving the taxi fare.

Velma intended to spend the day "acclimatizing" before her Wednesday presentation, but Baring swept her through a frenzy of meeting and greeting from breakfast to late evening. She was introduced to politicians and bureaucrats, among them Texas Democratic Representative James C. Wright and Republican John E. Henderson of the House Judiciary Committee, as well as Howard Cannon and Mike Mansfield, the Democratic senators who would cosponsor the bill in the Senate. Washington reporters happily pounced on a story that combined such disparate elements as a middle-aged secretary from Reno, the romance of the frontier, and the fate of wild horses. When Baring presented her at a press conference she was peppered with questions.

"Wild Horse Annie was here at last, and word spread across the capital range like wind whipped fire through sagebrush," wrote Frank Eleazer of United Press International. "Was this the Wild Horse Annie who single-handedly cowed the cowhands, outdrew the gunslingers, and hog-tied the Nevada Legislature in the interest of saving the vanishing Cayuse from the can? It was indeed. It was Wild Horse Annie, the nemesis of the dog food and glue factory moguls, the terror of the burro bootlegger, heroine of the mustang's last stand.

"I buckled on my fountain pen and galloped through the capital canyons to the office of Rep. Walter Baring (D-Nevada) where Annie had agreed to have a few words with a posse of pressmen. I was feeling uneasy about my citified suit and bow tie and the fact that I wasn't packing a gun. Annie, it developed, wasn't holstered up for the rendezvous either.

"I thought for a minute I had fallen into the wrong company. Here was a slim little lady in crisp linen sheath, kind of a blue-green I would say. She wore white pumps with stiletto heels and laid aside white gloves and white bag to shake hands. My 'hiya pardner' died in my throat. 'How do you do, ma'am,' I managed instead."[1]

That evening the organization Defenders of Wildlife held a dinner in Velma's honor. The event signaled important official recognition that the mustang was indeed a wild creature and worthy of protection. This group's approval was doubly significant because Defenders of Wildlife had been created in 1943 to further the science of endangered species protection. Most other animal groups concentrated on the politics of securing that protection. Velma was dazzled by what she referred to as a "star-studded affair" with the leading lights of the humane movement in Washington in attendance, as well as a coterie of politicians from Nevada. When she rose to speak, Velma risked a bit of oratorical parody.

"Because we are here together this evening, it is obvious we all have been exposed to and are afflicted with the same malady—a severe case of mustang fever. It is raging at high temperatures throughout the nation, is highly communicable, not only by exposure to a person already having it but also through the written word. Once having contracted it there is no cure."[2]

Rather than recite the history of wild horse abuse to the converted, Velma took a more personal tack, choosing to "indulge in a luxury against which I have rigidly schooled myself since early in this fight, and that is the luxury of sentimentality. Because it is expected of a woman, I have deliberately avoided it so that I could meet the opposition to our legislation with an objectivity and logic that has commanded respect, if not agreement." Velma's idea of sentimentality was to thank some of the offstage players, everyone from "my beloved executive," to Tex Gladding, to "my husband upon whose strength I've leaned and who has cooked countless meals and swept the floors to give me time to do all that has had to be done." She added a final word of thanks to her physician "who has somehow managed to patch me up, and with a skillful blending of the right proportions of go pills and slow pills, has kept me going."[3]

The next day, Walter Baring stood before the House Judiciary Committee and briefly introduced Velma Johnston of the Double Lazy Heart Ranch as a constituent, a friend, and Wild Horse Annie. "As you know," he deadpanned before the sixteen committee members, "this bill has received the attention of the nation and many of the members have received from hundreds to thousands of letters from their constituents." This elicited chuckles from congressmen whose offices had been inundated by letters of protest against wild horse roundups and support for passage of the bill. Baring uttered a brief prayer on behalf of horses and other animals, then turned the floor over to Velma.

In high heels and with her hair teased into a modest bouffant, Velma looked unusually tall. She was far enough from the half circle of seated committee members that they could not easily discern the disfigurement of her face, but no amount of makeup or artful positioning could entirely disguise the drooping eye or flattened chin and jaw. As she gazed steadily at the row of dark-suited men a tremble passed through her body, but this time it wasn't so much fear as anticipation. Nine years of hard work had brought her to this place and had prepared her to address some of the most powerful men in the nation. It certainly helped that she'd met quite a number of them over the previous two days. When her lips twisted into a smile she found many of them smiling back.

"Mr. Chairman and members of the Committee on the Judiciary," she began, "the fight for the mustang has come a long way in the past few years. From a room in the courthouse in Virginia City, Nevada . . . it has come to the capital of the nation—some 2,200 miles as the crow flies. From a mere handful of fifty or so firm believers in his right of survival, it has come to an awareness throughout the country of his desperate plight, resulting in a mighty plea on his behalf."

Velma traced her personal involvement, starting with the day in 1950 when she saw the mutilated horses in the back of the livestock truck, to the 1955 campaign in Nevada. She then described the cruelties of the mustang hunt, much of it gleaned from her interviews with ranchers and cowboys like Arne Bailey.

The old technique of rounding up horses with crews of hard-riding cowboys was too slow and too costly, so the airborne cowboy came into being. The mustangs are driven at break neck speed by planes from their meager refuge in the rough and barren rimrock onto flatlands or dry lake beds where the chase is taken up by hunters on fast-moving trucks and the mustangs are pursued to exhaustion. Sometimes they are burdened with heavy and terrifying devices which are attached to them by skilful ropers operating from the trucks.

Sometimes they are driven into box canyons from which there is no escape—other times into fan-shaped trapping corrals where the violent contact with the enclosing wires caused serious and painful injuries, occasionally resulting in death from loss of blood.

The horses are sometimes tied and left where they lie until sufficient are driven in to begin loading operations. Sidelining is one method of tying—a front and hind foot are tied together, and when the horse fights, because he will fight his confinement savagely, the legs are rope-burned until there is no hide left on them. To load them they are dragged up a ramp by saddle horses, in any position which the mustang drags best. Colts are left behind because they don't weigh enough to warrant their long haul to the processing centers. They have little chance of survival.

The requirements of the market are simple: the animals must be ambulatory and in quantity. The suppliers are paid by the pound—thus the more horses, the more money. Crowded into trucks for the long haul, loaded without regard to size, fighting as they will for release from their confinement, casualties are numerous and their condition reflects the roughness of their treatment.

What the officials have failed to take into account is the fact that the humane aspect has been completely disregarded and the public would have much preferred to have had necessary range clearance carried on at a price, provided it had been properly supervised, humanely carried out and intelligently planned.[4]

Velma then systematically dismantled any argument the BLM might make in favor of its amendment exempting the Bureau from its provisions. As she spoke, the committee members paged through Velma's report and studied Gus Bundy's wrenching photographs. "Our congressmen were visibly appalled," noted Ed Koterba, a reporter for United Feature Syndicate.[5] After almost two hours before the committee, Velma had made her case.

Then it was the BLM's turn. Gerald Kerr, a range officer based in Washington, argued for the agency's amendment. He assured committee members that the BLM believed there was "no need . . . nor intent to exterminate" wild horses. He portrayed the Bureau's range clearance operation as a benign housekeeping exercise. "The horses now described as wild are animals that were turned loose or escaped from their owners. This escape or release process is going on constantly. There is a general tendency for the wild herds to increase in numbers from this source and from reproduction. It is the purpose of the Bureau of Land Management to prevent the growth of these herds to such numbers as to provide serious competition with game animals and permitted livestock."

Kerr then repeated the BLM's long-held position that feral horses on public land were not "wild" unless they were proven descendants of the Conquistadores' mounts. "Wild horses, as such, do not exist on public lands today," he stated unequivocally. "The unclaimed and abandoned horses now using the federal ranges are remnants of extensive horse ranch operations which were conducted on the public ranges of the West until the early 1930s."[6] After Kerr spoke, a ten-paragraph supporting statement from Elmer F. Bennett, acting secretary of the interior, was read into the record, but no senior BLM management testified. The hearing took less than a day. The only surprise was the unaccountably weak presentation from the BLM, considering what was at stake.

Velma stayed in Washington for three more days to take in the sights, including tours of the White House and the Smithsonian Institution. Invitations came from all quarters and she felt feted and flattered by the attention. On Sunday, July 19, she returned to Reno, "somewhat the worse for wear" after a week of heavy drinking, parties, and dinners at some of the capital's best restaurants. "Tell Betsy, Jeanine and Nancy [Baring's office staff] that I may have been belle of the ball in Washington while they slaved, but I'm doing likewise as of this morning," she wrote to the congressman on her first day back at work. "Oh, well, such high living could bring on high blood pressure or any number of unpleasant things."[7]

Three days later, on July 23, the House Judiciary Committee voted unanimously to send HR 2725 to Congress. The nine-page report relied heavily on Velma's testimony, with many passages reproduced verbatim. It gave short shrift to the BLM's proposed amendment. "The committee has carefully weighed this suggestion, and has concluded that the amendment cannot be included. The insertion of a proviso of this sort would have the effect of all but destroying the effectiveness of the legislation. Its impact as a criminal statute would be seriously weakened by the fact that the Government would be empowered to engage in the proscribed activities. The provision for similar immunity for those granted federal permits is objectionable for the same reason."[8]

The committee also dismissed the BLM's contention that the mustangs didn't deserve protection unless they were descendants of the first horses introduced to North America. "The Department's view would apparently rule out horses which might be traced to stock which might have been used on ranches or farms in years past," the report noted. "Here again the approach of the Department has all but ignored the purpose of this bill which is to accord protection to any unbranded horse, mare, colt or burro running at large on the public land or ranges.

These horses exist in a wild state. . . . The testimony of Mrs. Johnston adequately shows that the horses existing in the wild have the physical characteristics and qualities which have long been associated with the horse known as the mustang. There should be no problem with identifying the animals entitled to the protection of the new section proposed in the bill."[9]

Over the next week, Velma received seventy-five letters of congratulations and encouragement as well as countless requests for interviews. NBC Hollywood phoned to ask her help in obtaining film footage of an illegal roundup. "Wonder what those people think with?" Velma mused to Walter Baring.[10]

There were few discordant notes in the otherwise perfect "symphony" Velma had orchestrated, then on July 27 *Time* magazine, the largest circulation newsmagazine in North America, credited her with taking the photographs that had illustrated her congressional testimony. A furious Gus Bundy was soon on the telephone complaining to Velma and to *Time*. "I must not have made myself clear to your reporter, Marion Buhagiar," Velma wrote to *Time*'s editor. "The pictures I used to document my evidence were taken by Gus Bundy, a local photographer, who went along on an actual roundup to obtain them . . . I have always been very careful to give Mr. Bundy the credit he deserves for the remarkable photographs."[11] Bundy, far from mollified, was now inclined to view these transgressions as intentional.

Aside from Bundy, there was only one other irritant. "Publicity has been just wonderful everywhere except in Reno," she complained. "I bet if I'd been found out in a juicy marital triangle, or had been discovered cheating at one of the gambling tables, there would have been enough reporters . . . to have covered it thoroughly."[12] Jock Taylor, editor of the *Reese River Reveille,* broke the silence with another wicked editorial scoffing at Wild Horse Annie's efforts to woo softhearted and ignorant easterners. "A foot and a half, no less, on the front page," Velma wrote to Baring. "At first, I thought I'd get Charlie to punch him in the nose, then I got to thinking how perturbed he must really be, and how he must have stewed in his own vitriolic juices to come up with that gem, and the humor of the situation struck me. We must really be gouging him deep! Maybe one of these days I will have the opportunity of getting a first class lady-like job done of putting him in his place."[13]

While Velma waited impatiently for the legislative process to unfold, the number of aerial roundups accelerated as operators set out to capture as many animals as possible while they could still use airplanes. Shortly after her Washington trip, she got wind of a large roundup in the planning stages. The rancher behind it, a woman, justified her actions by saying she intended to scoop up only the unbranded offspring of branded horses who were mingling with the wild herds. Of course, determining which offspring belonged to a branded horse, as opposed to a wild one, would be impossible, especially once the young were weaned.

"Damn these technicalities," Velma fumed to Baring, "as long as the word 'wild' is in the bill, without a definition, there will be this eternal conflict. As you will recall, on page two of my testimony, I have clearly defined mustang and wild horse as I wish the prohibition to apply. Am I tossing you an impossible curve? It is the only other loophole that I am trying to plug. I am certain that the flyboys are going to get every one they can while they can."[14] Baring telephoned to assure her that all such loopholes were plugged.

On August 24, HR 2725 passed both the House and Senate, leaving only the signature of President Eisenhower to make it law. Baring and Howard Cannon sent triumphant wires to Velma, who declared herself "of no earthly use to the insurance business the rest of the day."[15] Velma dashed off dozens of letters in celebration. "Bells are ringing—pulse is racing—stars are blinking on and off," she enthused. "It doesn't seem quite possible that the long, hard fight is nearly over—that an individual can still be heard by his government officials—that bureaucracy is not the Almighty that it thinks it is."[16]

Gordon Harris was the indulgent and admiring boss. "On Wednesday the telephone rang constantly with callers extending their congratulations, and if I did not have such a wonderful executive, I would have had to talk with my fans elsewhere, and on my own time. He is just as proud as can be, though, for he likes and admires a winner. . . . Surely hope Mr. Eisenhower takes care of his signing arm while out of the country!"[17]

President Eisenhower's signing arm was in good form despite a hectic, nine-day European tour, which concluded with the BBC's broadcast of his meeting with British prime minister Harold Macmillan, the first televised discussion between two heads of state. Eisenhower's mission was aimed at stiffening western European resolve in the face of the Soviet Union's increasing belligerence on the world stage. Back at the White House, letters were piling up from horse lovers of every kind, from bank presidents and businessmen, to factory workers and film stars. All were appalled at the slaughter of the wild horses and many incensed that a government agency, the Bureau of Land Management, had been facilitating the kill.

The most powerful pleas came from the children. "I think it is the most cruel inhumane thing I have ever heard of," wrote fifteen-year-old Terry Simmons from Des Moines, Iowa, in a two-page letter to the president. "Think how people would feel if men started killing dogs for money."

"Dear Mr. President," wrote Ellen Kaminski of Haledon, New Jersey. "You may not know me, but I know you. I love horses. If you want to get rid of horses, please send them to me. All of my life I have wanted a horse. Please don't kill the wild horses on the plains. Catch them and train them. Sell them and get money for them. But please don't kill them."[18]

While Europe pondered the possibility of the Soviet Union touching off a third world war, Eisenhower came home to attend to one of the last vestiges of the Old West. On September 8, 1959, he attached the presidential signature to HR 2725, which became Public Law 86–234. The press quickly dubbed it the Wild Horse Annie Law.

"Have you ever wondered how it feels to touch a star?" Velma wrote to Eugene L. Conrotto, editor of *Desert* magazine in Palm Desert, California. "I can pretty well tell you about it now. It is a combination of many things—of exhilaration over the successful accomplishment of a difficult job; of gratitude to all those who have helped to bring it about; of an inability to believe that the long, hard fight is actually over; of great pride in belonging to a country where it is possible to fight for that in which we believe, and to be granted the right to speak for it to the country's lawmakers.

"It is a combination too, of a deep humility for the love and respect that are written into the hundreds upon hundreds of letters that I have received . . . of a sublime belief in the great capacity of the human mind and heart for goodness and compassion when alerted to inequities of any kind; of profound joy, because children, little and big in their many different ways, responded to the dire plight of their animal friends — their letters of support, misspellings and all, are worthy of a special place . . . in the fight to right the wrongs done to those in the animal world; of a peace that comes with knowing that one small part of this earth is a little better for my having lived. How does it feel to touch a star? It feels real good."[19]

On September 12, Velma flew to Boston to receive the prestigious and rarely awarded Angell Memorial Gold Medal from the Massachusetts branch of the Society for the Prevention of Cruelty to Animals for her humanitarian work on behalf of the wild horse. All expenses were picked up by the society, which honored Velma at their annual gala. Velma didn't think anything could match the glow of her trip to Washington in July, but the award was an accolade from people she regarded as her peers, individuals with a broad and knowledgeable interest in animal welfare. An editorial signed by William Loeb, the owner and publisher of the *Manchester Union Leader,* exulted in her victory: "To this newspaper, this is a thrilling story because it represents what can be done where there is a will to succeed . . . Velma Johnston had neither money, fame nor influential friends, but she believed in her cause and her sincerity impressed those who listened to her. So now one of America's last wild resources, the untamed wild horses of the west, belonging to no man, can approach their water holes knowing they will not be poisoned. They can graze in their remote pastures knowing that no airplane will suddenly descend from the skies and hound them into a cannery. All thanks to the woman who was interested in injustice and decided to do something about it."[20]

The Boston trip was a one-day affair; Velma couldn't afford any more time off work. She was exhausted when the plane landed, yet eager to share every moment of the experience with Charlie. A welcoming committee including Gordon Harris, Tracy, and Ruthie met her at the plane. Velma looked around the tarmac, but their Buick

*Velma with Boston Mounted Police, 1959*

wasn't there. Velma finally tracked Charlie down at Saint Mary's Hospital. "He was very ill the day I received the invitation from Boston but did not tell me because he knew I would not go," she told Yvonne Spiegelberg, the U.S. correspondent for *Der Stern*, a popular German weekly newspaper. "He kept up the act until after my departure, then went to the doctor who diagnosed his condition as a severe case of herpes in the eye and head. He waited almost too long to go and the doctors have been battling to save the sight in his left eye and to keep the condition from breaking out on the right as well."[21]

Ocular herpes, like its sexually transmitted cousin, is passed from person to person through a cold sore on the lip or contact with the nose or mouth of an infected person. Though it can remain dormant indefinitely, outbreaks have been traced to stress, fever, dental surgery, or trauma, such as an accident. After years of bronchitis and the recent onset of emphysema, Charlie's weakened immune system offered little resistance to the virus. There was no cure or treatment available, but his doctors suggested an experimental serum. He began to improve, but slowly.

There is a strangely detached tone in the few comments that Velma

*Velma greeted on her return from Boston, 1959*
*(Right to left) Ruthie, Gordon Harris, Velma, Trudy,*
*and two unidentified women*

made to others about the terrifying illness that threatened not only Charlie's eyes but his life. In her fear of losing him, Velma fell back into the old habit of compartmentalizing her days. She had her paid work, her wild horse work, and now the work of taking care of Charlie. There are scant references to him in correspondence during this period. Her explanation of Charlie's condition to the *Der Stern* correspondent, a woman she had never met, is the most informative. Velma had difficulty talking about Charlie's decline with friends or family. None can recall her raising the subject of the advancing emphysema or this latest blow to a once-vigorous man.

Charlie recovered from the eye ailment, but he returned from the hospital considerably weakened. The California businessman who had purchased the Double Lazy Heart in June wanted Velma and Charlie to stay on as caretakers. Through the fall they pretended to each other that things were just as they'd been before, even as the work piled up.

Tom McCord cut the hay and neighbors stepped in to handle other tasks, but to a proud man like Charlie Johnston, their charity was worse than leaving the work undone. Velma's weekdays were spent in Reno though often she returned home midweek to check on him.

Being Gordon Harris's secretary gave Velma an insider's access to just about every property development in Reno. If Harris didn't have money invested in it personally or a hand in its insurance coverage, he knew the people who did. With Harris's help, Velma and Charlie found a building lot in a new subdivision, high on a hill at the north end of Reno. Below lay the grounds of the University of Nevada, also on a slight rise, and beyond it the city and the Truckee Meadows stretching down to the river. To the west they could see the Sierra Nevada Mountains.

"Our lot is on a bluff overlooking the entire valley in which Reno and Sparks are located, and it is so situated that nothing can ever be built to the south of us that will in the least interfere with the view," Velma wrote to Louise Huhne in August. "We are fortunate in having such a beautiful location, for Charles and I would be miserable living in a flat crowded area. Our lot is very large, and there will be room for a lot of landscaping, should he feel well enough to do it. It is only five minutes' drive from the heart of town and when the ache over selling the ranch subsides, I know we will like it. . . . On the lower level in the playroom, we are going to re-create the warmth and atmosphere of the ranch, and call it the Double Lazy Heart Room. It will be fun fixing it up, for we are just going to have it roughed in, and do the rest as we can."[22]

In the spring of 1960, Charlie and Velma took Ranger, Hobo, and Foxy to board at a neighboring farm near Wadsworth and moved into "the house on the hill," the only name they ever gave their Reno home. Charlie felt well enough to supervise the landscaping and set up a workshop in the garage with his tools neatly arrayed on one wall. Dubonnet, the last of the ranch cocker spaniels, had died in 1959. Charlie declared he wouldn't have a home without a dog and went to the animal shelter where he picked out Missy, a young tawny-coated cocker, who quickly took center stage in the household.

A typical postwar bungalow set close to the road, the house looked small from the street side, but with full two stories facing south and plenty of windows exposing the spectacular view, it was more than spacious enough. Velma threw herself into decorating and they took slow meandering walks through the adjacent fields, pausing periodically for Charlie to catch his breath. There were family visits, but Charlie and Velma rarely went out together. Still, they continued to talk about their long dreamed-of adventure. "We plan to play hookey the week of Labor Day and do the gold chain trail in California—travel the highway of the Mother Lode Country, and stop for the nights when the notion strikes us. For years we planned to do it horseback and never did, and now time has gotten away from us. We will never do it that way—so, will settle on it by automobile."[23]

Velma and Charlie missed the ranch, but life was unquestionably easier. Without the burden and frustration of chores he couldn't do, Charlie grew more content and his condition stabilized. He still greeted everyone with a cheery "it's a hell of a good day," though he wheezed as he spoke and sometimes coughed alarmingly.

Velma experienced a natural letdown after the federal bill was signed into law, but settling into their new home helped fill the void. In addition, the movement to protect horses and create an environment where the herds could thrive had developed some of its own life and momentum. For the first time Velma felt that her wild horse load was lifting.

In 1960, two former entertainers, John and Helen Reilly, who operated the Life of Reilly Lodge in Boulder, California, stepped forward to shoulder the administrative duties. With Velma's permission and encouragement, they created the International Mustang Club, later renamed the International Society for the Protection of Mustangs and Burros (ISPMB). The Reillys took on the burden of answering membership-related correspondence and sending out informational bulletins. Velma was the IMC's titular first president, but in those years she had little direct involvement.

The Reillys saw themselves as rank-and-file supporters, not leaders of a movement. Their interest and commitment were based on the fact that their daughter, Susan, successfully rode a mustang she trained on the show circuit. The Reillys had neither Velma's connections nor her political acumen, both of which would be essential to the next stage in the wild horse battle—the monitoring and enforcement of the new bill. Without enforcement, the Wild Horse Annie Law would be little more than window dressing for animal lovers. But as Charlie's health deteriorated, Velma withdrew from the front lines. She answered as many letters as she could, but gave few interviews and stopped issuing press releases. Contact with her closest political allies, Tex Gladding, Jim Slattery, Harold Cannon, and even Walter Baring, became infrequent.

———

EMPHYSEMA SUBJECTS ITS victims to a long and relentless decline. By mid-1962 Charlie had become an invalid tethered to an oxygen tank. He could still move about the house by himself, but as the months passed he failed steadily. Eventually he needed a wheelchair and even bathroom visits were impossible without assistance. His misery filled the house.

By the spring of 1963, Charlie could barely speak without doubling over in an effort to breathe. He refused to stop smoking, despite the danger of lighting up just inches from the oxygen tank. No definitive link had yet been established between cigarettes and cancer or lung disease, but it was clear that smoke irritated Charlie's lungs. A fit of painful coughing and gasping gulps for air accompanied every draw. Even when Charlie wasn't smoking, his breathing would catch and he'd start to smother with the oxygen mask in place. Velma, ever vigilant to the gurgling sound, rushed to open the valve that delivered more oxygen. She began to dread leaving him to go to work.

Every weekday morning Velma helped Charlie into his rocker by the living room window overlooking Reno. His bed was set up in the dining room, which also faced south, giving him a better outlook during the many hours he spent lying down. Trudy dropped by to fix him lunch and if he needed her, Velma could return from the office in minutes. When she came home in the evening, Velma poured herself a stiff drink and sat beside Charlie reviewing her day for him, just as she'd done every Friday night on her return to the Double Lazy Heart.

Velma and Charlie began watching television at night for the first time in their marriage. Westerns were their passion, especially *Bonanza,* with its location shots reminiscent of Nevada and the hills behind the ranch where they once rode the horses. Charlie got a particular kick out of *Gunsmoke,* noticing that when Marshal Matt Dillon, played by actor James Arness, went to draw his gun he always batted his eyes. Charlie laughed so hard each time he saw it, Velma thought he'd choke.

As the months of what he called his "incarceration" dragged on, Charlie struggled to keep up a conversation, so Velma chatted for them both. When his deteriorating eyesight made reading difficult, Velma read to him every day—newspapers, books, and poetry, especially Charlie's favorite, *The Rubaiyat of Omar Khayyam.*

When it was clear to both of them that Charlie's life was measured in months, he raised the inevitable. One day in the fall of 1963, speaking slowly and carefully and doing his best to smile from time to time, Charlie recalled the many joys of their years together. He stressed how much their work for the wild horses had meant to him and how proud he was of her bravery. Charlie urged her to remember that the struggle was for future generations, ensuring that they would have the chance to enjoy the wild horses as he and Velma had done.

When he finished, Charlie fixed Velma with rheumy but still blue eyes, and asked her to bring him his .38. First he asked, then he begged. Horrified, Velma refused. His entreaties became a daily event that wore Velma down emotionally as she tried to explain to her suffering husband that she just couldn't do it. When family members or close friends came to visit, Charlie implored them also to bring him his gun. "I lived through that awful eleven and a half months when Charlie was dying . . . when each of us acted out the grim drama and never once let the other know our hearts were breaking little by little . . . living each day as though we were not acutely aware that it could be our last one together . . . even setting out tulip bulbs while he watched through the window, both of us knowing he would never see them bloom . . . sitting night after night at his bedside giving out with gay chit-chat."[24] In January 1964 they celebrated—in advance—their twenty-seventh anniversary. "I brought to Charles, that horrible year, a loaf of bread and a jug of wine because we always had a 'thing' about Omar. He could not partake—only look—but it brought a smile."[25] A few days later she moved Charlie to Saint Mary's.

"I couldn't give him the loaded .38 but I could, and had the right, to give instructions that would keep them from prolonging a life that couldn't be saved. I sat at his bedside while his breathing became shallower and shallower, deliberately not sounding a buzzer that would bring a nurse to give him a shot that she would have had to give, then finally, when I knew that our twenty-seven years of togetherness was only a wonderful memory, I vowed that never again could anything hurt me. And nothing has . . . for I always remember the sheer hell it was during that awful time and I remember too; to be grateful for the legacy of courage Charlie gave me."[26]

Charles Clyde Johnston died on March 14, 1964. Even though it had been a year coming, Velma was devastated. Their union had been closer than most, perhaps because there had been no children. "The loneliest moment of a lifetime was when I was handed the flag from his casket, folded in that special three-cornered way it is done," she later recalled. "You see, contrary to what many people believe, I was never cut out to be anything less or more than a feminine female. For I loved doing all the tiddly little things dames do . . . sewing, keeping a nice house for Charlie, entertaining, lots of attention to grooming, baking cookies and most of all being a happy wife." In death Charlie returned to being Velma's comrade-in-arms. "Charlie was a fine partner in that fight, and when we thought we had it won back in 1959, we both heaved a gratified sigh and it was back to the cookie baking for me."[27]

Even as she grieved, Velma was forced to take a hard look at her circumstances. There had never been much money and in the previous decade any excess went to the wild horse cause. Now after the years of Charlie's illness and the extra expense of medications, oxygen, and doctors' visits, Velma was a fifty-two-year-old widow and flat broke. She sold her car and relied on Trudy to drive her to and from work. She also began moonlighting, doing payroll and accounting for construction companies, to supplement her full-time salary from Gordon Harris.

Velma never expressed disappointment or unhappiness with her "executive"—except for his early advice about writing children's stories—in any of the thousands of letters she wrote over the years. But there isn't any mention of his raising her wages to help her through this rough patch, though he made it clear that he disapproved of the moonlighting.

Nursing Charlie had taken a toll on Velma's own fragile health. As usual, she didn't confide in anyone, except perhaps Trudy, but others noticed she tired more quickly and she always seemed to be fighting off colds or the flu. She was also seeing her doctor for an undefined "heart problem," as she vaguely described it to family, and her teeth were giving her constant pain.

In the evenings, Velma sat looking over the sparkling lights of Reno with a whiskey or two and sometimes caught herself reviewing the day's events out loud as if Charlie were still listening. Habits that had once brought her great pleasure became underscored with sorrow. When she visited Hobo, happily pastured with a run-in shed for shelter near the Derby Dam behind the Double Lazy Heart, she couldn't even coax him over with carrots; he'd become accustomed to a life without humans. On top of that, the allergy to horses that had disappeared during the years at the ranch returned with a vengeance.

After the first unsuccessful, watery-eyed visit to Hobo, Velma dosed herself with allergy pills. She drove out to see him regularly, hoping to win back his affection, but he remained aloof. Her visits took her past the Double Lazy Heart, where she averted her eyes and put her foot hard on the gas. She had promised Charlie that she would have the horses put down if he died first because he didn't want them to become a burden to her as they aged. Now they were all getting on: Ranger and Foxy were nearly twenty and Hobo was well into his third decade. But as with giving Charlie his gun, Velma just couldn't do it.

Velma kept herself busy even as grief permeated every facet of her life. "Sometimes the rigid discipline I have over my mind slips a bit, and I remember too much, then I have to move the furniture, or spade up a place for a flower bed, or tackle some impossibly huge task. . . . When those moments of desolation take over, I know that the only antidote is work and more work."[28]

During the "horrible year" of Charlie's slow death and its aftermath, Velma had virtually nothing to do with the wild horse movement. In January 1965 she took the first step in an entirely different direction by accepting the presidency of the Reno branch of Executive Secretaries Incorporated.

# NINE

# The Lady in the Green Coat

E ARLY IN 1965 Trudy put the family home on Washington Street up for sale and moved in with Velma to share expenses and provide them both with company. Mother and daughter soon settled into a comfortable routine; Trudy looked after most of the housework and meals, Velma went to the office by day and did bookkeeping for others at night. Any leisure time was taken up with her duties as president of the Reno Executive Secretaries.

One day in March 1965, Trudy was watching a Giants baseball game when the telephone rang.

"May I speak to Mrs. Johnston?" asked a soft but assured female voice.

"Sorry, she's at work," responded Trudy. Willie Mays was due up and she didn't want to miss his turn at bat.

"Well, this is Marguerite Henry, calling from Illinois. When would it be convenient for me to call back?"

Trudy suggested the woman phone later that evening, then rang off.

"Marguerite Henry?" Velma asked when Trudy picked her up after work. "The name sounds kind of familiar, but I can't place it."[1] Velma thought hard all the way home; at the door, the answer came to her.

"Aha!" she exclaimed and hurried over to her bookshelves. "She's the lady who wrote all those books!"[2] Marguerite Henry was the celebrated author of dozens of bestselling children's books, some of which Velma had read to her sisters' children. She was surprised and intrigued that a famous novelist should be calling her.

---

HENRY WAS BORN Marguerite Breithaupt in Milwaukee, Wisconsin, in 1902, the youngest of five children. At the age of seven she caught rheumatic fever, which kept her housebound and often bedridden for five years, partly from weakness and partly from fear of the disease's quick spread. Without school or contact with friends, the years were tedious and she yearned for a pet, but her parents wouldn't allow it. Any sort of pet would have done, though a horse was her dream. "I used to get up in the morning, look in the mirror and hope that I looked like a horse," Henry once said.[3]

On Christmas Day 1912, her father presented Marguerite with a small red desk, a stack of writing paper, and a pitcher filled with pencils, sharpeners, paper clips, and scissors. "Dear Last of the Mohicans: Not a penny for your thoughts, but a tablet. Merry Christmas!" he wrote on the top page.[4] The next year Henry sold her first story, about a collie and a group of children playing hide-and-seek in autumn leaves, to a women's magazine for twelve dollars. "I was so overjoyed when they printed it, that I decided this was the most pleasant way in the world to earn a living."[5]

In May 1923, shortly after graduating from Milwaukee State Teachers College, twenty-one-year-old Marguerite married Sidney Crocker Henry, then a department store sales manager. Henry's writing career began with short stories published in the *Saturday Evening Post* and advertising copy for her husband after he opened his first store. Her first full book-length work was *Auno and Tauno: A Story of Finland,* published in 1940 and based on the experiences of two Finnish friends. In 1941 she launched the first of the sixteen-volume Pictured Geography series for children with *Alaska in Stories and Pictures* and *Mexico in Stories and Pictures.* She also ventured into biography with *Robert Fulton: Boy Craftsman* (1945), one in a series written by various authors on the childhoods of famous Americans. Henry's depiction of the restless, artistically inclined inventor was hailed as among the liveliest in the collection.

*Justin Morgan Had a Horse,* about the late-eighteenth-century foundation sire of the Morgan breed, vaulted Henry into the limelight in 1945. The book was a departure for children's literature at the time, with well-researched historical material presented in a style that was neither flowery nor condescending to young readers, though a strong moral tone underscored most of her work with clear divisions between good and bad and central characters struggling to do the right thing in the face of difficult odds. Henry successfully blended fact with dramatic invention to give the stories a compelling narrative flow while at the same time resolving any untidy conflicts in the actual events. With *Justin Morgan* Henry found her niche: "novelizing" the stories of real people for a readership predominantly of girls aged eight to fourteen.

Unlike many children's book authors, she didn't anthropomorphize the dogs, cats, foxes, and horses who were at the center of her books. There isn't a hint of Beatrix Potter or A. A. Milne in Marguerite Henry's works, no talking rabbits or morose donkeys. Instead, she directed the story line through the human characters who populated the narrative. The approach won her critical acclaim, several major children's literature awards, and commercial success. Virtually everything that flowed from Henry's pencil after 1945 became a bestseller, with many titles reprinted dozens of times by her publishers, Rand McNally. By the midsixties she was one of the highest-earning authors of her generation in any genre.

Henry's best-known work, *Misty of Chincoteague,* published in 1947, elevated her from a prolific children's writer of note to an internationally beloved celebrity. The *Misty* franchise expanded into a four-book series and gave rise to the first wild pony preservation society. By the early 1950s, an entire travel industry had developed around Chincoteague and Assateague, the two low-lying islands a few miles off the coasts of Virginia and Maryland, and the famous shaggy wild ponies that lived there. There were actually two pony breeds, each named after one of the islands, though both were found on the larger thirty-seven-mile-long Assateague, separated by a fence that splits the island between the two states. The ponies' origins have never been definitively determined, but whether they are the descendants of survivors from Spanish galleons wrecked in the waters surrounding the islands or escapees from early farms on both the mainland and the islands, they have thrived there since the mid-1600s. The *Misty* books were so popular that both breeds came to be known as Misty Ponies. In 1961, Twentieth Century-Fox made *Misty of Chincoteague* into a movie.[6]

Though she wrote on a vast range of topics, it was horses, particularly horses of myth and legend, that Henry returned to as subjects time and again. "It is exciting to me that no matter how much machinery replaces the horse, the work [a machine] can do is still measured in horse power even in the space age," she once explained when asked about her fascination with the horse. "And although a riding horse often weighs half a ton and a big drafter a full ton, either can be led about by a string if he has been wisely trained. This to me is a constant source of wonder and challenge."[7]

Henry knew from long experience that it was wise to approach a potential book subject carefully; she didn't want to spook a person by offering too much information or asking too much, too soon. As it happens this is also the best way to approach a horse, cautiously, respectfully, and with a little something in the pocket. Despite her fame, Henry had a pleasant, almost deferential manner on the telephone. When she and Velma finally spoke, she asked if Velma would be willing to be interviewed for a book she was considering writing. Henry was vague about the project itself, though she made it clear that she knew a lot about Wild Horse Annie.

In truth, Henry had already decided that Wild Horse Annie would be the perfect subject for her next novel. While browsing in a bookstore after finishing her latest manuscript, *White Stallion of Lipizza: The Story of the Lipizzaner Stallions,* she picked up a thin yellow-jacketed book called *American Wild Horses,* by the husband-and-wife team of B. F. Beebe and James Johnson. The name Beebe caught her attention since *Misty* had been based on the experiences of the Beebe family of Chincoteague. By the time she reached the last chapter, a description of Velma's crusade, she knew she had discovered the raw ingredients of a stirring story.

A biography of Velma—a living human subject—would be a departure for Henry and also a risk. Most of her children's books featured human characters but the central figures were invariably animals. The Beebe family, particularly Jeanette Beebe's niece and nephew, Maureen and Paul, inspired the story line of *Misty of Chincoteague,* but the title character and main attraction was clearly Misty herself. Shifting the spotlight to a human protagonist would be a challenge and might not sit well with readers who adored her books for their animal stars.

Henry was a relentless, almost obsessive, researcher. Misty was a real filly she had spotted during the annual Pony Penning Day when wild ponies were herded together on Assateague and swum across the Assateague Channel to Chincoteague, where weaned foals and yearlings were auctioned to support the local fire department. Clarence Beebe, Maureen and Paul's grandfather, had purchased Misty at the auction and afterward Henry asked him to sell her the filly for $150. Beebe agreed, providing she return the pony to Chincoteague for breeding once she matured. Henry shipped the foal to her rural property in Wayne, Indiana, where the filly lived while Henry wrote the book. Misty stayed on for ten more years. For *Brighty of the Grand Canyon* (1953), Henry rode the rugged trails of the Grand Canyon to get a feel for the terrain. The real-life model for Brighty, a small western burro, also resided at the Henry home. While animals in residence gave her firsthand research material, they were also compelling promotional fodder. Over the years, real-life Misty and Brighty appeared in hundreds of newspaper and magazine articles. Before she placed her first call to Reno, Henry had compiled a thick file of clippings on Velma Johnston.

Velma readily agreed to an interview and insisted that the author stay with them at the house on the hill. When Henry's flight arrived in Reno two hours late on a wintry March night, she found Velma and Trudy waiting. Henry's picture could be found on the inside flap of most of her books but she didn't presume Velma would recognize her. "I'll be wearing a green coat," Henry told her.

Narrow-shouldered, with an elegant long neck, Henry looked considerably younger than her sixty-three years. She was slender, though thickening through the middle, and her short dark-blonde hair was well cut. Henry was attractive, but not particularly striking, an advantage perhaps for someone who spent her career digging around in the lives of others. She and Velma were astonished to discover that both were wearing identical gold brooches in the shape of a horse attached to their lapels. Each had believed hers was unique; to find that a twin existed quickly broke the ice.

Marguerite Henry was endearingly self-effacing and she charmed Velma from the moment they met. The two women had much in common; both were childless and middle-aged, though Henry was a full decade older. Each had suffered prolonged, near-fatal illnesses in childhood. They doted on their pets and were passionate about their homes, their men, and their work. They were also strong-willed, well read, and softhearted to a fault when it came to animals. They shared several habits and small quirks, such as adding hand-drawn illustrations to their letters and sending greeting cards that could only be described as cute in the extreme. "Mole Meadow," as Henry called her property, was as important to Marguerite and Sid as the Double Lazy Heart had been to Velma and Charlie.

"I don't really think, Marguerite, that it is so strange that we are so close in our thinking. When you think of the very many things we have in common—and how it was destined that we meet—it just seems the most natural thing in the world that we would 'know' each other. I'm so glad our paths converged. I almost said 'crossed,' but then that would mean that each went on the way she was going—and this way, I don't really feel that we'll be out of contact again. Each may detour a bit, or get around a bend in the path from the other, but once in every

*Velma and Marguerite Henry*

precious while we'll be at a certain point together. Isn't it fun to think about it that way?"[8]

From the beginning Velma was slightly awed by Henry's almost regal demeanor, though the author dressed plainly and casually compared to Velma's stylish outfits. "I am constantly amazed at how beautifully you handle all your commitments and seem so unhurried and unruffled all the time. Do you have a secret formula?"[9] Henry's age and her childhood rheumatic fever, which may have permanently weakened her heart, made her cautious about her health. She paced herself carefully when traveling for research or promotion. She napped in the afternoon before an engagement and if she was giving a speech, she insisted that a private space be available before her presentation.

Henry claimed that beneath the serene exterior she had been a bundle of nerves when she first greeted Velma and Trudy. Velma was pleasantly surprised that such a famous and worldly person would be anxious about meeting her. "What amazes me is that you, of all people, Marguerite, would have heart thuds in the throat! That is for people with lesser poise, little charm, much uncertainty. You—who are the epitome of all that is gracious and assured, must surely know that people love you even before they meet you!"[10]

For her part, Henry discovered a smart, funny, and lively woman who liked both an evening cocktail and a rollicking party. But most important, Velma's life was custom-made for her young readers: She was a spunky heroine who had overcome profound odds. There was as well a built-in animal theme, though no particular horse stood out to serve as the leading character. Best of all, as in *Misty* and *Brighty,* Velma's story sent a clear moral message concerning preservation and protection. After writing *Brighty of the Grand Canyon,* Henry became an activist in the campaign to stop the flooding of the Grand Canyon, which would have destroyed the burros' habitat. She enlisted her fans, who numbered in the hundreds of thousands, to write letters of protest to their politicians. Henry particularly appreciated Velma's own letter-writing campaigns and she admired her courage in forcing herself into the glare of public scrutiny, despite a cruel disfigurement, to argue the case for the wild horses.

An infatuation often kindles between an author and subject in the process of researching and writing a biography. Like a romance, these relationships can ignite quickly or grow slowly, encouraged by patient tending. Henry had facilitated such affairs before. She had long been enamored of the story of Black Gold, the diminutive ebony horse owned by an Osage Indian that won the Kentucky Derby in 1924. "But that wasn't what made him great," Samuel Riddle, owner of the legendary Man o' War, had told her, piquing her curiosity. "His best race was his last when, with a foreleg broken, he finished on three legs and a heart."[11]

Unfortunately, the only person still alive with a connection to the undersized race horse was his Irish jockey and he refused to be interviewed. John D. "Jaydee" Mooney felt betrayed by an earlier movie script that portrayed him as a Chinese boy. "You won't catch me talking to any writers," he told Henry.[12]

Henry concluded that the best way to Mooney was through his wife, Marjorie. "I sat down beside her on the green grass there at the Aqueduct track, and we talked of many things. Mostly it was horse talk. Not of winners, but of the constant, every-dayness of training. The long hours—from sunup to sunset—with day never ending until each horse was bedded down. And then the worries in the night: the cough of the new colt, was it shipping fever? The exercise boy with the stained teeth, was he smoking near the barns? . . . As our friendship grew, I was invited to 'Sunday' with the Mooneys. What glorious Sundays they were! Marjorie's fried chicken, crispy brown. Her apple pie, oozing with juices. And afterward Jaydee loosened his belt and his tongue at the same time. Memories flowed unchecked. I could hardly wait for Sundays. Each seemed richer than the one before."[13] *Black Gold* was published to critical and popular acclaim in 1957.

Henry possessed a chameleon-like ability to blend in with disparate surroundings, to make those she observed and interviewed feel comfortable with the intrusion. And she was skilled at walking the fine line between fawning and gentle flattery. The technique beguiled Velma. During the week Henry spent with her, she visited Gordon Harris's office, met Velma's friends, saw the city sights, and trekked up to Virginia City to meet Tex and Marion Gladding and have a drink with Bill Marks in the Crystal Bar. She and Velma walked through the courthouse where Velma had made her first public declaration against the mustang roundups. Every night they sat talking over a pitcher of Bloody Marys. They enjoyed themselves so much that when she returned to Mole Meadow, Henry found her voluminous handwritten notes almost impossible to decipher. On a later visit, Henry issued an edict against excessive drinking, at least until the work of interviewing and note-taking had been completed.

Henry became close to Trudy too, affectionately calling her Ma Bronn. They both enjoyed gambling, a pleasure Velma didn't share. She liked the occasional hand of poker, but disapproved of casino gambling because she thought it was turning too many hardworking Nevadans into people who simply chased after easy money. So, after driving Velma to work, Trudy took Henry to her favorite casinos where they pulled on the one-armed bandits and played at the blackjack tables for hours. Henry enthused about the cooking skills of her "peanut butter mum" and was particularly fond of Trudy's chicken potpie. As she had done with the Beebes and the Mooneys, Henry slipped easily into Velma's life.

Though Velma had earned a degree of notoriety as Wild Horse Annie, she couldn't help noticing that she was suddenly accorded a much higher level of respect as "the lady who Marguerite Henry came to Reno to see."[14] One evening, a few weeks after Velma and Henry had stopped by the book department of Gray Reid's, Reno's department store, Velma dropped in again to make a few purchases. Her presence was quickly noticed. "Nothing would do but that I meet sundry officials, from the president on down," none of whom had previously shown the slightest interest in her.[15] "I must add here that you are so much in our thoughts here. Bill Rainey [proprietor of a book and stationery store] confided to me last week that he thinks of you many times every day; Mr. Harris actually called a client 'Mrs. Henry.' . . . You conquered this small part of the West as thoroughly as any military might did in the past. The others lost their lands—and we lost our hearts."[16]

Henry established a rapport with people that encouraged them to share confidences. When she met Bill Rainey, who had a crippled leg, he blurted out that he secretly wrote fiction.

"I wish I could have sent you the expression of utter and complete joy that Bill Rainey wore when he fairly burst into our office last Friday, with your letter in his hand. Not only did I not think he was limping, but he was walking four feet off the ground, with his head in cloud 9. And because you sent his little story to the *New Yorker*! . . . Thank you, Marguerite, for the extra measure of happiness you have given to those whom I love."[17] The story was ultimately rejected, but in the years following, Rainey never failed to ask Velma for news of Henry.

Velma now understood that being mentioned alongside wild horses in newspaper and magazine articles was one thing. It was quite another to be associated with a much loved and bestselling author. No amount of lobbying or crusading would give Velma the kind of cachet she enjoyed after a week spent in the company of Marguerite Henry.

Henry's impact on Gordon Harris was particularly instructive. He was so smitten on first meeting Henry that he insisted on hosting them for dinner at the Mapes Hotel, still Reno's finest. Gone as if it hadn't existed was his concern about the appropriateness of Velma's advocacy for the mustangs and he never again suggested that she would be better off writing children's stories. He frequently reminded Velma to inform Henry of some event or development he felt she should know about, even urging her to call Henry on the office phone from time to time. If invited, Harris would happily get on the other line for a chat.

In some ways, Marguerite Henry represented the person Velma might have become in different circumstances. One of Velma's unfulfilled desires was to write, and indeed children's books would have been her preference. In her letters and articles, she showed an untutored but adroit turn of phrase and an evocative descriptive ability, despite her tendency to florid prose.

On the Sunday before Henry's flight home, Velma telephoned the owner of the Double Lazy Heart to arrange a tour. It was not a casual decision; Velma still avoided talking about the ranch let alone driving in the vicinity. "Did it show through so very much, Marguerite? My love of the Double Lazy Heart Ranch?" Velma later wrote. "I thought I was getting so I could hide it pretty well! . . . Do you know that Charles and I always called it 'our cathedral'? For you to have called it 'a sacred Sunday'! You must be gifted with second sight."[18]

The evening she departed, Henry left a letter and gift for Velma to find when she returned from the airport. "Homecoming that evening lacked the joie de vivre that the preceding evenings had—but as you say, it just couldn't be 'goodbye.' . . . Oh, how glad I am that our paths crossed! That pot of roses is still beautiful—and is a sweet reminder of you. Also, the haunting fragrance that lingers after my bath in the bathroom. And thank you for that bit of thoughtfulness."[19]

If Henry left Reno with jumbled notes and a thick head, she also possessed an absolute conviction that she had a great book in hand. "I get goose bumps when you call it 'our story,' " Velma confessed. "And I too am hoping with everything I have that it will be one that you will be happy to do. I've no doubt that your ability will carry it successfully along."[20]

Henry also took away a signed contract giving her exclusive rights to the story of Wild Horse Annie in exchange for one dollar and a five-hundred-dollar consultation fee when the book was published. There doesn't appear to have been any discussion or formal understanding of the precise extent of Velma's involvement in the project or of how Henry intended to approach the material. Henry had full latitude to use or alter any aspect of Velma's life.

There was no burro or pony Henry could bring home to help her fashion the portrait of a mustang, but Velma gave her a print of a 1958 painting by Virginia City artist Cal Bromund of wild horses galloping across the Nevada landscape. "Tomorrow I expect to pick up the Bromund painting, all framed and ready to hang opposite my desk," Henry wrote Velma in early April. "Then it will seem as if I am actually breathing the clean pungent air of the desert and as if I am one with the wild fleeing herd. At other times as I look, I shall make believe that I am sitting at your dining room table, you on one side of me . . . 'Mom' on the other as we all feast on chicken pot pie and fluffy biscuits. Was anything ever so good? I feel so enriched."[21]

Guided by Henry's skillful probing, Velma began offering up details of her past. Henry was unfailingly intrigued and respectful. Hardly a letter she wrote to Velma didn't contain some demurral about the ability of a "would-be writer" to adequately tell the tale that she often referred to as "our story " or "Annie's story." "It's going to take a lot of

faith from everyone, plus prayers, that I may be equal to the significance of the story."[22]

Velma was convinced she'd found a kindred spirit; certainly Henry
was rapidly becoming a closer friend than anyone else then in her life.
Ruth McCord, who joined Gordon Harris's office to help with the typing, had been Velma's friend for more than fifteen years, but Velma
rarely wrote about her in letters and when she did, "Ruthie" was cast as
more a pal than a confidante.

It didn't take long for Velma to start feeling like an expectant
mother awaiting the birth of her child. "I'm so pleased that you feel the
story is a good one," Velma wrote to Avis Swick, who typed up Henry's
handwritten drafts and helped organize her research. "I've guarded it
zealously over the years, and though I've been approached by others to
furnish the material, I feared that it would suffer the fate of sensation-
alism and exaggeration. Goodness knows, it is sufficient without that,
and I know that it is in good hands with Marguerite."[23]

Over the next few months Velma directed a flurry of notes, recollections, thermofaxed magazine and newspaper articles and photographs to Henry. As the weeks passed, the correspondence mounted
up, confidences were exchanged, and the relationship deepened. "Here
I come with my little bag of questions. Such an insatiable hunger I have
when a story is in the making. My mind is eternally haunted by questions. For a long time now I have been trying to thread back through
the multifarious labyrinths of a life I have only recently known. Sometimes, not often, I am surprised and not a little frightened by my audac-
ity in thinking I can do it. . . . How can I tell you both how much your
answers mean to me? They are so rich in detail and fill me in [on] all
that I've got to know. Really, I get so excited when your letters come
that I can hardly wait to open them up."[24]

At the end of August, Velma wrote: "I too, wonder often how it
would be to try to live the life of another. Charles often said that we
should walk one moon in another's moccasins before judging him. . . .
It seems to me that is what you are doing now—walking many moons
in my moccasins so you can express yourself as I would. And it must be
so terribly difficult. Sometimes I can't even figure myself out and I've
walked all my life in these moccasins. And that is why I am so glad you

ask the questions! It even helps me get acquainted with myself. It isn't always easy, though, to convey just the right meaning, or thought."[25]

Henry responded in kind. "I'll be working hard for us meanwhile, walking in your moccasins. It was a wonderfully succinct saying of your Charles. I feel quite brave and daring, at times, when I try to be you. But much of the time I wonder how I can be so presumptuous. . . . Here's the rainbow: early in November I go on a speaking and autographing trip to Seattle, Portland & San Francisco. So about the middle of the month, if you're going to be home, I'll fly over for the day from San F. I couldn't possibly be that close without coming to my second family; to enfold you in my heart all over again. Chicken pie maybe?"[26]

Shortly after this exchange, Velma sent Henry an expensive pair of hand-tooled Paiute moccasins and later Henry reciprocated with an equally fancy pair for Velma. The moccasins and their significance became a touchstone. Their letters are studded with references to moccasins and they often featured in such gifts and mementoes as pottery, key chains, and postcards.

Henry followed a well-established work routine. She wrote her notes and observations in flowing longhand, adding possible bits of dialogue and description as they occurred to her. She often attached copies of newspaper articles or typed extracts from relevant books to her first draft. When she posed questions to Velma, Henry asked that each be answered on a separate piece of paper with the corresponding question reproduced at the top. Everything went into carefully labeled file folders. "I've never been able to work from a neat little outline," she explained to Velma. "I like to see the story life-size. Each one of the folders represents something important and [not] until they are stuffed full like a chipmunk's cheek, do I like to begin the actual writing. It's a fun way to work."[27]

Henry wrote the first draft by hand, editing as she went with much crossing out and scribbling in the margins. Then she turned it over to a typist. "Most authors, I believe, write their first draft on the typewriter. I feel happier with a pencil in my hand. It is almost like caressing the words."[28]

Though Henry intended the book to be a novel aimed at an adolescent readership, she was meticulous in her research into Velma's life, a process that involved lifting up corners of her past that Velma had assiduously avoided revisiting. In the fall of 1965, Henry casually inquired about the dogs at the ranch. Velma replied with three and a half single-spaced typed pages full of detailed and emotional recollections, later admitting that she'd cried for hours before, during, and after writing the letter. A passing inquiry about mining in the Virginia City area brought another carefully researched, three-page response.

Henry also asked for some small detail about the route Velma's grandparents had taken in their migration from the mining camp in Ione, Nevada, to California. Her request sparked a military-like mobilization by Velma to discover and then re-create the journey in reverse from Reno to Ione. Velma dragooned Dr. Everett Harris, Gordon's brother and a professor at the University of Nevada, into helping pinpoint the route her grandparents most likely followed. As with so many others she enlisted, Everett couldn't deny her. He drafted a ten-page report, complete with hand-drawn maps and precise descriptions of geography and terrain, mileage, travel time, as well as a possible day-by-day itinerary. Gordon Harris made numerous calls to friends in the mining industry seeking bits of information, and Ruthie McCord, who loved history, unearthed books relating to the pioneer trail, Nevada ghost towns, genealogy, and the silver-mining era.

Before Henry knew it, a full-scale expedition was scheduled to depart for Ione on October 24. The party included Trudy, who hadn't been back to Ione since she was twenty-one, and Aunt Mae, "Dad's only living relative and sister born in California when Dad was ten years old. She is seventy now and has not been in that area since she and Grandma journeyed out there in her early teens." Ruthie came, too, "bubbling over at the prospect of the trip."[29] Ancillary help was provided by Gordon Harris, who telephoned to check road conditions and issue periodic reports to the travelers en route. In one case he secured permission for them to travel on an abandoned stretch of the original road. His son, Gordon Harris, Jr., stood ready "to come to our rescue in the event the little blue Ford can't cope with the terrain and we find ourselves in the need of a knight in shining armor."[30]

There was only one missing element: "Marguerite Henry—who should grab a plane and be on hand for the 'wagons-ho' call on the 24th and if she can't, will be thinking every minute of the day that she would surely love to be! . . . Thank you again for reminding us that there is still a drop of blood of adventure in us yet!"[31]

What Velma saw as an adventure seemed like a very risky undertaking to Henry. "The map came this morning with your comments and itinerary. The more I studied everything, the more I worried. I can't bear to have the three of you exposed to the fall blizzards on the mountains and in the passes, nor the hazards of high altitude. Please stay home. With the map which is such a wondrously clear one, and with the notes from Dr. Harris' favorite engineering book on the Truckee River Route, and the book, 'Ghosts of the Glory Trail' and others of the period, along with your perceptive insight into Grandma and Grandpa's problems, I can do it with out endangering *you*."[32]

But nothing could dissuade Velma, who later reported on the expedition with a lengthy description of the sights on the route, a map, plus an assortment of pictures and her own suggested treatment of her grandparents' saga, together with many poignant descriptions of Ione. "The only public building is a general store, and it is impossible to describe the barrenness and bleakness of the interior." Though officially a ghost town, Ione still had a few residents. "Three old cronies were inside, and one of them was a veritable fountain of information, though he spoke with such an Italian accent that we could hardly understand him. We finally broke away from this one-man Chamber of Commerce, and headed for the cemetery. Of course, we couldn't find any evidence of Rena's grave, so we put our flowers at the headstone of a 'mother' who had died in 1882 at the age of 42. It was one of the few we could read."[33]

In November, at the end of her promotion tour for *White Stallion of Lipizza,* Henry made good on her promise to pay a side visit to Nevada. "Rushing off in your direction!!! Should arrive Reno Thursday 6:22 P.M. Flight 810 United. Please be my guest at Mapes or wherever for dinner. Now if you've something planned please don't hesitate to call or write, tell me not to come."[34]

Then Henry dangled a tempting morsel. "I may read you some of the manuscript!? In any event let's not do any partying this time for the simple reason that there is too much at stake. We'll have to do a lot of pow-wowing—just us three. Here are some horrendous questions I've been accumulating."[35]

Offering Velma a taste of the manuscript was rash. Like many authors, Marguerite Henry couldn't bear having anyone see her early drafts, let alone the subjects of her work. Either she had second thoughts or she was advised against it by her publisher or by Avis Swick. Shortly after Henry returned from Reno, not having shown Velma any of the manuscript, Swick wrote to reassure Velma that all was well.

"After typing the first few chapters of the new book, I just had to start this letter 'Dear Velma' or 'Dear Annie' for I feel as if I know you so well. You might like to know that Marguerite's worries about whether she could actually 'do' the book were only part of her modesty and not to be taken seriously. She has a story—an exciting, touching story that will be one of her best. I can hardly wait to read each new chapter. She has made Annie so understandable and warm, so human and lovable that readers will thrill to her just as I have. When Marguerite saw my reactions to the story, she said 'O, I wish Velma knew that.' And this is why I am writing you."

Then Swick gently tendered the explanation for Henry's failure to share the work-in-progress with Velma. "Of course at this stage of the manuscript it is so very rough that no one may see it yet. But it is the next few drafts—the rewriting, the refining, the smoothing—that she truly enjoys, and so do I. And while we are doing them, letters will continue flying off to you with queries on details of places and things and people.

"Don't you worry a bit about this story—but do be patient as you can, waiting for a glimpse of the manuscript. Marguerite is working like a beaver—resenting every interruption which takes her away—but it will take many months more of work. I'm sure you'll be pleased and thrilled with the result as it's going to be a masterpiece!"[36]

In early December, Henry herself wrote with an update. "I had exciting fun doing the Virginia City scene in the courthouse. Have only a few questions for the next 'go-around.' Deadline on the book is June 1. Rand McNally is setting a production date of October 20, 1966. So my own schedule is to do another draft in January, another in Feb, & another each month til I have to 'let go' on June first. I always hate to let go; I'm like a dog with a bone, or a child with a beloved teddy bear. Parting is more'n sorrow, it's desolation. You mentioned that perhaps it was too late to send me a printed transcript of the hearing in Washington. But that is not the case at all."[37]

Just before Christmas, Velma and her mother visited Mole Meadow in Wayne, Illinois, a horsey suburb just south of Chicago. It was her first trip since Charlie's death. Henry once again offered an enticement. "When you stop off in Wayne, I'll let you read this draft. I usually do 6. These I love to do! It is only the first draft that is difficult (understatement)."[38]

This time Henry did allow Velma to read a short passage from the early part of the manuscript. The experience was simultaneously uplifting and traumatic, so much so that it took Velma an uncharacteristically long time to write to Henry after her visit. When more than two weeks passed without a word, Henry telephoned.

"Thank you for calling," Velma wrote after their conversation. "It made us feel so very beloved! And to have you say we are missed! Can you believe that last year we did not even know each other? It seems as though you have been part of our family always, and now we have Sid. You always leave such an empty spot in our lives when you go. It takes quite a while to get back on an even keel again.

"I think much about the book. And I am so grateful to you for making the little girl who is Annie Bronn a courageous person. You know, she never wanted sympathy—and she's never changed. How well you described her without making it maudlin! Wish I could have talked more to you about it, and let you know for sure how pleased I am. The simple reason I didn't is that I was pretty 'shook up' and didn't want to come unglued in front of you and particularly Mom. I still don't know how you could so successfully crawl inside my skin and think and do as I have done. Perhaps we are closer than we ever thought possible."[39]

The manuscript may not have been the only reason for Velma's reticence. She was proud, sometimes to a fault, but Velma was not an envious person, nor was money a motivating factor in her life. However, she was too sensitive not to have suffered a few pangs while with the Henrys. They were an unpretentious couple, though clearly quite wealthy. Sid's "five and dime" had grown to seven Chicago department stores and Henry enjoyed a considerable income from her writing. Sid golfed regularly, they belonged to a country club and dined out frequently, all alien to Velma's frugal lifestyle.

But it was Sid and Marguerite's obvious affection for each other after forty-two years of marriage that most reminded Velma of what she no longer had. "There was such a lost feeling when you two went hand-in-hand toward the plane, and I was glad I had my desk to come back to, else I could not have got through that forlorn afternoon without weeping," Velma wrote after Marguerite and Sid visited her in Reno in May 1966. "Only wish Charles could have known you both. How he and Sid would have clicked! And in the special way Sid looks at you, I see again the loveliness that was mine too."[40]

# TEN

# Out of Cold Storage

V ELMA'S SPIRITS LIFTED dramatically in the months that Marguerite Henry rummaged around in the Bronn family history and Velma's early memories. Henry's probing functioned as a kind of therapy, allowing Velma to revisit the happy events and impressions of early childhood, including the once-warm relationship with her father. There were the scars of polio, physical and emotional, but there were also the comforts of her marriage, Charlie's devotion, and the joys of the dogs, the horses, and Double Lazy Heart. Where once she spoke only of what she had lost, Velma began to look to the future. References to Charlie and their life together did not disappear entirely in her letters, but they became less frequent.

By 1966 another voice was asserting itself in her correspondence — that of Annie. Velma began referring to herself by that name, subtly trying on the persona Henry was creating for her. She had read only a small portion of the draft manuscript, but it was enough to give her a clear idea of how Henry intended to portray her. Velma knew the signature features of a Marguerite Henry novel: a noble creature, a gallant champion, a struggle against terrible odds or a nefarious villain, all wrapped up in a happy ending. She began modeling her life on the heroine she was about to become.

In January 1966, Velma's term as president of the Reno chapter of Executive Secretaries, Inc., came to an end. Gordon Harris, who accompanied Velma to the ceremony honoring the departing officers, insisted afterward that she write to Henry with all the particulars. "The well-dressed sir, calling for the lady in the rustly evening dress, the high hair-do (especially on one side) and the evening wrap. Then to the hotel . . . the social hour, the dinner, etc. The gentleman on my left a bishop in the Church of Latter Day Saints, the lady on my right the incoming, gracious president. Lots of stimulating, interesting conversation."

Instead of the usual farewell gift of an inscribed inkwell, quill pen, and gavel with a tiny diamond in the handle, the chapter presented Velma with an inkwell surrounded by jewelled pears at the base and a ruby-encrusted quill pen. "The first jewelled pen ever presented in the chapter," a delighted Velma wrote to Henry. "There was another 'first,' too: a standing ovation—and Annie knew she must have been dreaming, when those important, successful, wonderful executives and their ladies paid her that tribute. In an organization of Executive Secretaries, since the individuals are only representatives of their executives, no personal recognition is usually given or expected. Each only does her best to represent her firm in a way to make her executive proud. And that is why last evening was so very different from all of the 'pinnings of past presidents' that preceded it."

She ended the letter still in character: "Such wondrous things have happened to the little girl who was Annie Bronn—the little girl whose heart broke when she looked in the mirror and a face all askew looked back at her. Lots and lots of love to you—and thank you for taking her out of cold storage."[1]

Later that month Charlie's mustang Ranger died, prompting Velma to fulfill a commitment that had been haunting her. "I promised Charles that if I were the one to survive, I would see to it that the horses were put down rather than that they pass into other hands. He was to do likewise," she explained to Henry. Ranger and Foxy had been living on the country property owned by Velma's sister Betty Jo and her husband, Roy. They had volunteered to take care of the horses and Velma jumped at the offer. But the Larsons were soon to move to Fresno, California. "They can't take Foxy at this time, and plan to leave him in the care of a little neighbor girl. You know how that goes! I asked my sister to have him put down, but she says her little girls are too disturbed already about having to change schools and having lost Ranger, for they loved to ride the horses.

"So . . . Foxy won't be in the care of the little neighbor girl too long after they move. Two of 'our boys' will go with us to Newcastle and I'll arrange for the veterinarian, etc. It is fitting that the boys (giants of young men now) who shared the fun at the ranch also help me with the sorrow, and they wouldn't have it otherwise. I must grow up to be a big girl for the day! They will expect it of me."[2]

That left only one unfulfilled promise. "I visited Hobo last Monday after work," she reported to Henry in August. Hobo was now twenty-seven years old. "In more than six years, I had not been closer to him than we were that day you were here with us, Marguerite. He had not been caught for three and a half years, and eluded all his pursuers. His host and hostess doubted that I could even get close to him, but when I got within his hearing out in the pasture, I began calling all the special pet names I had for him. He looked up from his grazing, gazed a moment at me, then came right to me. I had brought carrots, but had to break them up into pieces to feed him, as some of his teeth are missing and it is getting very difficult for him to eat. We had a lovely mutual admiration time of it! And I am glad so glad he remembered me.

"Gordon Harris made the arrangements for the veterinarian to put Hobo down and to have him buried. "[He] insisted that I go and tell him goodbye, and I am so grateful that he did, for Hobo looked satin sleek, and his eyes were clear as ever. Hobo will be buried by the river, surrounded by the bare brown hills, in the area where he had spent the most of his life."[3]

Velma unpacked Hobo's silver bridle and mounted it over her fireplace. The Double Lazy Heart door knocker, however, remained stowed away in a basement closet.

Velma gingerly began socializing again outside of work and the activities of Executive Secretaries, Inc. Trudy suggested she organize one of her lavish theme parties and together they outdid themselves with a Vegas nightclub–style bash that filled the house with two dozen gaudily costumed guests, many of whom were so inebriated at the end of the night they simply slept where they last sat down. Those who were still mobile unrolled sleeping bags and camped wherever they could find a clear spot of floor. In the morning Velma and Trudy threw together a hangover breakfast.

In late February, as she expected, Executive Secretaries offered her a seat on the national board. The appointment would be the pinnacle for a career secretary, second in importance only to the post of national president. "It would mean star-spangled years (five perhaps) of recognition in the business world, some glamorous trips, and of course some work too."[4] It was the kind of success Velma had dreamed of as a girl, a triumph that defied all predictions. Before Marguerite Henry appeared, Velma would have accepted without hesitation. Now, after nearly a year of reliving her past and the fight for mustang protection legislation, Velma once again heard the call of her "wild ones."

"It seems that I have some value in the world of humane work, and God knows, everyone who can contribute somewhat to alleviating the harsh lot of animals in this world is badly needed. I couldn't effectively serve two masters, besides my very precious one at the office, so I elected to follow the course of humanitarian work. You see, since I am not a family any more, with Charles gone, I must have something constructive to fill the aching void, for I am not the kind who can sit passively and not live life to the fullest."[5]

The first thing a newly committed Velma did was put the touch on Henry to appear at a fund-raising horse show she had been asked to coordinate. In 1963 Velma had helped create the Animal Welfare League of Nevada, an organization dedicated to building an education center and shelter for abandoned small animals. She served as president for the first two years until Charlie's illness put an end to her active involvement. In 1965 the group staged a popular fund-raiser at the Reno Coliseum, and its success prompted the Comstock Arabian Association to approach the league with an offer to stage an even more ambitious show. They would underwrite all expenses and share half the profits with the league.

"We can't lose any money," Velma explained in a letter to Henry. And the partnership "would give us access to another bracket of people in the area when the time comes. I'll admit I'm being selfish in asking you to come, for it could mean only another trying event in the many, many you have gone through before. However for us it would mean the opportunity to have an attendance far beyond any number that we could achieve for ourselves without you. . . . If it sounds like out and out exploitation of our friendship, it is. But being the dear friends that we are, I know you will tell me if you don't care to do it."[6] Henry accepted and was the headliner at a well-attended event.

Velma realized what she had missed in those years of absence from the wild horse movement, the limelight. Henry's book promised to thrust her back into it and if she was to stay within its glow, it would be children who would keep her there. Though they had played a role in the passage of the 1959 Wild Horse Annie law—mostly saddle club members and horse-mad girls who gathered petitions and wrote letters—Velma had never actively sought their support. But Henry believed fervently that the best way to guarantee humane treatment of animals was to mobilize young people.

There was still much to be done to protect the wild horses. In 1962 a 435,000-acre refuge of sorts had been established on the Nellis Air Force Base practice range northwest of Las Vegas by order of the secretary of the Interior, Stewart L. Udall. But the Bureau of Land Management had neither the funds nor the manpower to oversee it properly. And though the 1959 Wild Horse Annie law appeared strong on paper, it provided no means of enforcement or penalty for violators, who were growing ever bolder. With Henry's encouragement, Velma made a calculated decision to focus her energies on those who would, in just a few months, be reading about her in the pages of Henry's book. They might become the catalyst for better legislation.

"I had the honor of making Annie's role one with which children could identify completely and satisfyingly," Marguerite wrote as she neared completion of the manuscript. "The work you did could not be minimized; they had to understand the special kind of courage it took, the days of despair, the days of hope, the endless work. I feel now as if a great responsibility has been lifted, a responsibility which I had to discharge to all hurt creatures that feel pain just as we do."[7]

If Annie was to become a role model for the young, Velma herself would need a little cosmetic work. No longer did she volunteer information about the days when she and Charlie acted as their own law by freeing captured wild horses, and she asked Henry to alter or delete certain details she'd earlier provided.

"The gentlemen who visited me last evening from Sacramento are officials of the Humane Society of the United States and following our lengthy discussion, it is more important than ever that the humanitarian image of me be kept intact," she wrote to Henry in April 1966. "I know you will not overlook making changes in the purple dyed rabbit & chicken bit, for it would be quite hurtful under the circumstances. . . . This is terribly important to me, for as I indicated some time ago, I have cast my lot (as of last night) in with this movement to an even greater extent than heretofore."[8]

The "purple dyed rabbit & chicken bit" was a reference to the common pet store practice in the fifties and sixties of dyeing bunnies and chicks at Eastertime. Velma told Henry how she and Charlie did the same to thrill the children at the Double Lazy Heart's Easter egg hunts. A law had just been passed in Kentucky forbidding the use of dyes, which often sickened the animals, and other states, including California and Nevada, soon followed suit. If Henry wrote about it, Velma worried she might appear cruel in the eyes of readers, not to mention hypocritical on the issue of animal abuse.

Through the spring and summer of 1966 Henry continued to fire questions and requests at Velma. "Could you rush me some kind of picture of Mr. Richards? Even a snapshot of him standing would do. But a portrait would help too."[9] The book was to be illustrated with line drawings based on available photographs or Velma's descriptions. Henry's usual illustrator, Wesley Dennis, was committed to another project, but his replacement, Canadian Robert Lougheed, was just as accomplished. His work had appeared in *National Geographic* and *Reader's Digest* and he was the designer of Mobil Oil's famous flying horse corporate logo. Among the photos Lougheed used as reference for Henry's book were three taken by Gus Bundy, though no credit was given to him for the originals.

Velma was underwhelmed when Henry told her in March that the book would be titled *Mustang: Wild Spirit of the West.* "It seems so colorless compared to those of your other books," Velma complained. She chivvied Henry to come up with something better. "Let's all be thinking, huh? Something on the order of: 'Here is your Freedom, Mustang'; or 'That They May Roam Free.'" Velma's suggestions all reinforced the notion of someone, namely Wild Horse Annie, actively rescuing the mustangs of the West. Henry put Velma in her place, informing her that the publisher had issued ballots to his staff to vote on the title. Velma couldn't resist expressing surprise that people who knew nothing about wild horses, or her, would choose the title. Henry firmly told Velma that titles are all about sales and publishers know more about that than the subjects of their books.

Velma's disappointment with the title was overtaken by a new worry that she might have damaged their friendship with her criticism. On top of that was her sadness at the inevitable end of Henry's research and their almost constant contact. She wrote to Henry and wondered if their relationship would continue.

Henry penned her reply on United Air Lines stationery while flying home from Washington, where she and Sid were guests of Jim and Kathryne Slattery. "You asked, Velma, will the book ended mean our friendship ended? Once a person grows dear to you, you can't turn that feeling off any more than you can turn off a memory, or the sun from shining. I hope you won't ever be able to turn me off. . . . A friendly spark or two makes it all the more endearing and enduring."[10]

"How badly I put that question!" Velma quickly responded. "Will the end of the book mean the end of our friendship? It didn't come out at all the way I meant it. . . . Actually I can't imagine how anyone as busy as you are always would have time to spend on the luxury of friendships, and I just didn't get my thought across. I've almost dreaded the passing of time that brought ever closer the absence of bulging envelopes of questions—of notes of sheer exuberance—of the time spent sharing of reminiscences so very precious. And perhaps not to look forward to the sight of a plane skimming onto the field with a special guest or guests alighting. You see all that was going on in my mind when I asked that question—and I'm not usually so bungling with the spoken word. The ties are much too strong, I know, and so very special."[11]

The spark Henry referred to was the tiff over the book title. Velma got the message. "Woe is me! I did not mean to upset you with my remark about balloting, etc. I would be presumptuous to assume that any of us would know more about the saleability of titles than Rand McNally . . ." Velma now declared *Mustang: Wild Spirit of the West* a wonderful title. "And I am so glad that my beloved West is brought into the title. Maybe you thought that I felt it should have had a name linking it more closely with me as an individual. But that is not true, for there has never been the slightest desire for personal aggrandizement . . ."[12]

Finally, on Monday, October 3, 1966, Velma held an advance copy of *Mustang* in her hands. Its 224 pages of text were lavishly illustrated with nearly a hundred of Robert Lougheed's drawings. The dedication read, "to Wild Horse Annie in whose moccasins I have been walking these many moons," above a sketch of Paiute moccasins. It took Velma three days to respond. "I have my emotions under control now," she wrote to Henry on October 6, "which was far, far from the case last Monday from the moment I received *Mustang* until late into the night when I finally was able to get to sleep. I was at the salt mine in body, that day, but certainly not in mind—and the tears kept spilling out. . . .

"It is beautifully written, Marguerite. What a loving, loving tribute to Charlie! And as for my dad—who grieved from the time of his son's death until his own that the Bronn family name would die with him— how proud he would be of the touch of glory given to it . . . I am so glad that I was able to have a copy before it is released to the public. I needed the extra time to get used to the strange new feeling it gave me. There's so much, much more I could say. How skillfully you've pictured Annie Bronn—not pitiful nor tragic—but different."[13]

Velma shared her copy widely. "Monday, I called Bill Rainey and told him my book was here. He came immediately to the office 'just to touch it' he said." While Rainey read, Velma had to whisk out a box of Kleenex to avoid getting the pages "spotted" with tears. "I asked him to take it home last night to read. When he returned it today, he could hardly speak without emotion. . . . Both the Harris men, senior and junior, looked carefully through it, but neither would read it, except for the last five or six pages, until his own has come. Mr. Harris Senior wept."[14]

*Mustang* quickly became a bestseller and drew critical praise. *Publishers Weekly* called it "a sure-fire block-buster" and the *Bulletin of the Center for Children's Books* declared it "engrossing as a story of the preservation of wild animals and truly moving as a story of a dauntless woman."[15]

Velma threw herself into promoting the book as if she had written it herself. When Henry came to Reno on her book tour, they made appearances together and jointly autographed copies. Velma carried copies with her and sold them at every opportunity, sometimes ten or fifteen at a time. Bill Rainey provided the inventory and Velma returned the receipts to him. She also kept a close eye on reviews. When a generally approving reviewer in the *New York Times* remarked that Velma's role in the bill's passage was "not well-known" and that the "highly fictionalized biography" was most suitable for the "age ten to fourteen category," Velma took umbrage.[16] The reviewer's comments seemed to diminish her life's work. "I just can't agree with the reviewers that put it into the age ten to fourteen category," she complained to Henry. "If they could listen to my phone calls and read the letters, they would find that the adult readers are legion."[17]

Though Henry based *Mustang* on fact, the *Times* reviewer was essentially correct in her characterization of the book as a fictionalized biography. She could not have known the extent, of course, since this was the first time any aspect of Velma's personal life had appeared in print. But Velma had come to identify so closely with the Annie of Henry's creation that she protected not only the character, but also the details of the story, even those that differed from the actual events.

The book spanned the period from Velma's birth to the passage of the Wild Horse Annie law in 1959. The main events and a number of key figures, such as Walter Baring, James Slattery, and Tex Gladding, feature in the book very much as they did in real life. It was with the particulars about Velma herself that Henry took the most liberty.

In *Mustang,* Annie Bronn is afflicted by polio, but it strikes her at the age of five and lasts nearly seven years in the book, though the disease was well known to kill or maim its victims within a year. Henry sends Annie to San Francisco at eleven to be treated with the full-body cast, as happened in real life, and she emerges with facial disfigurement, though the author doesn't describe the severity of it and the illustrations give no hint. Hobo is a gift to Annie from her father when she is released from the hospital. The Lazy Heart Ranch initially belongs to her parents before Charley (not Charlie) Johnston, a "neighbor boy," buys it from them. After proposing to eighteen-year-old Annie, Charley, aged twenty-four in the book, changes the name to the Double Lazy Heart.[18] At one point Henry has Charley playing the harmonica. "Charles Johnston never played a harmonica in his life," his sister declared, highly miffed. She was also affronted by a passage that claimed that her brother "wasn't one for poetry." On the other hand, Velma's family was thrilled with *Mustang* from start to finish, despite the fact that the Annie of the book was not the Velma they knew.

*Mustang*'s heroine quotes the Bible frequently; she certainly doesn't party, smoke, or drink. And though she has a job, it's clearly not a career. Like the heroines of many young adult novels of the period, Annie seems as mature in the early chapters at twelve as she is later on as a married woman. Henry played up the frontier origins of her characters for an urban and suburban audience: Annie's mom uses words like "figger" and "mebbe," and she is very much the submissive housewife compared to "Pa," who is a dominant character through the book. Annie wraps her tongue around hillbilly expressions that no one in the Bronn family would have used. Just before she is scheduled to go to Washington, Annie tells Charley she's not going. "Because—because if you must know," she sobs, "I'm plain scairt."[19]

Marguerite Henry knew that young girls then and now are attracted to quests, especially those involving animals. A warm heart, strong principles, and a man, first a father then a husband, to lean on composed an ideal Henry heroine. The real Annie would have been too great a departure for writer and reader. In the end, *Mustang* really isn't about Velma Johnston but about the battle to pass the federal bill to protect mustangs and burros from being hunted to extinction. Velma was content with that and delighted at Annie's portrayal.

Few authors before or since have demonstrated Marguerite Henry's dedication to maintaining a readership. Even after decades as a successful author, she rarely refused an interview request or public speaking opportunity, sometimes flying across the county for a single engagement. Her correspondence in general, but especially with young people, was voluminous and she amassed a mailing list of thousands of names for a newsletter that she wrote, printed, and mailed out several times a year. A high-quality, four-page production on glossy stock, the newsletter carried photographs and drawings reproduced from her books and was a chatty collection of inside material related to her subjects, practical tips on horse care, and soft-sell promotion of her titles.

The front page featured a letter addressed to her readers with news related to her latest release. After *White Stallion of Lipizza* was published, the lead story explained that while there wasn't an authorized branch of the Spanish Riding School in the United States, the Tempel Mill Creek Farm near Wadsworth, Illinois, owned by Mr. and Mrs. Tempel Smith, boasted 160 Lipizzaners. "[The horses] are learning classical dressage as their ancestors did. Ten years ago Mr. Smith bought a few mares and stallions from the school in Vienna and shipped them to his farm in Illinois to start his own herd. Experienced riding masters came from all over Europe to train the stallions in the 'Airs Above the Ground' and in the graceful steps of the quadrille."[20]

The two center pages in every issue were devoted to answering readers' questions.

Dear Marguerite Henry,
Please tell me how to stop thinking, dreaming and drawing horses?
Beth Weston, W. Long Beach N.J.
*Dear Beth—Why stop?*

Dear Mrs Henry,
What do you do for a horse that a bumblebee has stung?
Narcy Recker, Ellsworth, Minn.
*Dear Narcy—As soon as possible, apply wet baking soda or plain old mud pack. Pond mud is especially good. If the swelling does not subside, call your veterinarian at once to give an allergy shot.*[21]

The final page offered the background story about how one or other of her books came to be. The newsletters were masterpieces of age-appropriate marketing: The writing was direct and engaging with the personal tone that bound her readers' loyalty year after year, book after book.

During a second publicity visit to Reno, Henry attended one of Velma's sessions with children and came away impressed with her "quiet delivery, studded with facts and your logical, sound solution to the [wild horse] problem."[22] Her obvious affinity for children and Henry's flattering appraisal prompted Velma to follow the author's example. She cultivated youngsters of every age group, not forgetting teenagers, understanding that no contact was too slight or fleeting to make an impression.

"I met a darling little girl, through her father, who brought her to meet me. She's not little really—5' 10" tall—and the kind of little girl Charles and I would have been proud to have. That's where I was playing hooky last Saturday—with her and her horse in the morning (I took my pill), then she came home with me for lunch, and we worked on scrapbooks, hers and mine. She's fourteen going on fifteen and it seems that Wild Horse Annie has put the frosting on her cake."[23]

Within six months of *Mustang*'s publication, Velma was making two or three appearances a week before gatherings of children at libraries, horse clubs, and schools. She was acutely conscious that it was not plain Velma Johnston who addressed them, but Wild Horse Annie, more real to them than Velma ever could be. "I did a program for six- to twelve-year-olds at the library, and entertained them with true stories about the life at the Double Lazy Heart Ranch. I wore the 'dude' outfit that I wore to the airport last October. Only with 'our' moccasins, which the children always ask me about thusly: 'Are those really the moccasins that Mrs. Henry walked in?' And I can truthfully answer them yes!

"I did the same program for first- to sixth-graders at an assembly also. As props at both programs, besides *Mustang,* I took Hobo's bridle, which they touch with the same reverence they would touch a holy object; the 'humane' branding iron from the Double Lazy Heart; and my spurs which I always wore when I rode Hobo and I explain that they were not worn to hurt Hobo but to discipline him if he should jump sideways on a trail etc. I also take Charlie's picture, for the kids invariably say they wish they could have known him. At the conclusion of these programs, I autograph until my arms almost fall off! Then when I leave, as it surely must be with you too, I feel like the Pied Piper of Hamlin, so many of the youngsters follow me wherever I go."[24]

Velma continued to polish the Annie brand. "It is only the clean and noble side of life at the ranch I tell them about—not the times we whooped it up! This clean, noble public image of Girl of the Golden West that I have become is surely having a reforming influence on me. Once in a while I rebel, and that is why I had such a ball at the Mardi Gras last week when I went as Nevada's most famous madam. Wore half-inch long false eyelashes, managed a 40-inch bosom measurement, cinched in my waist, borrowed gobs of rhinestone jewelery to go with what I had, and for an evening became a different kind of Girl of the Golden West. Even then was terrified when a reporter took a picture, until I could convince him that it just couldn't be used in a newspaper account of the party."[25]

When Velma recounted the story of her family, Charlie, and the mustangs she followed the script exactly as written by Marguerite Henry. Why confuse those who'd read the book? She incorporated the fiction that Hobo had been a gift from her father and that she and Charlie had known each other since childhood. So often were such "facts" repeated that even the family became confused; her sisters believed she'd contracted polio at five. In the book Henry described a weekend dude ranch for children at the Double Lazy Heart, a business Annie and Charley operated to pay the bills. Though there had been plenty of children at the ranch, there was never any suggestion of paid lessons or trail-riding fees. Yet a number of family members thought that Velma and Charlie did, indeed, operate a dude ranch business. The life of Annie Bronn described in *Mustang* crept into newspaper, magazine, and later nonfiction book accounts of Velma Johnston's exploits, but she never corrected the errors.

Speaking requests became so numerous and far-flung that Velma drew up a curriculum guide about her wild horse crusade as an aid for teachers when she was unable to travel to their schools. She covered the bulk of her travel expenses herself, which limited her school appearances to those within easy driving distance, though at least twice she went to northern California to speak. She was still working full-time but Gordon Harris, now enthusiastically supportive, allowed her time off for her talks.

Velma's presentations weren't always delivered to the converted. The Nevada State CowBelles, many of them wives of members of the Nevada Cattlemen's Association, asked Velma to address their regional convention in March 1967. Cattlemen had always been among her most vociferous opponents. "I can't back off now, or they would think I'm afraid of them. Besides, if I play it just right, I may get the wives on my side of it. It's a challenge, believe me, and I break out in a cold sweat whenever I think of it."[26]

Velma needn't have worried. "CowBelles are like anyone else, I found, and the talk went superbly. I mean it was received superbly. Although, I didn't pull any punches on the atrocities and the reason behind them, I bore down considerably on the need for management and control, which is what I have always emphasized. I am sure I gained lots of support and a full measure of understanding where before there might have been criticism. Also sold several copies of *Mustang*."[27]

Velma poured out her daily preoccupations in letters to Henry as she would in a diary. "Wild Horse Annie keeps Velma so busy that there's not much time left for fun—or dates," she wrote to Marguerite early in 1967. "I've got to reschedule some of my activities, I'm afraid. Romance (?), well . . . maybe. You would approve! . . . This isn't exactly the way I had planned my life but we'll see. So much of me will always belong to Charlie! I just think that maybe there's not enough that doesn't on which to build a new life."[28] Ultimately she was right; though there were a few passing references to dating or to a man escorting her to one event or another, romance remained in her past.

Velma believed that her friendship with Henry had blossomed into a partnership of two women—peers equally respected in their fields—who as friends do, helped advance each other's interests. Velma would promote Henry's book and the author would publicize Wild Horse Annie's continuing efforts to protect the wild horse, and so Henry did.

"Wild Horse Annie, who fought to save the Mustangs, is on the warpath again," Henry reported in Newsletter Number Four, published early in 1967. "Three men were caught chasing wild horses by plane right in her home state of Nevada. They were accused of 'buzzing' the herd with screaming sirens and tin cans rattling from long ropes. For eight miles—from Antelope Summit through Long Valley—they drove the horses at heart-aching speed, trapping them at last in a corral built of bulldozed cedar trees."[29] The piece accurately described the entire event, omitting only the names of the perpetrators. Henry included an appeal to "the boys and girls of our nation" to write to their government representatives and insist that the 1959 Wild Horse Act be upheld in the forthcoming prosecution.

Henry had encouraged Velma to view the research and even the writing process as a collaboration, a professional technique that she had used to great advantage in the past. In this case it was underscored by her genuine warmth of feeling for Velma.

Nonetheless, Velma had been sheltered from the true dynamics of the relationship between subject and biographer. Friction often arises over the degree of ownership that the subject claims of the final product. On the one hand the work is the author's creation, on the other it is the subject's life. Velma was certain Henry felt as she did, that they were cocreators, a team. Henry, the consummate professional writer with more than fifty years' experience, thought differently.

In late March 1967, Henry received word that *Mustang* had won a prestigious award for juvenile literature from the National Cowboy Hall of Fame in Oklahoma City. "Dear Mr. Faris," she wrote to the executive vice president on April 2. "Your exciting letter telling of the Western Heritage Award for *Mustang* was the nicest Welcome Home!

*Velma with Reno businessman William R. Luce at the*
*release of a mustang bourbon decanter in 1967*

All of us in any way connected to the book—Robert Lougheed, Rand McNally, and our long-suffering families—are overjoyed. Mr. Cobb has asked me to join him in Oklahoma City for the Award ceremony and I am looking forward to it with great pleasure. My flight number is 539, American Airlines, arriving at 1:35 P.M. on April 14. Would someone please make reservations at the Skirvin?"[30]

On April 4, the National Cowboy Hall of Fame issued a press release announcing the prize. In an undated letter to Velma around the same time, Henry neglected to mention the exciting news; instead she told Velma she was taking a trip to Oklahoma City to speak to a group of teachers and librarians who select books for school libraries. "I'm trying my best to sound learned. 'Taint easy for me. The one thing I do love about making these talks is that it gives me the chance to weave in something about us. Then I am in your moccasins again and loving it. Ears burn?"[31] Marguerite goes on at length about how Alex, her dachshund, was bitten by a horse, but says not a word about the literary prize.

On April 14, 1967, Henry accepted the juvenile book award at the annual ceremony hosted by the National Cowboy Hall of Fame and Western Heritage Center. Seventeen western states were members of the Hall of Fame and the gala black-tie event featured dinner, entertainment, and a keynote speech by Will Rogers's son. Marguerite accepted the trophy, a replica of a Charles Russell bronze, *The Wrangler.* Named as recipients with her were Robert Lougheed, the book's illustrator, and Sanford Cobb, vice president of Rand McNally. Velma Johnston was not mentioned.

Exactly why Marguerite Henry kept Velma in the dark about the award and the ceremony is unclear; perhaps she knew that Velma would have expected an invitation and for whatever reason didn't want her there. In any case, Henry underestimated Velma. With connections everywhere, it took less than a week to begin unravelling the story.

"What a coincidence your mentioning your trip to Oklahoma City," Velma wrote on April 20. "I just heard by letter from a friend in Los Angeles that a friend of his had returned from a vacation there, and had seen *Mustang* in the Cowboy Hall of Fame. I wrote to a fellow member of Executive Secretaries in Oklahoma City asking her to verify it for me—and maybe you know it already. If that be the case, I am glad it is the book about Annie instead of Annie herself who is there, for I understand you must be deceased to qualify for a spot in the Hall of Fame. I'm not quite ready to go yet—too many pieces of unfinished business."[32] Velma must have sensed that something was amiss, but she clearly didn't have all the details, such as the fact that the book would have been displayed in the Hall of Fame because of its recent honor.

The next letter from Henry may have been a hasty attempt to cover up her transgression in the face of Velma's careful overture, or it may have been written out of a guilty conscience and crossed in the mail with Velma's.

"Will wonders never cease?" Marguerite exclaimed in another note sent in April. "I came to Oklahoma City ostensibly to speak to the Oklahoma Reading Council and it turns out to be a double-barrelled affair! The National Cowboy Hall of Fame is located here and once a year they and the Western Heritage Center . . . have a gala black-tie dinner at which trophies are presented to an outstanding motion picture, a TV program, documentary film, magazine article, adult novel and juvenile book that presents the true West. Now for the good news: 'Mustang Wild Spirit of the West' won the last category."[33]

Henry described the presentation of the trophy and the setting of the museum and gallery on Persimmon Hill overlooking the city. "Seventeen state flags flood-lighted, and fountains and new-springtime-green willow trees lighted to high heaven. And within the gallery are more Remingtons and Russells and Leighs than I ever dreamed of."[34] It was the sort of evening Velma would have adored, a gathering of politicians, producers, and writers together with the stars of some of her favorite television westerns. Lee Majors, then costar of ABC's *The Big Valley,* and Amanda Blake, Miss Kitty the saloon owner on *Gunsmoke,* both accepted awards.

On April 26, 1967, Velma wrote to Henry with congratulations on her "Oscar." "I am so glad for you, and how richly you deserve this recognition." At the bottom of the letter was a poignant postscript. "When I received the pen with which President Eisenhower signed the bill, I remarked to Charles: 'Someday we will be in the National Cowboy Hall of Fame because of this, honey!'"[35]

In early May, likely via her Executive Secretaries colleague in Oklahoma City, Velma learned definitively that Marguerite Henry's version of events wasn't truthful and that she had known of the award well before she casually wrote to Velma about her speaking trip.

Velma may have gotten past her distress at not being invited to witness *Mustang*'s honor, but knowing that Henry deliberately lied about it, then lied again to cover up, was a dreadful blow. Velma regarded Marguerite as her best and most important friend; she assumed Henry felt the same. The episode demonstrated that the divide between author and subject, between a wealthy, international celebrity and Velma Johnston of Reno, Nevada, was very wide indeed.

Velma picked up the telephone. There is no record of the fateful call, but it can be reconstructed from Marguerite's response and Velma's ensuing letter. The conversation started off as "solely congratulatory," in Velma's words, but quickly deteriorated. "About the hurt feelings that spilled over," Velma wrote afterward. "It seemed to me at the time that everyone connected with the book was privileged to be in Oklahoma City, where it received honors dear to our hearts, except I who was responsible for its being eligible to be judged on a Western heritage basis.

"To me whose life is an integral part of it all, it would have been a star-spangled recollection to last for all time just to have been a witness to honors bestowed on you at that particular place because of your superb and absorbing telling of this Living Western Legend that has its roots deep in the heritage that is mine.

"It would also have been the opportunity to observe with pride that which will become a special tribute to the memory of my dear ones— Charlie, Dad, Grandma, whose bountiful love enriched my life and spills so generously from the pages of *Mustang*."[36]

Velma's outburst went on to include what she later referred to as "non-essentials": "How could you do this to me after all I've done for you" complaints about how much autographing she had undertaken on the author's behalf, her efforts to sell and promote the book in her speeches, and answering extra mail because Henry had written about the illegal roundup in her newsletter and had requested that children lend their pens to the cause.

Henry didn't disguise her annoyance in an uncharacteristically graceless response. Her note had a remarkably cool undertone and she made no attempt to apologize or otherwise ameliorate Velma's wounded feelings. Nor did she offer an explanation of why she not only didn't invite Velma but didn't tell her about the award until her hand was forced. Henry completely brushed off Velma's "non-essentials." "Many, many authors, or others involved in books, frankly pass up their fan mail. John Ciardi had an article in the *Saturday Review of Literature* telling of the contents of his waste basket, admitting that he refuses to take time to answer the fan mail that floods his office. Munro Leaf is another author I know who never answers a fan letter. The Beebes down in Chincoteague don't either. They send it to me! If you want to do the same, I shall certainly understand.

"As to the autographing, you need feel no compulsion whatever about doing it. Why not frankly explain the situation—that your working hours belong entirely to Mr. Harris, and the rest of the time you need to yourself, and that you in no way benefit from the time and trouble it takes. I'm so sorry I mentioned the violation of the Mustang Law in Newsletter #4 for I know it must have meant added letters for you as it did for me. I promise not to let you in for any further involvement."[37]

Henry then compounded the hurt by assuming that Velma's distress centered on money. "I told Rand McN (the book's publisher) about your telephone call and they feel that they can't make an exception because the same situation exists with Gibson White of 'Born to Trot,' and the Mooneys in 'Black Gold' and the Beebes in 'Misty' and 'Stormy' . . . not to mention their connections on the many other books they publish. Because I feel sorry about the extra burden I have added to your life I shall personally send you $250 whenever a new edition of twenty-five thousand shall be printed, $150 for fifteen thousand, $100 for ten thousand and $50 for five thousand. But as far as getting Rand to take any action I can't do it."[38]

Velma tried to patch things up by apologizing for her emotional telephone call. "It should have been postponed a week," she admitted, "because by that time my hurt feelings would have been all healed and forgotten and would not have come through as whining to you. . . . It could only have been an oversight—not on the part of you from whom I have received only thoughtfulness and consideration—and I should not have let my feelings come through to distress you. In a way, the oversight is understandable, since your books have almost always been of four-footed heroes and heroines who do not wear their hearts on their sleeves, and I'll bet there are times when you wish that I walked on hooves or paws instead of in moccasins."[39]

The insinuation that Velma was no different from any of Henry's other book subjects, coupled with the offer of money, chilled Velma. She had developed a strong sense of proprietorship over the wild horse issue and she had a healthy ego, but she was never interested in money for its own sake and hated to ask for it or hint that she needed it. "I am sorry that you were put in the embarrassing position of speaking to the publishers in my behalf for there was no intention on my part of conveying to you anything of a financial nature. From a business standpoint they must draw the line somewhere and I have never expected anything from them other than the usual courtesy that goes hand in hand with good public relations. . . .

"How dear and generous of you to offer additional financial consideration. Thank you—but please know that I am thoroughly satisfied with the arrangements that you made with me when I signed the release: the $500 for my technical help (which was my pleasure to give) . . . I couldn't accept any more from you and would be hurt if you sent it along."[40]

Had Velma accepted the additional money Henry proposed, it would have amounted to a sizable sum over the years. Though not a blockbuster on the scale of *Misty*, which has sold more than 2.5 million copies to date, *Mustang* has sold an estimated six hundred thousand copies, and still averages sales of about ten thousand copies annually.

The incident was never mentioned again but the relationship between the two women foundered. Though they wrote to each other on friendly terms for many years and Henry continued to support the wild horse movement, the intimacy was gone; there were no more invitations from either side, no more moccasin mementoes. The frequency of their correspondence gradually dwindled until it ceased completely in 1971.

# ELEVEN

# The Battle of the Pryor Mountains

D URING THE YEARS Velma cared for Charlie and in the months after his death, a wild horse controversy percolated in the remote Pryor Mountains region of southern Montana and northern Wyoming. Its 145,000 square miles of bowl-like valleys, steep peaks, and deeply carved gorges were home to thousands of wild horses when the first white settlers arrived in the 1890s. Before then, the Crow Indians, as legendary in their passion for horses as the Apache, Nez Percé, and Sioux, kept large herds. The Crow horses, like most of the earliest Indian ponies, were descendants of escapees from Juan de Oñate y Salazar's exploration of the lands north of the Rio Grande in the early seventeenth century, their bloodlines diluted by the heavy-bodied Canadian horses, the English Hobby horse, and the smooth-gaited mountain breeds of Kentucky and Tennessee.

The horses of Meriwether Lewis and William Clark also contributed to the Pryor gene pool. Their expedition, sponsored by Thomas Jefferson, left from St. Louis on May 14, 1804, to explore the newly acquired western territories and search for a continental water passage. The party set out in three riverboats down the shallow, muddy Missouri River until they reached the mountains in Montana. There they negotiated with the Shoshone for the horses they needed for the overland leg of the journey; some bore Spanish brands.

On the return trip from the West in July 1806, Lewis and Clark assigned Sergeant Nathaniel Pryor and two men under him to lead their remaining twelve horses to the confluence of the Yellowstone and Bighorn rivers in Montana where they would meet up with the rest of the company making the trip by water. Problems controlling the horses had plagued the expedition all along. Extra guards, hobbles, and crude corrals didn't stop the horses from wandering off at will, especially at night. And the situation grew worse for the shorthanded Pryor when a herd of buffalo appeared near their camp. "The horses, trained by the Indians to hunt, immediately set off in pursuit of them and they surrounded the herd with as much skill as their riders would have done," Pryor reported to Captain Clark.

Not long after that incident the three men woke one morning to discover all the horses missing. In his report Pryor listed the horses as stolen, though some speculate this claim was a wiser choice than admitting they had simply drifted away while he and his men slept. Stolen or strayed, the Spanish-branded jennet-type horses lent their genes to the herds that populated the Pryor Mountains—later named after the sergeant—both in the wild and in Indian bands.

Folklore holds that the Pryor herds might also be descended from one of the last great clashes of Indian and white in North America, the 1876 Battle of the Little Big Horn. Only two horses, Comanche, an officer's mount, and one other, were known to have been left alive after the carnage, but there may have been more. It certainly would have been possible for a horse from Custer's Last Stand to make it from the confluence of the Reno and Big Horn rivers to the mountains some sixty miles away, and stories persist of uninjured mounts of both Indian and white armies joining the wild herds in the Pryors.

By the end of the nineteenth century, the Pryor Mountains horses had developed an appearance quite distinct from the smaller, narrow-bodied Nevada mustangs. In conformation they most resembled the French-Canadian horses of the fur trade *voyageurs,* crossed with the jennet types of the Spanish. Stocky, with small heads and thick necks tying in to low withers and deep chests, the Pryor mustangs sported long, thick manes and sloping hips with extravagant tails. Even more striking was the spectrum of their color: deepest blue roan, almost purple from a distance, red roan with brown heads and hen-speckled coats, dun, grullo, and dark golden palomino. Paint-splashed sabinos and overos stood out like bright songbirds in a shadowy forest, while sorrels, coppery like new pennies and set off by flaxen manes and tails, gave an impression of creatures from a fantasy.

In 1894, the family of Bessie Tillett, then a girl of five, arrived in the southern Pryor region. An estimated twelve hundred horses in various small bands inhabited the territory surrounding the ranch settled by her parents. Much of the country where the horses roamed was high desert. With three to five inches of rainfall annually in the foothills, palatable vegetation for livestock was scarce. Scattered throughout the range were lush depressions, carpeted with meadows of grasses, purple pasqueflowers, blooms of prairie smoke, and the startling upright heads of pink shooting star. Beyond the oasis of green, rock lurked close to the surface, making it far from ideal cattle country. In the higher altitudes, rainfall nudged thirteen inches annually, but most of the terrain was too rugged for livestock.

After passage of the Taylor Grazing Act in 1934, the Tilletts, like other ranchers who had been using public land to graze cattle and sheep, took out permits from the Grazing Service, later the Bureau of Land Management. By the 1960s the Tilletts' TX Ranch encompassed over nine thousand deeded acres along Crooked Creek, running through Montana and Wyoming, with an additional sixty-five thousand acres leased from the BLM. They needed every acre of forage to bring one thousand head to market each year.

Ranchers and the Crow Indians who refused to stay put on their reservation cut out the odd wild horse for their own use. Occasionally a rodeo supplier captured a few for a bucking string; the Pryor horses were known to be among the buckingest creatures on four legs. When Bessie was still a girl, mustangers came through the area hoping to score a good number to sell for glue or hides, but they had little impact on the wild horse numbers.

It all changed after World War II with the sudden growth of the pet food industry and the advantage of airborne pursuit. By 1946, the wild horse population in the Tilletts' area had dropped to an estimated 140 and they decided to act. Though the TX Ranch had a permit to graze only twenty horses, Bessie and her sons, Lloyd and Royce, declared that all the wild horses on their owned and leased land belonged to them, which in those days was enough to ensure that no one would touch them.

"Just to look at them was good," Lloyd explained. "And we were fed up with the treatment they were getting, the same as we'd be madder than hell if some s.o.b. came in and bulldozed these mountains. God knows enough from America's past has been wasted without tearing down what's left. They're magnificent animals. They don't deserve to end up in cans."[1]

The population of wild horses on the Pryor Range remained relatively stable and unthreatened for the next fifteen years, until February 1961, when President John F. Kennedy, responding to the cattle-ranching and hunting lobbies, directed the Department of the Interior to put into place anti-erosion measures designed to improve forage capacity, particularly on land that had already been badly degraded.

These were welcome words in the corridors of the BLM, where attitudes toward wild horses had changed little since passage of the 1959 Wild Horse Annie law. With what they took to be the president's blessing, the BLM began targeting wild horse herds for range clearance. The Pryor Mountains region was high on its attack list, though it was an odd choice. According to the BLM there were at most 200 horses, 140 according to the Tilletts, and they moved through a vast area that even the BLM acknowledged was largely unsuitable for livestock.

The man assigned to rid the Pryors of wild horses was Dante Solari, Velma's old nemesis. Solari had lost every round against Velma from 1955 to 1959, but he had nonetheless climbed the promotion ladder from local range manager in Nevada to district manager for the entire Pryor Mountains area. He was stockier and balder in 1961, but still the bulldog Bureau man through and through.

Solari's boss, Harold Tysk, who backed him unconditionally, vigorously denied that the BLM had anything to do with horsemeat ending up in dog bowls. "Perish the thought!" the thin, bushy-browed state director told a reporter. Nonetheless, Tysk was also careful to assert that the BLM had no control over what "other people" might do once they had a permit. "If whoever takes the horses off the range wants to sell them to canneries, that's his business." Like Solari, Tysk had no time for the roundup opponents. "I think this whole thing is an emotional issue whetted by Walt Disney movies," he declared.[2]

As in Nevada, the damaging effect of wild horses on the public grazing lands was a matter of opinion, not fact. The BLM had done no surveys or comparison studies in the Pryors—at least none it chose to make public. A 1951 report written in conjunction with the Bureau of Land Reclamation surfaced later; its authors concluded that the wild horse's territory was possibly suitable for timber but not for grazing livestock.

Shortly after President Kennedy's directive to the Department of the Interior, Solari announced that the Pryor horses had to go—all of them. His rationale was virtually identical to the one he offered Velma in 1950: Because wild horses were degrading the rangeland, hardworking stockmen would lose their livelihoods unless the BLM stepped in.

Lloyd Tillett scoffed at Solari's assertion. "If this was real grass country, I'd have to agree it's in pretty bad shape. But unless climatic conditions change considerably, this Pryor area will always be some of the worst damn range in the state . . . semi-desert really. Hell, there's not enough forage in a lot of these red foothills to stop erosion whether any animal is grazing or not . . . drought and terrain are the villains, not horses."[3]

The herds claimed by the Tilletts were spread throughout the southern portion of the Pryors on land designated by the BLM as "extremely poor." The area was scored by canyons and punctuated by steep summits, with the occasional plateau supporting scattered trees that followed the path of seasonal runoff. The horses lived mostly above four thousand feet where little forage existed except dun-colored rabbit brush and mountain mahogany bush, plants favored by deer.

Water, like grass, was scarce. Only two spring-fed water holes existed on the range's southern boundary across the Wyoming border. But the horses had found another source in a mine tunnel on the southwest edge of the range. Some bands traveled ten miles from their grazing land to the tunnel, where they uncharacteristically queued up for water. Normally when two herds converge, the stallions square off. In this case, one herd waited patiently while the other entered the narrow entrance one horse at a time. Sometimes it was so dry the horses had to linger until their hoofprints filled with water before they could drink.

It wasn't just one disgruntled ranch family that opposed Solari and the BLM. Influential naturalist Dr. Harold McCracken, then director of the Buffalo Bill Historical Center at Cody, Wyoming, and the leader of many research expeditions for the American Museum of Natural History, directly challenged the BLM's claims. "The horses stick back in the mountains in places too rugged for cattle to graze," he pointed out. "Cattle couldn't survive under those conditions, so they stay in a gentler area. You could put a thousand horses up there and still have no conflict." McCracken neatly summed up the stakes. "If the BLM moves against that herd in Montana, it will be one of the greatest disgraces to conservation and to our heritage since the slaughter of the buffalo. And if they get away with it, the same people are going to do the same thing in other areas."[4]

Faced with such criticism from an expert, most bureaucrats would have backed away. Not Solari. He recycled the standard BLM line, repudiated by Congress in 1959, that these mustangs were not wild, merely untamed and feral, and too far removed in time from America's first horses to claim any genetic link. In fact, to suggest such a thing, Solari declared, was to perpetrate a fraud. He also continued to insist that the horses were degrading cattle, sheep, and deer forage. He had the backing of the Montana Fish and Game Department, which wanted to introduce mountain sheep to the southern Pryors, even though knowledgeable hunters maintained that any mountain sheep deposited in the Pryors would waste little time relocating southeast to the grassier Bighorn Mountains.

After warning Lloyd Tillett for two years that he'd better get rid of "his" horses, Solari ordered to him to round up and remove any in excess of the twenty specified on the TX Ranch grazing permit. The Tilletts responded by wrapping the Bureau in red tape. Since the horses ranged back and forth across the Montana-Wyoming border, they pointed out that state law required brand inspectors from both the Montana and Wyoming brand boards to ensure there weren't any branded horses among the herd. And who was going to pay the expenses for that operation?

While Solari wrestled with this complication, three riders appeared one day at the TX Ranch. Claiming they were sent by the BLM to offer a deal, the men informed Lloyd Tillett that they had standing offers for the horses, including one from a Montana mink farm: four cents a pound for dressed or butchered horsemeat. The value of the herd amounted to roughly twenty-five hundred dollars, more if sold to canneries, which were paying six cents a pound for horsemeat on the hoof.

Tillett, a lean figure with a face weather-lined beyond his forty-six years, had a soft way of talking but his eyes quickly turned hard when he heard something he didn't like. He told the men they'd better vamoose or they'd have a fight on their hands. The Tilletts had no intention of relinquishing their claim to the herd.

On December 15, 1965, the BLM notified the Tilletts that 134 of their horses were grazing on public land illegally and so were liable to monthly trespass fines of two dollars a head. The family calculated they would owe as much as seventy-two hundred dollars if the BLM fined them for all the time the horses had spent on the range since the original eviction order more than two years previous. "Once the horses have been removed to the satisfaction of this office," Solari wrote, "we could meet with you and make final disposition of the trespass case."[5]

Solari's assistant, Birrell Hirschi, later conceded that the BLM intended to drive Lloyd Tillett into an impossible financial corner. The agency anticipated that he wouldn't or couldn't pay the fees, which would give the Bureau license to corral the horses and charge him the roundup costs as well. Tillett ignored what he considered a BLM bluff until February 1966, when the Bureau suspended TX Ranch's cattle-grazing permits, citing improper fencing. It was the decisive blow. Without public land for spring grazing, there would be no choice but to herd the cattle onto the ranch's privately owned summer pastures. "A hundred and forty cattle eating summer grass in the spring can do more damage than 3,000 later on," Tillett told a reporter. "And if the feed ran out before fall, it could cost us $4,000 to $5,000 in lost weight when we went to market."

After more than two years of skirmishing with the BLM, the Tilletts abandoned their ownership of the horses, making them unclaimed property and subject to clearance by the Bureau. They asked for a single concession, that the horses not be shot. State Director Tysk refused to make any guarantees. The horses had a few months of grace left, because the BLM and their mustangers couldn't negotiate the mountains in the middle of winter.

Although Velma had been aware of the Pryor Mountains standoff since 1964, she had neither the energy nor the inclination to get involved in the wake of Charlie's death. But in early 1966, as she rededicated herself to the wild horse movement, she began inserting herself into the dispute. By spring she was fully engaged. "The ruckus in Wyoming and Montana has certainly created a furor, and I don't believe the BLM can afford to ignore it," she wrote in April 1966. "I am hoping now that [Secretary of the Interior Stewart] Udall will set up some sort of a meeting whereby this sort of thing can be avoided in the future. This impasse is really of no benefit to anyone—and I am afraid that if it is left to go on for too many years, people will lose the fighting spirit and give up. However it really doesn't look like it at the moment judging from the copies of letters and telegrams that are being sent to me. Bless those red-blooded Americans!"[6]

Velma's goal was to have part of the Pryor Range declared a federal wild horse preserve, similar to the one in southern Nevada. This time, though, she envisioned a civilian management committee to monitor the horses and their habitat. Velma reconnected with Walter Baring and set in motion another letter-writing campaign to government, media, and supporters. Though she'd been offstage for a few years, Wild Horse Annie still resonated with the press. Soon newspaper articles were appearing across the West. At *True* magazine, editorial memories of the response to "The Mustang's Last Stand," published ten years earlier, had not faded, and the editors sent journalist Charles Remsberg to Lovell, Wyoming, the closest city to the Pryors.

As public awareness mounted, it occurred to members of the Lovell Chamber of Commerce that they could cash in on the wild horses as a tourist attraction. A planned road and recreation area would soon be taking tourists into the famous ice caves to the north, right past the horses' territory. In truth, the herds frequented such remote country that spotting one from a car was extremely unlikely, but the idea of safari-like wild horse excursions attracted both attention and support.

The Chamber of Commerce formed the Pryor Mountain Wild Horse Association and hired its own range expert to contest the arguments of the BLM. The association has been spelled Pryor Mountain and Pryor Mountains in various official and unofficial documents.

"There's a lot of history out here in the West," pointed out Floyd Schweiger, a Lutheran minister and spokesman for the association. "Right around here we have mountain men's huts, cliffs with Indian writings on them, places where you can still pick up arrow heads used to kill buffalo. The horses are part of all of this. We must preserve our historical legacies for the generations to come."[7] Schweiger was infuriated that the assessment of wild horse damage to the terrain was to be made by BLM personnel, not ranchers or hunters who knew and worked the land. He also suspected that Bureau officials were informally encouraging stockmen to shoot stallions. He had seen gunshot Pryor horses loaded on to flatbeds destined for the Red Lodge Zoo in Montana, where the carcasses would be cheap food for the zoo's big cats.

The first national publicity appeared in April when the *National Observer* and United Press International picked up the story. Fearing a rekindling of the public outrage that propelled Velma to Capitol Hill in 1959, the BLM hastily announced a one-year moratorium on the wild horse clearance while officials conducted a range inventory. Dante Solari promised the Tilletts that their grazing rights would be restored and the trespassing fines forgotten and that the horses themselves wouldn't be molested until the survey was finished in the spring of 1967.

Velma smoothly folded the Tilletts' five-year-long conflict with the BLM into her own cause. "Remember the Tillett family rebellion against the Beeyoorow earlier this year?" Velma wrote to Marguerite Henry in October 1966. "And the one-year reprieve that we won for the wild ones? Well, the faint rumble of war drums is echoing on that front and faintly discernible battle lines are now being drawn . . . I took my flu bug to bed early last night, and just as I was drifting off into a marshmallow soft cloud of drowsiness, the insistent ring of the telephone brought me out of bed. It was a writer for *True* magazine calling from Lovell, there on an assignment to write that phase of the mustang war. All roads lead to Annie, it seems, for he learned from the Tilletts that I had tangled with Mr. Solari when he was field man for this district."

Velma hadn't lost her touch; she converted Remsberg during their forty-five-minute conversation. "Now," she reported gleefully, "if *True* comes out with a strong article against the methods employed by the Beeyoorow in deciding when there is an over-abundance, etc., etc., I'm going after the Department of the Interior stronger than ever for a refuge in every state, two in some."[8]

Remsberg called on Velma several more times for background information. At one point he confessed his amazement that she had prevailed in the past while facing the same strong-arm tactics Solari and the BLM were using against the Tilletts.

Despite the Bureau's apparent retreat, the Tilletts were far from confident of ultimate victory. "The BLM has just backed away from the issue to let things cool off. Then when everyone has forgotten about the horses, they'll move in for the kill. If anyone kicks, they'll have a slanted survey to offer as justification," Lloyd predicted. Dr. McCracken agreed. "Unless some very drastic action is taken, I am convinced the BLM intends to move against these horses as originally planned."[9]

The self-described "chief ramrod" of the Pryor Mountains' range inventory was Solari's assistant, Birrell Hirschi, "a muscular young blond" as one reporter described him. The survey methodology was simple: Hirschi and a team of BLM employees made visual comparisons of vegetation in two areas, twenty-four miles apart. One site was frequented by the horses, the other was not. "We will figure these findings against what the BLM thinks is a proper range to see how it stacks up," Hirschi explained.

Unsurprisingly, the BLM survey confirmed what the agency had contended all along: The wild horse area had far worse erosion, poorer vegetation density, and less variety and distribution of wildlife. But Charles Remsberg of *True* proved to be an enterprising journalist. He unearthed aerial photographs of the two sites that showed the horses' territory consisted of extremely rough terrain marked by steep canyons, while the other area was comparatively gentle rangeland. Hirschi was forced to admit that topography alone would "tend to affect the difference in range conditions."

*True*'s article, published in April 1967, ridiculed the BLM with dry humor, portraying the agency in general and Dante Solari in particular as heavy-handed bad guys in a high-noon showdown with a rancher who embodied the spirit of the independent West. "[This] should go a long way in helping us get further refuge areas under the control of a board that includes civilians," Velma exulted. "I'll bet the day will come when Solari will wish he had never heard of a wild horse."[10]

When Velma was on the scent, she couldn't restrain herself. She resurrected Gus Bundy's photographs and distributed them to various reporters, "loaning" a set to Doris Cerveri, an experienced journalist and the author of four books. Cerveri's article appeared on May 19, 1967, in the *Nevadan,* the weekend magazine of the Las Vegas *Review-Journal,* at that time the largest daily newspaper in Nevada. The accompanying photographs were reproduced "courtesy of Velma Johnston." An angry Bundy telephoned Cerveri, insisting she or the newspaper pay him six dollars for the use of the photos. After the money arrived, Bundy wrote the *Nevadan*'s editor, Bill Vincent, sarcastically thanking him for the "token" payment and demanding the attribution be corrected.[11]

But Velma steadfastly stuck to her interpretation of the photos' status. "It is most regrettable that once again the proper credits for your superb photography were omitted," Velma wrote to Bundy, with a copy to Vincent. "I had loaned the photos to Mrs. Doris Cerveri with the request that she first obtain, as a courtesy, permission directly from you for their reproduction in the article. . . . Since I had already had the written permission from the owners of the prints to use them in any manner I saw fit, and they are now mine through gift from *True* magazine, there was actually no requirement that you be contacted for your permission. However, I have always felt it was the courteous thing to do and that is how I explained it to Mrs. Cerveri.

"I do hope the foregoing will clarify the ownership of the pictures in question, and you can be sure that I shall continue to do my best to see to it that you receive the credit you so richly deserve. I am sure you will agree also, in view of the foregoing, that no payment needs to be paid to you for their use at any time, and I, of course, have been permitting their use gratis."[12]

Bundy must have been furious at Velma's claim of ownership of his photographs and her blithe statement that he should be consulted only as a courtesy. But he gritted his teeth and wrote a restrained reply, insisting again on his absolute ownership of the photographs. "Rather than go into more detail concerning your beliefs, I urge you to contact *True* magazine in order to clarify for yourself on what basis they allowed you to have copies for which they bought only 'single-use' rights. This will save you (and *True* magazine) further embarrassment and a lawsuit for damages."[13]

Bill Vincent stepped into the role of gentlemanly protector, much as Professor McKnight had done eight years earlier. "In view of Mrs. Johnston's letter of June 1 it seems to me, rather clearly, that it would behove you to send Doris Cerveri an apology and a check for the $6 you conned from her. The photo credit, which you or anyone else deserves, will be carried as planned in next Sunday's issue of the *Nevadan*. But in light of your browbeating of Mrs. Cerveri, a copy will not be sent to you by me. You can get your own copy. Goodbye, Mr. Bundy." Vincent added a note to the copy he sent to Velma. "The above only partially expresses my feelings, but Bundy should get the idea. We have had many comments about the story and your work. You have many friends here now."[14]

Velma was now content to simply ignore the situation. "Many thanks for the blow you struck in defence of the weaker sex," she responded to Vincent. "You by now have received the copy of Mr. B's disagreeable letter to me. I don't plan to contact the picture editor, nor anyone else, about my right to use the photos, unless it becomes absolutely necessary, but I rather imagine Mr. Mason was fully aware of the magazine's rights of ownership before he sent the pictures to me."[15]

Fed up with Velma's stonewalling and Vincent's "libellous" letter, Bundy wrote to *True* himself. Editor Douglas S. Kennedy responded, "You have every right to complain if Mrs. Johnston is using your pictures anywhere in the world. Mr. Mason has not been with *True* since 1960. I think he meant for her to promote her campaign noncommercially, with the use of your pictures. At any rate, he had no right to give her even that permission. As far as *True* is concerned, they are your pictures and we bought only one-time reproduction use."[16]

Armed with indisputable proof, Bundy wrote to Velma again. "It is with deep reluctance that I write this letter to you. Hopeful that you would do the proper thing voluntarily I have held off from this drastic step until this time." Bundy demanded the return of all of the photos and negatives in Velma's possession and forbade her using them without written permission, "since your acts no longer permit credence in your abuses being the result of innocence or ignorance. . . . It is sad that of all the groups and individuals working towards the same legislation each in his own way, only you have abused my permission for use of my photographs in order to secure this legislation."[17]

Still protesting that she was innocently involved in this "unpleasantness," Velma turned the matter over to her lawyer, William C. Sanford, Sr. "It has occurred to me that Mr. Bundy's photographs would not have realized for him the financial gain they have had it not been for Wild Horse Annie's fight that made the public aware of the treatment of the wild ones. . . . Incidentally, I have never used the photos commercially, and the only remuneration I have ever received over the years for anything was the $250 for the story for *True,* $1 for the release of my life story to Rand McNally and $500 from the author of *Mustang, Wild Spirit of the West* for my technical assistance and the use of my files. The rest has been expense and there has been lots of that. I'm not complaining, understand, but it is quite possible that Mr. Bundy thinks I'm getting rich off the royalties."[18]

Unabashed by the incident, Velma referred to Bundy as "a nasty little man" in a letter to a friend and later airily dismissed the matter as a tempest over a vague, unwritten law of copyright. But she did stop offering the photographs to journalists and she never again included them with press releases.

In December 1967, eight of Bundy's images were added to the National Cowboy Hall of Fame in Oklahoma. There is no record of how the Hall of Fame obtained the photos in the first place, though Bundy must have had his suspicions. It was galling to have his work displayed, in the words of the *Nevada State Journal,* as "part of an exhibit tracing a Reno secretary's campaign to save wild horses from an eventual fate as pet food. . . . The pictures will join the original paintings used to illustrate the book about Mrs. Johnston's fight, the original black and white sketches of the paintings, the pen with which President Dwight Eisenhower signed the Wild Horse Bill into law, and the notes Mrs. Johnston used to argue before congress."[19]

It was a final indignity for Gus Bundy, but he appears to have been reconciled to it. He hadn't won a single skirmish with Velma in his decade-long battle with her, and he wasn't likely to win this one. As a result of Velma's willful appropriation of his work, Bundy hasn't received full payment or credit for his extraordinary photographs to this day. "[Velma] displayed a series of horrifying photographs that had been published in *Life* magazine and have since become iconic," states an otherwise authoritative book published in 2008, describing Velma's 1959 presentation to Congress.[20] The passage goes on to describe Bundy's photographs in some detail but his name appears nowhere.

# TWELVE

# A Perfect Storm

E ARLY IN 1967 Velma's informants told her that at least two thousand wild horses had been captured illegally and secreted in various locations in central Nevada and northern California, awaiting
shipment to slaughterhouses. The news rankled on several levels. In
the eight years since the passage of Public Law 86–234, not a single
charge had been laid against violators. So far the Wild Horse Annie law
had proved to be a paper tiger and Velma was desperate to find a test
case to give it teeth. She had hoped the Pryor Mountains battle might
spit out a convictable bad guy, but the only culprit that emerged was
the BLM itself, and not even Velma thought that taking the Bureau to
court was practical. Still, she believed it was critical that someone—
preferably a large operator—be charged and prosecuted.

Laying charges under the act, let alone mounting a successful prosecution, required that the perpetrators be caught red-handed with
their airplane and the captured horses. This was a formidable problem since the roundups were conducted in the most isolated locations
and the planes were in the air only briefly. Once the horses were harried out of their hiding places and buzzed toward the trap, the plane
peeled away and disappeared, usually landing miles away. And who
would lay the charges? The BLM had neither the inclination nor the
budget. Deputy sheriffs and state brand inspectors faced the difficulties of distance and timing and the very real personal risks of accosting
armed men in the middle of nowhere. Finding an enforcement officer
who shared Velma's aversion to planing and was willing to lay charges
and testify in a test case was as arduous a process as getting the bill
passed in the first place.

Then in mid-January 1967, Velma received an unexpected call from

Stanley F. Routson, supervisor of the Bureau of Livestock Identification, the brand inspection arm of Nevada's Department of Agriculture. A rancher complained that some of his branded horses had been captured with a group of mustangs. "They were all taken in an aerial roundup, that was clear enough," he told Velma. "I was called in to check for privately owned stock. Well, they all turned out to be unbranded. But I have to tell you, Mrs. Johnston, I had to order them all slaughtered to put them out of their misery."[1]

There was so much blood, Routson couldn't tell what had caused their injuries until after the horses were put down and he was able to extract buckshot from the wounds. "Eyes were shot out and lips hanging down where they'd been shot off," he said somberly.[2] The horses had been contained in a concrete-walled pen at the slaughterhouse in Newark and the mustangs' hides were torn and gouged from their frenzied battering against the walls in an effort to escape. Routson's disgust with the brutality of the crime was exacerbated by his frustration at not being able to apprehend the perpetrators, even though he knew the horses had been illegally chased by airplane. He vowed to Velma that he would do everything he could to get them.

Routson secretly gave Velma access to his department's records, which allowed her to confirm a ruse she'd long suspected: Mustangers would often slip one or two of their own branded horses in with a shipment of wild horses. This gave the capture a quasi-legal aura, since the BLM had ruled that "the rancher may use any method he wishes . . . including driving the animals with trucks or airplanes . . . as long as they belong to him. [Wild horses and domestic horses] may be grazing side by side. If someone intends to round up their own animals, he may accidentally take wild horses at the same time."[3]

Routson believed the thirty-nine horses he examined were part of a group of some 150 that had been targeted by Julian Goicochea, a large-scale sheep and cattle rancher with BLM grazing permits for seventy-two square miles of range in eastern Nevada's White Pine County. Goicochea had the ear of senators and congressmen and sat on the BLM's powerful White Pine County Advisory Committee. He was just the sort of big fish Velma was hoping to catch.

On Friday, February 7, 1967, Routson received a report of horses being run by airplane in Indian Hills south of Carson City. The plane—which had crashed during the roundup—was tantalizing evidence. Unfortunately when Routson got to the scene, he found eight mares, one stallion, and a colt, all branded. There was no sign of mustangs and the man behind the roundup wasn't associated with Goicochea.

Later that same day, however, Archie Robison, sheriff of White Pine County and one of Routson's contacts, struck gold. Robison had received a phone call at eight-thirty the night before, informing him that horses were being planed in the Newark–Long Valley area of White Pine County, 270 miles east of Reno. Most of that country is so desolate it was hard to imagine lizards surviving, let alone herds of wild horses. Even the dunes of Long Valley moaned: When the humidity, wind, and temperature conditions were right, the sand grains emitted an eerie song.

At eight the next morning, Archie Robison, along with Shirley George Robison, a district brand inspector and his distant cousin, set out in a four-wheel-drive Jeep Wagoneer. The two men were an ideal combination from a law enforcement point of view. At the time there were 138 brand inspectors in Nevada charged with overseeing Title 50—the issuing, recording, and inspecting of brands, and enforcement of Nevada's brand laws. Their authority did not extend to enforcing a federal law such as PL 86–234, but sheriffs did possess that authority and could make arrests.

The Newark–Long Valley area was vast but the point of capture had to be accessible by trucks to haul out the horses. The officials wound their way up the west slope of Antelope Summit and along progressively rougher roads until they hit a sheep trail just before 10:00 A.M. "I spotted a plane about a mile to the north which was starting to circle and lose some altitude as though it were working over some horses," Shirley Robison later testified. "We observed it from this position for a few minutes as it dived and circled but were unable to see the horses, so we moved up over the summit and found a better vantage point, and from there we were able to see seven head of horses coming off the mountain."[4]

The airplane, with a howling siren mounted to its wing and strings of tin cans jangling over the side, dove sharply as the pilot strafed the horses. Archie and Shirley watched as five horses, including a colt, were harried down the mountain. Two of the original seven disappeared from sight. The colt eventually tired and was left behind. The plane drove the horses into a long V-shaped funnel fashioned of cedar trees, much like the prada developed more than half a century earlier by Pete Barnum. The horses tore through the funnel and into a small corral. The gate clanged shut while the plane went back for the colt. The whole operation took about ninety minutes.

At the corral they found two ranch hands, a gate tender and the hazer, who had waited on horseback some distance from the trap to catch any mustangs that tried to cut away from the herd. The men admitted they had been working for Julian Goicochea for the past three weeks and that the horses were being chased out of the mountains by plane. The sheriff and the brand inspector drove to the airstrip after the plane landed and arrested the pilot, Ted Barber, along with Art Cook, a rancher neighbor of Goicochea. A search turned up a sawed-off shotgun in the plane. Both men admitted they worked for Goicochea but protested that all necessary permits were in place and, in any case, Goicochea owned all the horses. He was just rounding up his own property.

Using a Polaroid camera and making detailed notes, Shirley Robison documented five horses found at the corral:

1 Black Stallion, no brand and no other identifying marks or white hairs.

1 bay mare, no brand; left hind fetlock white, same foot black and white.

1 filly bay, left front foot and right hind foot white, white star in forehead, unbranded.

1 light bay filly, left hind foot and leg white stocking about one foot up, white spot on outside of the right front foot at top of hoof, white blaze face, unbranded.

1 steel gray mare, branded, CA right shoulder and C on right thigh; this mare was bleeding from eight shotgun pellet wounds which

Mr. Barber admitted having inflicted by shooting from the plane to help control and turn them.[5]

The two officials gathered sufficient evidence to justify convening a grand jury and, based on the testimony, the FBI laid charges against Julian Goicochea, Art Cook, and Ted Barber. The trio faced a maximum penalty of a five-hundred-dollar fine or six months in jail. The only real weakness in the case was that one of the five horses was branded. Routson set out to prove that branded horses were a rarity among those taken off Goicochea's land. He took five men with him to White Pine County to revisit the holding facility in Newark. There, in the same concrete-walled corral, they found nine horses—a shipment from Goicochea—standing knee-deep in slop. As they approached, the fearful animals careened around the pen, filling the air with flying mud, the smell of blood, and the sounds of their rattling breath and the splat-suck of hooves driving in the muck. It took Routson's men all day to rope and examine the horses for brands. Routson's investigation eventually uncovered 158 horses shipped by Goicochea to the slaughterhouse, only four of which were branded.

Velma rejoiced at Routson's findings; here, finally, was a legal test of the Wild Horse Annie law with irrefutable evidence on the prosecution's side. "This will be an important case, as it is the first one where there are witnesses to the actual planing, pictures of the operation, a federal grand jury indictment, and a person (Mr. Routson) who is determined to go ahead with it," she wrote to Helen and John Reilly, her mainstays at the International Society for the Protection of Mustangs and Burros. "So many times the roundups (illegal) have been observed; the ones who report it to me refuse to give their names, or decline to testify. I am hoping that the trial will get nationwide publicity."[6] In a letter to another supporter she wrote, "I am sure there will be a conviction—unless money or power or both can weasel them out on technicalities."[7]

The defense lawyers were Andrew Demetras, one-time district attorney for the White Pine jurisdiction where the offense took place, and his partner, Paul Richards. Prosecuting was Assistant U.S. Attorney Julien Sourwine, a young lawyer from Washington, D.C., recently appointed to Reno. He knew little about wild horses, the BLM, or the fine points of the act itself, but Velma educated him about brand and permit issues and loaned him reference material from her extensive library.

On February 22 Velma learned that in response to a motion from the defendants, the trial had been moved from Las Vegas to Goicochea's home turf of Reno. "Congressman Baring is here in Nevada, and I'm in contact with him through his sister," she wrote to a Humane Society official. "He stands firm on this, and Cannon can hardly do otherwise, as he co-sponsored the bill. . . . I'm resting easy about the whole thing at this time—and only hope that the defendants do not change their plea to 'guilty.' I want them to stand trial—with lots of publicity."[8] Velma was so sure of the ultimate outcome, she considered the trial a mere formality. The statements and evidence supplied by the witnesses were impeccable and their credentials unimpeachable.

On the first day of the jury trial, July 5, 1967, Sourwine carefully laid out the prosecution's case, and vigorous cross-examination by the defense failed to shake his witnesses. When the defendants took the stand, they admitted they had used an airplane to facilitate the roundup, but stuck to the story that Goicochea owned the horses and that they were all branded. Goicochea testified that he'd cleared out all the wild horses in 1958 and then allowed a hundred head of his own horses, as well as fifty head belonging to his codefendant, Art Cook, to graze in the area. By the end of the first day in court, it appeared that conviction rested on the question of whether the horses were branded. Velma expected the sworn statements of the sheriff and the brand inspector, who testified that only one of the five horses had been branded when they inspected them, coupled with Routson's statement that there were only four branded horses among the 158 horses Goicochea had captured over the period of his investigation, would carry the day.

The next morning, the defense called a surprise witness, Ed Garavante, a deputy brand inspector from the Fallon area, sixty-two miles east of Reno, and a rancher for over forty years. He testified that in the winter months when the mustangs grew long coats, the only way to determine if they were branded was to shear off the coat to expose the branded area beneath. Art Cook was then recalled to testify that he took the five horses in question back to the Goicochea Ranch and sheared them. All five were branded. Cook produced pictures of sheared horses with brands clearly visible and entered them into evidence. There was no way to tell from the photographs if they were fresh brands or even if they were the same horses.

Richards and Demetras then proceeded to shred Sourwine's case. Inexplicably, Sourwine failed to recall Stanley Routson, Garavante's superior in the service, for rebuttal. Routson would have testified that shearing a horse was necessary only if a brand could not be precisely identified. Branding forever altered the growth of the hair, making it fairly straightforward to determine if a horse was branded. He would also have reminded the court that only four of the 158 horses captured by Goicochea's crew over a period of weeks were branded and that none needed to be sheared, even though all were inspected in January with full winter coat.

The jury deliberated just a few hours before bringing back a verdict of not guilty. Sourwine's inexperience appears to have played a role, but so, too, did Velma's. She was overconfident and ignored what she knew, that ranchers close ranks when the government comes knocking and even public servants will rally around a powerful man like Goicochea. The difference between making money and losing one's shirt in ranching in Nevada was access to grazing licenses. No one ranching within the BLM's White Pine County Advisory Committee jurisdiction could afford to get on the wrong side of one its prominent members.

Velma also failed to give Sourwine information that would have neutralized Garavante's testimony. When Goicochea claimed that the BLM Advisory Committee had met on December 16, 1966, and determined there were no wild horses in the area, Sourwine could not challenge him. But Velma had a copy of a letter from the acting director of the Department of the Interior to Walter Baring dated March 21, 1967, stating, "Bureau personnel in Nevada have been aware of a considerable number of both licensed and unlicensed wild horses on Mr. Goicochea's public range allotment."[9]

Why the woman who never left anything to chance slipped up so badly on this occasion is hard to explain, but it could be attributable to pressures and distractions in other areas of her tightly compartmentalized life. While she juggled preparations for the trial, the Pryor Mountains situation, and several other wild horse emergencies, a crisis arose at the office. Gordon Harris suffered a heart attack in late February and was ordered to take three weeks' bed rest in the hospital.

"It is like trying to keep a flea tied down, as you can well imagine. . . . He's going to be alright, if we can just keep him from getting so tense about everything. Ruthie, Jr. [Gordon Harris Jr.] and I are running the office, and for a while it was really a challenge, but by putting in a few extra hours each day, and confining lunch hours to minutes, we are doing real well."[10] Harris insisted that his clients not know he was hospitalized, necessitating quite a bit of "fast talk" from Velma. All the while she continued to moonlight in the evenings and on weekends, though both Harris and Trudy urged her to give it up.

Velma was so distressed by the Goicochea verdict that she could hardly speak about the case except to admit that "I lost so much that day—so very, very much."[11] After a month of contemplation, she was ready for a more objective postmortem. Her relationship with Marguerite Henry was no longer close but there was no one else to whom she could unburden herself. "I've cooled off considerably over the trial, for I know that nothing is accomplished in hot-headed emotionalism, and my making myself sick over it. . . . In talking with a friend of one of the jurors, I learned that it was poor presentation of evidence against the criminals and failure to bring out some points strongly enough. I understand that the jury was convinced of guilt at the end of the first day, but then 'had no alternative' after the witness was brought on who swore that the only way to tell if a horse is branded is to shear it. I still think they could have used their collective heads and realized this was not true."[12]

Velma misjudged the complexity and subtlety of the American legal system. It wasn't that Garavante's testimony was so convincing, rather that it introduced doubt. And although Velma didn't hesitate to whip her outlanders into action, she couldn't bring herself to do this with Julien Sourwine. She was just enough of a secretary to acquiesce to a man who held a status similar to that of her boss. Velma also saw young Sourwine as a member of her team and she was loath to criticize anyone she'd anointed as a fellow crusader. Seven months later she laid most of the blame on Sourwine but was never able to admit to her own mistakes. "I feel that the failure to obtain a conviction of the trio last year was in large part due to lack of horse knowledge by the deputy U.S. attorney who prosecuted the case," she wrote to Christine Stevens at the Society for Animal Protective Legislation. "My attorney also agrees, and hopes that we can get a U.S. attorney sent out from Washington who knows about horses when and if we get sufficient evidence for an indictment and arrest. . . . Maybe you can help us from Washington when the time comes."[13]

About one of the opposing attorneys, Paul Richards, who'd turned the tables on the prosecution so deftly, Velma wrote grudgingly, "a competent slickaroo if I ever saw one, and I'm only sorry he wasn't the prosecuting attorney! I can't like him though."[14]

The trial wasn't a complete loss: It brought necessary exposure to the mustangers while demonstrating the difficulty of getting a conviction under the 1959 law, and it highlighted the weaknesses of local law enforcement. Despite their willingness, neither Archie Robison nor Shirley Robison was trained or equipped for such situations. They had arrived on the scene without the resources to impound the horses, for example, and so were forced to leave the evidence with the very men they intended to charge. Ultimately, Velma did enjoy something of a last laugh when Goicochea's lawyers had to file suit against him to collect payment of their five-thousand-dollar legal bill.

Midway through that hectic year, a drama similar to that of the Pryor Mountains began unfolding in the rugged and spectacular high country near Grand Junction, Colorado. There the BLM threatened to clear out the wild herds that had populated the Little Bookcliff Mountains since the seventeenth century. When Velma leaped in with her usual multipage, single-spaced letter demanding information and justification from the BLM, she was completely nonplussed by the Colorado district manager's cordial response. He assured her that the Bureau had no imminent clearance plans and that he would keep her informed of events. A second letter arrived from the Reno district manager, offering to assist her in any way possible and promising to pass along any news he received about the Little Bookcliff herd.

Velma had always thought she could work with the BLM if the

agency would only meet her halfway. And when the Little Bookcliff herd joined the Pryor mustangs in generating more bad publicity for the BLM, she actually expressed some sympathy for its predicament. "It is too bad the Bureau has brought about this unenviable situation for itself by its very bad public relations in the past and its policy of evasiveness, denial and downright defiance. It is such a waste of time and money, this eternal bickering, and having to stand off the Bureau incident by incident. If only a permanent program can be worked out that will guide all future decisions," Velma wrote to a fellow wild horse activist.[15]

In November 1967, the BLM surprised Velma again with an unprecedented invitation to come to Washington and participate in discussions about the Pryor Mountains situation. She couldn't afford to take time away from work, however, and asked Tom Holland and John McCormack, president and vice president respectively of the recently formed National Mustang Association in Utah, to take her place. The combative Holland was unimpressed with the three alternatives the BLM put forward for the Pryor horses: completely remove all horses; reduce the herd to thirty or thirty-five horses and manage the range and watershed accordingly; or chop the herd to a token dozen horses in order to allow "maintenance of a healthy deer herd and later reintroduction of Bighorn sheep when forage conditions improved sufficiently."[16]

Velma's nascent sympathy for the Bureau dissolved when she read McCormack's report of the meeting. "The BLM is confusing the term 'preserve' with another term, 'permit to exist,'" Velma complained to Lynn Augustine, a former investigator for the Humane Society. "Although they issued a news release indicating that the mustang will now receive help, I can see no evidence that this is their intention. They plan to select certain areas in which they will 'permit limited numbers of mustangs to exist.' There was no talk whatsoever of setting this land aside specifically for the use of the mustang, nor is there any program to provide any form of protection for those few which are permitted to remain. To the general public, this would appear to be setting aside a preserve for mustangs, but in reality it opens the door for the removal of all mustangs from the vast remaining public domain."[17]

Still, Velma was guardedly optimistic that the Pryor imbroglio could be settled to the benefit of the wild horses. "The terms of the BLM are not generous," she wrote to Christine Stevens, "but they are at least an indication that there might be a starting point for a reasonable approach to the situation. It is when we reach this point that a massive publicity campaign will be important."[18]

Holland and his colleagues in the National Mustang Association believed the worst, and they were right. Sometime in February or March 1968, the BLM upped the ante by beginning construction of an elaborate horse trap situated on one of the few springs in the arid Pryor Range. When the horses came to drink, they would trip an electric eye that automatically shut the gate behind them. The trap was massive: ten feet tall with posts set three feet into the ground at six-foot intervals and capable of holding all two hundred horses thought to be on the range.

Into this simmering situation strode Hope Ryden, a slight thirty-

*Chuck Wagner (left) and Lloyd Tillett at the Pryor Mountains*
*horse trap built by the BLM*

two-year-old former fashion model, now a rising documentary film-maker for ABC Television News. One of the few women in the news documentary field, Ryden was necessarily forceful in her pursuit of any story. She'd received a tip from John Walsh, a special agent for the International Society for the Prevention of Cruelty to Animals, about the imminent capture and slaughter of the Pryor mustangs. Walsh had previously directed her to stories on starving sled dogs in Alaska and animals drowning in the flooded jungles of South America, both of which became subjects of Ryden documentaries. After nearly succumbing to hypothermia in Alaska, Ryden swore off doing any more endangered-animal stories. But once she heard about the Pryor Range fight, Ryden recognized that the horses were part of America's legacy and their story transcended local interest.

Ryden's first call was to Dean Bibles, the BLM district manager in Billings, Montana. Such was the power of network television news that she could pick up the phone and get an interview with the top man in the region on her first try. It had taken Velma eighteen years of dogged perseverance to gain that kind of access. Bibles fed Ryden the familiar BLM line about destruction of forage and soil erosion while likening the feral, not wild, horses to common pests. He emphasized that the Pryor herds were starving.

From the beginning, Ryden was struck by the contradictory facts cited by both sides. The BLM said there were 200 horses, the Tilletts said 140, and when pressed the BLM claimed the actual number was not known. The BLM said the horses were starving, the Tilletts said otherwise. The BLM maintained the horses weren't wild, Harold McCracken said they were. Ryden was also surprised by the agency's punitive attitude, as if the Pryor horses were pawns in a personal range war. "If Tillett wanted to keep the excess horses," Bibles told Ryden, "he could do so by decreasing the number of cattle he runs on his allotment. But he must make up his mind what he wants . . . more horses or [more] cattle. A rancher using the public lands cannot have his cake and eat it too."[19]

To Ryden it was a "hell of a story" with obvious heroes and villains. Television isn't the best medium for making a complicated argument, but it is powerful when covering a well-delineated dispute. Even better from a filmmaker's perspective, the Pryor Mountains and the people involved offered dynamite visuals. "The first night I booked into a motel in Lovell and was visited by Lloyd and his brother Royce," Ryden said. "The two looked spiffy in their mud-caked boots and big hats, straight out of central casting. I hadn't expected John Wayne but this was better."[20]

When the BLM toured Ryden through the Pryors, they came across "only a single horse staring at us."[21] Later, guided by the Tilletts, Ryden filmed numerous bands of horses, all in good condition. Only two were thin, both mares with new foals. For one sequence, Ryden posed three of the Pryor Mountain Wild Horse Association members, Reverend Schweiger, Chuck Wagner, and Lloyd Tillett, near the edge of Devil Canyon Overlook, a thousand feet above Bighorn Lake. The breathtaking drop-off made it appear that the edge of the world lay just behind them. The three men spoke simply and clearly about the beauty of the horses, their historical importance, and the fact that they definitely weren't starving. In addition to the reels of film the crew shot, Ryden took a photograph of Tillett and Wagner dwarfed by the massive timbers of the BLM horse trap. She estimated the materials alone cost thirty-five thousand dollars, enough to feed two hundred horses for eight years.

As part of her research Ryden spent four days in Reno with Velma. The two women were friendly yet maintained a distance as the veteran, Velma, suggested direction and offered advice to Ryden, the novice. Velma was accustomed to taking the media in hand, but Ryden responded differently than the mainly male writers who had previously made the pilgrimage to Wild Horse Annie. Ryden had a considerable ego of her own and wasn't about to defer to anyone. And while she admired Velma's intelligence and remarkable energy, Ryden also felt that Wild Horse Annie's reputation was overblown and she bluntly, though privately, described Velma's face as "a fright." Velma, in turn, believed Ryden would be a valuable addition to the wild horse fight but she worried that the journalist's aggressive approach might undo what she had spent nearly two decades trying to construct.

After Ryden edited her Pryor Mountains documentary it sat in ABC News's offices for more than a month, an unusually long delay for one of her timely stories. Behind the scenes, the BLM was working to keep it off the air. Ryden's assertiveness had gotten under the agency's collective skin and senior officials worried about how the Bureau would be viewed by a national audience. They demanded a viewing of the documentary before it was broadcast. The BLM's complaints prompted ABC executives to summon Ryden to the screening room, "where the entire upstairs (meaning all the big shots at ABC) were seated. This was quite out of the ordinary. I had covered stories on such subjects as dictator Papa Doc Duvalier in Haiti and union busters in Chinatown factories and never been subjected to a review."[22]

ABC did turn over an advance copy of the documentary and a friendly BLM staffer in Reno whispered to Velma, who in turn alerted Ryden, that the Bureau was out to "get the producer and ABC."[23] The BLM scrutinized the tape, searching for errors or actionable claims. The intimidation alone might have been enough to keep the story off the air, but then *Newsweek* ran an article on the Pryor herds that spotlighted the use of wild horses as dog food and drolly referred to the BLM's three options for the mustangs as "Remove, Remover and Removest." In the same issue, Jack Kroll reviewed the Broadway debut of *Hair,* commenting that it made "any musical on the Broadway boards look like high noon in a Christian Science reading room."[24] *Hair* was all about freedom from authority. What better real-life example could there be than the wild horses of American history against the dictatorial designs of government?

ABC finally aired Ryden's documentary during the evening news on July 11, 1968—awkward timing for any government department with reactionary tendencies. Antiwar sentiment was pushing the federal administration toward withdrawal from Vietnam; American flags were being burned, by Americans, in protest against the war. Reverend Martin Luther King, Jr., and Senator Robert Kennedy had been assassinated just months before, and mobs of demonstrators threatened to disrupt the 1968 Democratic National Convention. Americans could not stomach the sight of another of their country's symbols being willfully destroyed.

The six-minute documentary was the first national television coverage of the plight of wild horses. Millions of viewers were captivated by the distinctive long, thick manes and tails, the dazzling colors, and the sheer majesty of the horses the BLM intended to bring to slaughter. Contrary to the Bureau's claims, they didn't look at all like animals on the brink of starvation. The public's response hit the BLM with the force of a double-barreled kick from the hind end of a mustang.

Quickly the BLM announced that a limited number of surplus horses might remain in the Pryors if they were "sponsored." Velma thought the proposal unworkable and ridiculous: "I am going to start a movement to require that every herd of animals at large—elk, deer, etc.—be required to have a sponsor." Still she offered her support to the Pryor Mountain Wild Horse Association, which wrote to the BLM offering to sponsor the Pryor horses.

That summer Ryden, who had taken a leave of absence from ABC to write a book about wild horses, "rattled" around Washington, D.C., as she put it. She enjoyed easy access to the senior elected and nonelected officials she wished to interview, and she gave interviews herself. "Having left my job as a journalist, I now felt free to be outspoken about my personal views," she said.[25] On August 6, 1968, Ryden, along with two of Velma's allies, Pearl Twyne, president of the American Horse Protection Association, and Joan Blue, its vice president, met with Boyd Rasmussen, national director of the BLM, in his Washington office. The three women presented an intimidating triumvirate. When Rasmussen complained to them that no one had come forward to sponsor the Pryor wild horses, the women forcefully contradicted him, citing the Pryor Mountain Wild Horse Association's proposal. Rasmussen claimed not to have known of it and, in any case, he doubted the offer was serious.

Ryden further increased the pressure on the BLM in a meeting with Senator Clifford Hansen from Wyoming, telling him that the BLM was waffling on the sponsorship provision. "I would appreciate knowing if such an offer was officially made to the BLM, and if so, when it was made and what the Bureau intends to do with the offer," Hansen wrote to the BLM on August 13. "Your careful consideration of the Association's offer would, in my opinion, serve the best interests of all."[26]

Back in Nevada, Velma did her best to discreetly coordinate and direct the new activists in the wild horse movement while she once again lobbied for stiffer federal legislation. At her instigation, Walter Baring introduced a bill to make the wild horse an endangered species. If passed, it would stop the BLM—with its selective definition of "wild"—dead in its tracks in the Pryor Mountains. But Congress didn't sit again until September 4 and time was running out.

The BLM completed the horse trap on August 20. Once it was in operation it would take mere days to capture the bulk of the Pryor herds. Baring gave Velma a stack of his office stationery and a list of people to write to in his name and told her to start typing. He would sign whatever she wrote. He also put Boyd Rasmussen on notice that he would be calling a meeting of the Public Lands Committee, a body he chaired, and asked him to be prepared to answer questions raised by a constituent, Mrs. Velma Johnston.

Aroused by reports from Velma, Hope Ryden, and others, the powerful Humane Society of the United States rumbled into the fracas. On August 22, HSUS lawyers sent a registered letter to Secretary of the Interior Stewart Udall demanding that the BLM halt its activities until a management plan was announced and publicly debated. "We do not want to discover next week that these horses have been destroyed and are already on their way to the cannery. Thus it is not unreasonable that we must ask for your assurance by noon tomorrow, Friday, August 23, 1968. This lacking, we are presently prepared and have no alternative except to seek judicial relief."[27]

It is a mark of the disarray within the BLM that the deadline from the Humane Society, which had a formidable legislative and courtroom-victory record, came and went without response. On August 27, the HSUS, armed with reams of information provided by Velma and Hope Ryden, appeared before a United States district court judge for the District of Columbia to request that the court enjoin the BLM from trapping and destroying the wild horses on the Pryor Range.

The U.S. Justice Department, arguing on behalf of the BLM, stated the Bureau had no plans to trap or destroy the wild horses, a claim backed up by sworn testimony from BLM personnel. They specifically denied the existence of a horse trap. The Humane Society lawyers promptly produced Hope Ryden's photograph of the Pryor trap, whereupon, according to witnesses, the BLM officials "paled." Because the Justice Department gave assurances that no action would be taken without public announcement and debate, the court ruled that an immediate injunction wasn't necessary. However, the judge left standing the Humane Society's complaint, allowing it to be reopened on short notice.

The story of wild horses versus big government caught the attention of Pegeen and Edward Fitzgerald, who had been broadcasting a husband-and-wife chat show on WOR Radio from their apartment overlooking New York's Central Park since 1937. The program, a combination of book and movie reviews, news of the day, commentary, and occasional spousal bickering punctuated by the purring of their many cats, had a national audience of up to two million listeners. When the animal-loving Fitzgeralds flailed the BLM on their show, the Bureau blamed Hope Ryden, who happened to live in New York, not far from the Fitzgeralds. Velma quickly set them straight. "I furnished that material on request and have so informed the [BLM] attorney in Washington; furthermore, I stated that if there was anything not factual in the material, I would eat the paper on which it was written."[28]

It amounted to a perfect storm of public condemnation for the BLM, heightened by the antiauthoritarian and antigovernment sentiments already rampant in the country.

On the evening of September 5, Velma went shopping for lamp shades at Weinstocks', a Reno department store. The sales clerk who served her had a day job as the longtime secretary to the BLM's Nevada state directors. The two exchanged "girlish chit chat about this and that." In her notes, Velma hints that their conversation might have strayed to the subject of why the secretaries of high-ranking executives found it necessary to supplement their incomes with evening work. Eventually the woman mentioned that Velma had caused the Bureau "an awful lot of extra work." Velma responded that the BLM had "caused me extra work too and that it is unfortunate that we cannot all sit down at a council table and talk this all over, and perhaps arrive at an equitable settlement of the whole situation."[29]

At ten-thirty the following morning, Assistant Nevada State Director Gerald Brown telephoned Velma and invited her to lunch. Velma calculated that there had been just enough time between the start of the workday in Nevada and Brown's call to her for a telephone call to Washington. Brown would never have initiated a back-channel meeting with Wild Horse Annie without express approval from his boss or from National Director Boyd Rasmussen.

Brown was ingratiating on the telephone, telling Velma that he'd heard a great deal about her and was eager to get to know her better. A few hours later, he called for Velma at the office and escorted her to the Coach Room, the posh main-floor restaurant in the Mapes Hotel. Velma later characterized it as a "two-hour, half-pack-of-cigarettes luncheon." As they casually discussed Percheron horses, a heavy draft breed, and the Spanish-bred, dancing Lipizzaners, Velma pondered the Bureau's motives. "I was dying to ask him if he had drawn the short straw, but I was a lady and pretended it was the pleasure of my company he sought."[30]

Finally, Brown volunteered that the BLM was in a predicament and believed it was being unfairly portrayed as the villain in the wild horse drama. Velma nodded sympathetically, even though she'd worked very hard to cast the Bureau in that very role. She did concede that some of the publicity might be unfair but pointed out that since the BLM administered the public land, it was only natural for them to be the target of objections.

Brown spoke to Velma as he would to an admired colleague, telling her he had read much of her writing and that John Mattoon, chief of the BLM's Office of Information in Washington, had told him that Wild Horse Annie was one of the BLM's best supporters. Velma worked hard to swallow a laugh. "I said I wouldn't go quite that far, but that I did appreciate the Bureau's position."[31] Brown revealed that Mattoon had actually suggested Velma might be helpful in solving their wild horse problem. At this point, Velma understood that something more than lunch was going on. She even wondered if the BLM had somehow known that she had intended to buy lamp shades at Weinstocks' and had set up the secretary to serve her.

Velma gathered from Brown that the BLM was deeply concerned about Baring's endangered-species proposal and more than a little alarmed by the juggernaut the wild horse movement was becoming. To test the waters, Velma "expressed the hope that I would have wisdom enough to properly direct the powerhouse that is developing in the realm of congressional action." Brown responded by saying "he wished he could be as sure of everything else as he was of that." Velma couldn't resist pointing out, subtly, that she held all the aces. Brown readily agreed. "The Bureau doesn't know which way to turn," he said meekly.[32]

Polite sparring ensued about the depletion of forage and the need to reduce the number of horses. When Brown mentioned that the BLM would "gladly designate areas of the public lands where wild horses could be redistributed," Velma perked up. She didn't like the idea of redistributing the horses, but this was the first time anyone from the BLM had hinted there might be a viable solution in the Pryors that didn't involve destroying most of the horses. Brown went further by stating that the BLM was willing to address the research inadequacies in the Pryors with an in-depth study of the mustang's habitat. Velma insisted that a management program—that is, a culling of the herds— should not proceed until the study was completed and evaluated, and

*Velma, 1969*

that a citizen advisory committee was essential. Once again, Brown agreed. Velma reminded him that this was precisely the plan of action she'd advocated a decade earlier.

After lunch, Velma and Brown strolled back to her office, where, like old pals, they examined the recent correspondence she'd received from average citizens, elected officials, and sympathetic groups supporting the wild horse. Brown left with a stack of materials, including back issues of the newsletter published by the ISPMB.

On September 12, 1968, the Bureau of Land Management, prodded by Secretary of the Interior Udall, who apparently knew a self-inflicted public-relations disaster when he saw one, announced the setting aside of a thirty-one-thousand-acre wild horse and wildlife range in the Pryor Mountains. "It is essential that we move ahead immediately to designate these lands to provide federal protection for this national heritage," declared Boyd Rasmussen, "and as quickly as possible to establish long-term management for both horse and wildlife, including a mule deer herd."[33]

Then came the caveat. Rasmussen announced that the BLM had no plans to trap or round up horses, but he did reiterate the Bureau's perennial concern "that the total numbers of animals—horses and big game—may not be in balance with food available to them." He added the dubious contention "that something must be done to halt continued soil and watershed problems which have been brought about by intensified competition between horses and wildlife for food."[34] Interestingly, he made no mention of cattle, the primary foragers in the area.

However, Rasmussen did offer the BLM's first official recognition of the mustang's value. "We all recognize that these horses are a national asset, and the Pryor Mountain herd is suitable for management of the wild horse so important in Western history." In another first, he announced a special advisory committee to oversee the management of the range and "advise us of a suitable method to arrive at a balance between the horses and deer and the food available to them."[35] Velma, stepping firmly out of the back room and into the situation room, was named to the advisory committee.

On the face of it, the decision to create a wild horse range, coupled with a special advisory committee, signaled a new era for the Bureau of Land Management. In fact, the BLM, after years of resistance, was simply conceding the battle in the face of a tsunami of change washing over public institutions at the local, regional, and national levels. Public participation and citizen involvement were the catchwords of the day. The idea that citizens had a right to participate in the planning of their society—be it constructing public buildings, managing parks, operating schools, or delivering programs—had taken hold. Smart bureaucrats quickly adapted to the new environment. The quality of social and environmental planning was no worse with voters' input; many argued it was better. Either way, the public was much happier with the results when they were consulted.

Though the BLM had been forced to open the door to their former adversary, there might be advantages in doing so. Opponents could be co-opted by the system or neutralized by the demands of exhaustive consultation. But Velma had fifteen years of strategic maneuvering with the BLM on her résumé, and she had no intention of being diverted by new tactics.

# THIRTEEN

# Trapped

V ELMA'S APPOINTMENT TO the Pryor Mountain Wild Horse Advisory Committee legitimized almost two decades of work on behalf of wild horses and cemented her status as the leader in the burgeoning animal protection community. No longer could she be dismissed as a middle-aged secretary with a soft heart and a bee in her bonnet or, worse, as a kook. She revelled in this tangible recognition of her achievements and influence, and she welcomed the chance to work alongside like-minded scientists, activists, and rangeland specialists. Operating as a lone wolf, as she had in the early days, actually ran counter to her nature. Though she was ambivalent about the BLM, sometimes believing it was corrupt, other times simply misguided, she had never ruled out the possibility of working with the Bureau if the circumstances were right.

Apprehension underpinned her exhilaration as the board's first meeting, scheduled for October 16, 1968, drew close. Even though she had been steeped in wild horse issues for years, she called on Dr. Michael Pontrelli, an assistant professor of biology at the University of Nevada, to give her a three-week crash course in animal biology so she would appear knowledgeable to the wildlife, soil, and ecology experts who were her colleagues on the committee.

Four months earlier Pontrelli had written to Velma, soliciting funding for summer research into the habitat and biology of wild horses by one of his graduate students, Steven Pelligrini, the son of a local rancher. It would be part of a larger study, the first of its kind, into wild mules and horses. Pelligrini had already spent weeks in Velma's library preparing a literature review for his thesis. Velma sent out an appeal to members of the International Society for the Protection of Mustangs and Burros and to other animal welfare organizations asking for contributions. She expected Pontrelli's work would "prove the importance of these animals in a material sense and provide a definitive evaluation upon which to base a permanent management proposal that will be equitable to all concerned."[1] She raised three thousand dollars in donations, of which seven hundred dollars remained after Pelligrini's summer fieldwork.

The inaugural gathering of the Pryor advisory committee comprised six packed days of site inspections and meetings in Billings, Montana. After landing at Billings, she was taken directly to a lengthy introductory session. The next morning, BLM officials herded the eight committee members onto a small plane for a two-hour aerial tour of the Pryor Mountains rangeland, after which they joined a military-style truck caravan and, with twenty BLM personnel, embarked on a ground inspection. Velma carefully positioned herself for the best views, beside the pilot in the plane and in the front passenger seat of the truck. She also took a flight in a helicopter, which reaffirmed her opposition to herding horses by air no matter how careful the operator might be. Any horses within sound of the whapping blades stampeded in terror.

Over the next two days Velma and her colleagues saw more than forty wild horses, all of which looked healthy. On the first day they stopped for lunch at the abandoned mine shaft near the Tillett ranch that served as one of two main water sources for the herds.

"It was hard for me to believe that wild horses would go into so confined an area, but I saw for myself, from their droppings forty feet within the entrance of the shaft, where untold numbers of them regularly water—sucking the precious drops of moisture from the oozy mud on the floor of the shaft. Observers told me that the stallion mounts guard outside while his mares and colts go inside; and only when they have finished and emerged does he go in for his water. Another day there would be a different band, but the same procedure. Apparently they have their own rules in their desperate game of survival, for no conflict at this precious source has been ever noted."[2]

Velma and Pearl Twyne were the only women on the board or among the attending BLM personnel. "Mrs. Twyne and I learned later that all the men expected us to hold them back; that they groaned in anguish at the prospect of a couple of vaporish females aboard. It turned out that one man fainted during the tour; another needed a button sewn on his shirt; another, an extra pack of cigarettes; still another ran out of matches. Mother Johnston had all the essentials, including a wee silver flask of whiskey."[3]

Velma was thankful she'd brushed up on biology when she was introduced to the two academics on the committee, its chairman, Dr. Wayne C. Cook, head of the Range Science Department at Colorado State University, and Dr. Frank Craighead, an expert on wilderness preservation and management who had done pioneering work tracking grizzly bears with miniature radio transmitters. She immediately warmed to Cook when he sharply corrected a BLM official on the type of grasses the horses were eating in the Pryor Range.

The rest of the board members represented one faction or another in the dispute over the Pryor herds: Frank H. Dunkle, director of the Montana Fish and Game Department; Clyde A. Reynolds, mayor of Lovell and a member of the Pryor Mountain Wild Horse Association; Pearl Twyne, president of the American Horse Protection Association, whom Velma had brought into the wild horse fight in 1959; and George L. Turcott, a BLM representative from Washington. Some members of the wild horse community weren't impressed with Turcott, but Velma came to appreciate his genuine concern for the horses.

The only board member who worried Velma was rancher William G. Cheney, executive officer of the Montana Livestock Association and an acknowledged authority on livestock brands. Some of his critics claimed he was personally responsible for virtually ridding Montana of wild horses; certainly, he was everything Velma disliked in a man: pushy, abrasive, and anti–wild horse. On the first night, "Guess who they sat me across the table from! My arch enemy Cheney, who has been causing most of the ruckus in Montana and about whom I've said some pretty harsh things. We spent the next two hours glaring at each other."[4]

Unknown to Velma or the other committee members, the BLM had asked wildlife specialist James R. Hall to observe the Pryor horses and their feeding habits and behavior and provide the first empirical information about the herds. His year-long research project was already well under way when he gave the committee a preliminary report. During one of his first encounters with a Pryor herd, Hall had been astonished to see a stallion eating sagebrush. "After closer inspection it was determined that the animal was smashing the sagebrush with his front hooves so that he could get at the undisturbed grass . . . the stallion was the only animal that exhibited this grazing behavior."[5] A month and a half later Hall revisited the herd and found that the mares had adopted the stallion's technique.

On another occasion he spotted a band of five wild horses gingerly picking out grass from between clumps of opa, *Opuntia polyacantha,* a plains prickly-pear shrub with yellow flowers and a profusion of thorns. He theorized that because foraging among the shrub must have been difficult for sensitive noses, there was likely a scarcity of forage in the horses' normal grazing areas.

Hall wasn't experienced with mustangs, and he quickly discovered that field studies of wild horses were quite different from those of botanical species. One day late in his research work, Hall was following a blue roan stallion with two mares. With the wind in his face he was able to creep unobserved to within seventy-five feet of them. "The stud let out a loud whinny and ran down into and across the Big Coulee. At first I thought I'd spooked him but the other two horses did not move." Hill took advantage of the stallion's absence to move in on the mares for better photos. Shortly the stallion reappeared with a sorrel mare, one the biologist hadn't seen before. "He was whinnying and neighing and nipping at the mare's flank as if attempting to force her back across Big Coulee. She was kicking and biting at him."[6]

Not realizing this was the classic behavior pattern of one stallion stealing a mare from another, Hall crept closer to the feeding mares, snapping pictures as he went. A few minutes later he found himself between two rivals. "The blue stud came thundering back down the coulee with a black stud in hot pursuit. Every time the blue stud would slow down, the black stud would bite him in the flanks and attempt to strike him with his hooves." The blue stallion stopped when he reached his mares. "Rocks and dirt were flying from the black stud's hooves as he pawed the ground and whinnied loudly. His dilated nostrils and the foam dripping from his mouth were very evident as he was less than 90 feet away."[7]

Eventually the weaker blue roan submitted with bowed head. When one horse surrenders, the aggressor usually breaks off, but the black stallion was still agitated and he cast around for another combatant. He zeroed in on the scientist. "When he spotted me, I knelt slowly and picked up a couple of good sized rocks," Hall wrote. The stallion closed the distance between them. "I threw a rock at him and yelled loudly when it struck him on the side. I then decided to take the offensive and ran toward him a few steps and heaved another rock. The total effect of my actions was somewhat less than good; he appeared more angry now than when I had started my attack. It was then I concluded that the best thing I could do was remain still in hopes that he would forget me. After about five minutes of screaming and pawing, the black stud moved downhill. I then started to move slowly back away. After gaining the screening of a few juniper trees I made a fast retreat."[8] In his final report, Hall recommended future researchers pack a sidearm, but he made no comment on the wisdom of provoking an angry stallion by hitting him with a rock, then charging him on foot.

After a second meeting in Billings in March 1969, George Turcott suggested the committee convene the following June in Washington so that the new secretary of the interior, Walter J. Hickel, could hear its views firsthand. Velma had been to Washington before, but as a supplicant, not an insider. That summer, against the backdrop of the Department of the Interior's richly paneled conference room, she had as many as twenty-five BLM staffers to provide assistance. Director Boyd Rasmussen, whom Velma had once called a stuffed shirt, was always accessible. After so many years of operating on a shoestring while she battled the BLM, she lapped up the perks. If she asked for a document, it was produced; if information from a specialist was needed, that individual appeared. "Having been involved in office procedures all my business life I can only guess at the tremendous amount of time and effort that went into the preparation for our meeting, for in addition to the on-the-site assistance, we have been furnished with a prodigious amount of study material, including maps of surveys made under the best available methods of study."[9]

Still, Velma was well aware of the danger of being compromised, and she took care not to reveal her primary objective, which was the establishment of wild horse refuges throughout the western states. "That part is off the record, though, and will come as somewhat of a shock to those who think I'll probably shut up if we get the Pryor situation settled satisfactorily."[10]

Despite the BLM's solicitous treatment, Velma found the stiff formality and clenched demeanor of the staff in Washington heavy going. "I wore a black lace garter above my knee, with a tiny pistol in its tiny holster. I let it be seen quite frequently, with the comment that I was afraid what might happen to a gal in the big city at the mercy of bureaucracy. It was fun to unseat pomposity in a chain of command where each person, fearful of what his immediate superior might think or do to him if he didn't do the same thing, was most restrained. It took some of the grimness out of the thing."[11]

Velma stayed with Pearl Twyne at her horse farm in Great Falls, Virginia. It meant a commute to the meetings but also relief from the stifling heat and humidity of the capital. After a lifetime in the desert Velma found herself drenched in perspiration from morning to night.

Sixty-two-year-old Twyne, recently retired from a position in the Department of Agriculture, had been combating animal abusers since the early 1940s when a stray dog collapsed in front of her house. She had been appalled when the individual who came to rescue the animal simply tossed it into the trunk of his car, slammed the lid shut, and drove off. Twyne formed the Animal Welfare League of Arlington in 1944, serving as its president until 1967, and she was instrumental in forming the American Horse Protection Association in 1966.

Twyne and Velma were a natural fit, not only because they both loved a good party and enjoyed challenging the status quo, but because Twyne also knew horses and, like Velma, had hands-on experience with them. She had spent nearly thirty years pushing for a ban on "soring," a technique used to force the characteristic, high-stepping gait of Tennessee Walking Horses on the show circuit. Trainers made the horses' hooves and fetlocks painful by burning them with irritating chemicals, wrapping chains around their feet and inserting barbs under their shoes so that the only relief was to jerk their knees up sharply to avoid the pain.

In 1964, Twyne descended on the Carolina Walking Horse Celebration in Raleigh, North Carolina, with a vet, a lawyer, and two policemen in tow, intending to inspect the horses for abuse. "Had she come dressed in burlap, worn tennis shoes, flashed an axe and cried, 'Praise the Lord and pass the ammunition,' she could not have caused greater trepidation," a *Sports Illustrated* writer observed. "A hundred angry men, who had come to the state fairgrounds . . . to show their Tennessee Walking Horses, clustered around Mrs. Pearl Twyne. She wanted to have a look at the horses; they wanted to have her bull-whacked. Or worse.

"'Get her out of here,' said one, beginning a chorus.

"'If she steps into my stable,' said Jimmy Norris of Fayetteville, N.C., 'she'll never step out again.'

"'Nosy old bitch!'

"After retreating under a police escort from the enraged, cursing spectators, Twyne commented to a reporter that she didn't mind so much being called a bitch, " 'but I do object to being called an old bitch. That's just not true.'"[12]

On the evening before the final day of meetings, Twyne hosted a garden party for sixty-five guests. Boyd Rasmussen showed up with plastic bags bearing a Department of the Interior insignia on them and the motto "You mustn't be a litterbug." He passed them around to the gathering, joking that his new town house needed landscaping and he'd appreciate everyone bringing a bag of manure to the last meeting.

Velma and Twyne couldn't resist taking him at his word, and the next morning they filled two bags with steaming-fresh manure. They arrived at the session ten minutes late. Before the committee's official adjournment and a press conference to announce its recommendations, Velma stood up and thanked Rasmussen for his confidence in the group and asked him to accept a token of appreciation. She reached under the table, pulled out the two sacks of horse manure, and plopped them down in front of the director. "And let the record show that the only two members who carried out your instructions were the distaff appointments." Embarrassed silence greeted her gesture until Twyne piped up that they were sorry they had been late for the meeting that morning but they had to wait on the horses. "Bureaucracy nearly fell off its respective chairs," Velma later wrote, "and I think the Director had completely forgotten his humorous instructions of the day before.

Anyway, gales of laughter rang out from that room that probably hadn't even witnessed a smile in the years since it had been built."[13]

The advisory committee made eleven recommendations relating to the management of the Pryor herds, most of them remarkably similar to those Velma and a single range advisor had proposed in 1959 to support the Wild Horse Annie bill. The BLM believed the Pryor horses numbered two hundred and the committee emphasized that "every effort should be made to retain at least 100 horses." Should the size of the herd need to be reduced, "branded, claimed, old, sick, and deformed animals should be removed first," and any roundups should be handled in small groups with no more than one stallion or herd to a corral. The committee also suggested that two new water sources be established and that a fence be built to separate the horses from a proposed recreation development adjacent to the reserve. Finally, the committee urged the Department of the Interior to establish a permanent advisory group; all of the current members volunteered to continue to serve.

Everyone seemed pleased, especially Velma. "We came out of it smelling like roses," she declared. Rasmussen bestowed certificates of appreciation and Walter Hickel pronounced himself satisfied. "I'm firmly convinced that the public interest is always best served when people can sit down together and seek mutually acceptable solutions based on the very best information available. I am sure the distinguished members of the special advisory committee on the Pryor Mountain Wild Horse Range have done this."[14]

Even William Cheney had apparently softened, declaring the wild horse a national treasure, though later he told the *New York Times* that while livestock ranchers would accept this particular wild horse range management control program, they "don't like to see too many precedents set."[15]

On September 15, 1969, Secretary Hickel officially accepted all the committee's recommendations without reservation. "Because the Bureau of Land Management's ultimate boss—the American public—has asked it, a herd of wild horses will be maintained in the Pryor Mountains. And the BLM has accepted this challenge to provide a permanent and healthy home for these wild ones—creatures that J. Frank Dobie so aptly termed 'the wind drinkers.'"[16] Velma thought the hyperbole was a little excessive considering that, until recently, Bureau officials had done everything they could to ignore public opinion.

But even the best minds, armed with the best information available and possessed of the best intentions, could not compensate for the continued lack of knowledge about wild horses and their behavior. Two key elements of the committee's recommendations—fencing the range and establishing two additional water holes—proved disastrous.

A thirty-two-thousand-acre sanctuary, one thousand acres more than orginally planned, sounded impressive for just two hundred horses, but much of it was too rugged and canyon-riven, even for the tough Pryor mustangs. Within two years, the palatable and nutritious forage—Indian ricegrass, needle and thread grass, blue bunch wheatgrass, winter fat and various salt bushes—had been denuded. Even species that wild horses rarely ate had been nibbled out of existence. "What is truly significant," noted Montana State University range specialist Dr. Carl Wambolt in 1971, "is that the desirable forage species are flourishing just outside the boundaries of the wild horse range. The contrast between inside and outside the horse range boundary is astonishing, especially when it is remembered the fence has been standing only two years. The contrast is very apparent at both low and high elevations. This then tells us that this artificial restriction, in the form of a fence, imposed on the horse population of the range has restricted their natural occupation area. The result is an overstocked condition within the current horse range. Horses that historically grazed what must have been a significantly larger area are now penned up in a pasture with natural freedom of mobility impeded. This has been especially harmful as a number of former wintering areas are now cut off from the horse population."

The two new water holes made a bad situation worse, since they drew horses onto what had been their traditional winter pasture during the summer months where they consumed forage that was critical to their sustenance through the winter. "If the wild horses are allowed to continue to punish the forage species on the range . . . a massive die-off of starved horses will occur. Even more tragic . . . it will be many years before the vegetation will return to a level at which it will be able to support a horse population again."[17]

Wambolt recommended either rigidly controlling the horse numbers, which had actually dropped to 170 and included a number of branded animals, or dismantling the horse fence and the two artificial watering holes, in effect reversing the recommendations of the Pryor Mountains advisory committee.

———

DURING THE MIDSIXTIES, mustang protection groups sprang up across the country, spurred by the wave of publicity Velma had instigated in 1958 and 1959 and fed by burgeoning public concern for the environment. Though she felt a strong sense of personal ownership of the issue, Velma welcomed other groups and individuals, as long as they cooperated with her and worked toward the same goals. She liked to say that "all roads lead to Wild Horse Annie when the wild horse matter is pursued," but increasingly these new players were galloping off in other directions.

Velma had brought Pearl Twyne and Christine Stevens of the Society for Animal Protective Legislation into the Pryor fight. Both had lent their support in the late stages of the campaign for the 1959 Wild Horse Annie bill. They were important recruits, representing well-funded eastern organizations with excellent access to and experience within the corridors of power.

Then there was Hope Ryden, who made the influential ABC news documentary in 1968. After her 1970 book, *America's Last Wild Horses,* rocketed to the top of the national bestseller lists, Ryden quit her job to devote herself full-time to the wild horse movement. Velma found Ryden's strong personality off-putting. "She not only wears people out physically, but mentally as well," she complained in 1968. Many people over the years had said the same thing about Velma. Ryden deferred to Velma to a degree, but she clearly saw herself as Wild Horse Annie's equal.

Joan Blue, founder of the Animal Welfare Institute and a vice president of Pearl Twyne's American Horse Protection Association, was another influential figure. She also made the pilgrimage to Reno and Trudy showed her the city's sights while Velma organized an outing that spotted five mustang bands in the Virginia City area.

Another horse group, the National Mustang Association, head-quartered in Salt Lake City, Utah, had formed in 1965 "to enable as many Mustangs as possible to remain truly wild and roaming free."[18] Tom Holland, the NMA's president, lived in Las Vegas. The association had been peripherally involved with the Pryor Mountains situation but first came to national prominence during what Velma called "the Nevada emergency."

Late in February 1969, unusually heavy snowfall and fierce winds combined to create impenetrable snowdrifts that trapped wild horses in blind canyons and their familiar redoubts. Many were starving and a number had already died. The worst-hit areas were the Pinenut Range, eighty miles south of Reno, the Kawich Range in Central Nevada, and a third near Mount Grant in the windswept Great Basin.

Residents of the Pinenut area had the situation well in hand with donations of hay and the free use of a helicopter and pilot. All they needed was money for gas. Velma took up a collection and contributed some of her own money; ISPMB members came up with the rest. In the remote Kawich Range the situation was considerably more serious, prompting the BLM manager in the district to ask for Velma's help. One of his field men, flying over the area, counted about two hundred stranded and starving horses. He had already contacted Nellis Air Force Base, whose personnel agreed to drop hay for the animals, but someone had to supply the feed. It wasn't part of the air force's mandate to buy hay for starving horses, nor did the BLM have a budget for that kind of emergency expenditure. Velma called Tom Holland in Las Vegas, the closest contact she had to both the base and the hay, to ask if his organization could provide the needed funds. He told her the NMA's kitty was empty.

Time was short, horses were dying, and the plane was standing by. Velma decided, with Michael Pontrelli's blessing, to dip into the remaining research funds from his student's summer project. But the BLM couldn't accept private funds directly, so Velma sent six hundred dollars to Holland and the National Mustang Association to purchase the hay.

Shortly afterward, the crisis at Mount Grant became equally grave, with many horses already dead or dying. Fortunately, the Pinenut Range residents had again found hay, a helicopter, and a pilot, but they were short four hundred dollars for gas. "I had no more funds to respond to their appeal so I telephoned to the National Mustang Association in Las Vegas asking for $400 that was badly needed for the Mt. Grant rescue operation, as I had been informed that there had been considerable financial donations made to that organization. The president refused to send the money. Hay, they would send, yes. Hay we had. Money we did not." Basically Holland told her to whistle for the money.

Velma did a little sleuthing and was infuriated to find that the NMA had indeed received substantial donations from fund-raising related to the Kawich Range hay lift. Furthermore, they had auctioned off bales of excess hay purchased with the money Velma sent, and then kept the proceeds. She chose to let the matter lie. "In the final analysis there was comparatively little to be gained by any action I would take, and a lovely image (of which there are much too few nowadays) of mankind's better self would have been blemished. The matter was relegated to the limbo where all unpleasant happenings belong."[19]

Velma may have swallowed her anger for the greater good, but she would not soon forget. The NMA used her money to garner publicity for itself and then, when she needed it to feed more horses, refused to give it back. On top of that she now faced the prospect of restoring the research funds out of her own shallow pockets. That's when another wild horse devotee stepped forward. Judy Lynn, a thirty-three-year-old country singer with her own national television show and one of the first country stars to appear regularly in Las Vegas, anted up the six hundred dollars.

Aside from the NMA's maneuverings, the wild horse rescues appeared to be a success. But Michael Pontrelli was concerned about the hay lifts. The only other known operation of its kind had resulted in all the horses dying from mold on spoiled hay. Tough as mustangs are, they have sensitive digestive systems, like all horses. At Velma's instigation, the BLM flew Pontrelli to the horse ranges in Nevada where the hay lifts had occurred. He discovered six horses in the Pinenut Range which had died from eating moldy hay and more dead from exhaustion after concerned residents tried to drive them out of the area where they had been trapped by snow. "Only one animal was left alive from the herd and he was standing guard over the dead. The snow was melted enough and this animal could have left. It left only reluctantly and it probably returned soon after we had gone. It was not done with malice. So little is known about wild horses that people tend to act simply out of concern. Too often the animals suffer."[20]

Not long after the hay lift episode, Tom Holland surprised Velma by dropping into Gordon Harris's office, their first face-to-face meeting. The Pinenut Range Association had organized a fund-raiser in Lake Tahoe, and since Holland was seen as the hero of the hour, he was an honored guest. The tall, handsome Holland was striking in his Stetson and western dress, though even his fellow NMA board members agreed he could be crude and offensive. "We chit-chatted about everything under the sun except the actual issue and mutual dislike." Holland proposed a merger of the NMA and ISPMB, which Velma privately vowed would never happen. He also suggested they join forces to draft a new federal bill to plug the loopholes in the 1959 Wild Horse Annie law. That, at least, she could endorse.

As their conversation drew to a close, the NMA secretary traveling with Holland produced a camera and asked if he could take a picture of Holland and Velma together. Velma, already irritated that the NMA had appropriated her name and photograph for their fundraising materials without permission, would have nothing to do with it. "Hah! I must look naïve. I made all the feminine excuses I could think of why I couldn't just then (hair not done, no fresh make-up) but I did catch the secretary aiming the camera at us anyway and ducked. [Holland] took the hint and covered the camera up with his 10-gallon hat at that point. Did that faze our hero? Not a bit. He only jovially commented that there would be lots of professional camera men at Lake Tahoe that evening."

Velma telephoned Pontrelli, who was planning to attend the benefit, and explained her predicament. He recruited four of his fellow academics. "When I arrived I was introduced to my body guard. Every step I took in that jam-packed, beautiful place, I was surrounded by five pairs of broad shoulders. No one but no one could have gotten a picture of anything but wide black-clad backs."[21]

Two months later, Velma was shocked to learn from a Washington source that Senator Frank Moss of Utah had introduced a wild horse bill based on information provided by the National Mustang Association. She was aggrieved that another organization would propose a federal bill without seeking her counsel. When she and the board of the ISPMB scrutinized Senator Moss's bill, S2166, introduced on May 14, 1969, they found a new and frightening threat to wild horses. In the group's July/August Bulletin Velma identified the offending passage:

> Subsection (a) of Section 2 calls for the rounding up of wild horses on lands under the jurisdiction of the Secretary of the Interior; with a view to separating from them any Spanish barb and Andalusian wild mustangs which he determines should be conserved, protected, restored and propagated; thereafter placing such Mustangs on selected lands under his jurisdiction. I am unalterably opposed to any reduction of wild horses based on bloodlines . . . the elimination of all but the Spanish barb and Andalusian would result in virtually wiping out all of the wild horses in our country, and this would not be tolerated either by those working closely on their preservation and protection, or by the vast army of individuals who support such a program. The public expects the wild horse to continue to be a part of the western scene, and because it is a horse, running free and untamed, the public is quite satisfied with its mixture of origins, since it does not contemplate going into the horse breeding business.[22]

Velma believed that the NMA was playing into the old BLM argument that a wild horse wasn't wild unless it carried Spanish blood. Clyde Reynolds, Velma's colleague on the Pryor advisory committee and the mayor of Lovell, offered an alternative bill, which Senator Clifford Hansen of Wyoming agreed to present. The bill was so well written and inclusive that Velma suspected some unknown sympathizer or sympathizers within the BLM had had a hand in its drafting. Shortly after the ISPMB announced its opposition to the Moss bill and support of the Hansen bill, "The wrath of the officers of the National

Mustang Association [came] down on my head."[23] Both John McCormack and Kent Gregerson, vice presidents of the NMA, sent letters accusing her of not understanding the situation and dividing the wild horse protection movement.

Velma responded to the NMA criticism with a five-page letter. "Probably the worst thing that could happen to the future of the wild horses would be a division in the ranks of those fighting to save them, and it has been my aim and purpose to endeavour to avoid that possibility at all costs. It still is. My comments on the bill were solicited by a number of Congressional offices that have long been aware of my intense interest in a protection and preservation program . . . I very carefully avoided the negative approach in that commentary, with one single exception—I oppose a bloodline determination. Even there I used the words, 'if that be the intent.'

"I did not at first realize that Mr. Holland and you were the originators of the bill for a number of reasons, among them the fact that it did contain the Spanish barb and Andalusian qualifications for preservation. I refer you to your letter written following your meeting with BLM personnel in Washington which specifically set forth that 'There are several points I feel are important to you, and your readers. One of these is the NMA position on mustangs. Where we speak of 'protection' for mustangs, we refer to *all* wild horses in the Western States.' It came to me as somewhat of a surprise to learn that your positions had changed on that point."[24]

Privately Velma worried about the growing prominence of the National Mustang Association. "I'm handling the NMA people with kid gloves these days," she wrote to Hope Ryden on October 10. "And taking a lot of crap from them in order to keep this thing from erupting to the disadvantage of the horses. If only one of them had the good sense to contact some of the rest of us at the time their legislation was being considered, it would have been simpler."[25] At the same time she realized she couldn't turn her back on the NMA. "While I do not believe that our two organizations should merge, I have felt for a long time that we could and should work together on this," she wrote to John and Helen Reilly at the ISPMB. "We are strong where they are admittedly weak; in administration and publicity. They are strong where we are weak: members who are competent to work 'in the field' and have first-hand knowledge of the situation in that regard. Also I think they are a little better financed. However, I still withhold a final opinion until we have had a meeting."[26]

———

WHILE VELMA WAS trying to avoid a schism within the wild horse ranks, she continued to hunt for a case that would test the 1959 act. Since the bitter outcome of the Goicochea trial in 1967 her pursuit of a prosecution had become almost an obsession. She chased down every conceivable lead, constantly pressing her network of spies.

On January 20, 1968, Velma received an anonymous tip from California that 600 horses, most of them unbranded mustangs, were about to be rounded up near Lander, Nevada. Shortly afterward she learned that a different operator had caught and transported 725 horses out of Nevada, 469 of them unbranded wild horses. Most of the horses went to slaughterhouses, one of which was owned by the rancher behind the roundup. Frustrated at not having a man on the ground in that area, Velma hired Lynn Augustine, the former investigator for the Humane Society and a one-time FBI special agent, to gather evidence for a citizen's arrest.

"I'll be moonlighting the rest of my life to pay for it, but we have to have a conviction to make believers out of the violators," Velma wrote to Marguerite Henry. "When we build our case, I'll be able to publicize it from the rooftops, but at this point even Mom doesn't know the circumstances — only that I'm mixed up in something that she's afraid I'm going to get hurt at and she's pretty grim about the whole thing."[27]

Velma referred to herself as "Girl Friday" in her letters to Augustine and addressed him as "Chief." And though she paid him out of her own pocket, Velma also inveigled him into giving her many days of investigation work at no charge. Over the next two years, Augustine tracked numerous reported incidents and located several witnesses, none of whom were willing to testify. Based on information from her spies, she estimated that in 1968 and 1969, some four thousand wild horses had been captured in Nevada and shipped to California slaughterhouses.

Velma was so anxious to nab a perpetrator, she sometimes allowed her eagerness to overrule her common sense. Once she became embroiled in a messy family quarrel involving a Washoe County rancher who had been illegally catching mustangs with an airplane for years. It was a highly profitable operation; the rancher also owned a slaughterhouse and apparently dabbled in cattle rustling, which was rampant along the California-Nevada border. The man's son-in-law came to Velma offering testimony against him for illegally catching mustangs, but the witness was also implicated in the capture and, since he'd served time for cattle rustling, was hardly a credible source. What's more, he and his wife were suing her father for their share of the illegal proceeds. For many months Velma doggedly pursued the case, interviewing other witnesses and reviewing reports, before she belatedly came to the conclusion that the whole affair was a dangerous waste of time.

Though Velma made no progress toward a prosecution, her efforts were clearly worrying the mustangers. She felt it was no coincidence when one of the most famous of them moved into the building where Gordon Harris had his offices. Jerry "Chug" Utter took over an office lease and hung out a shingle for C. C. Utter Real Estate. He did have a real estate license, but only one listing was ever associated with the company during the time he spent in the building. Velma knew him as an airplane pilot who claimed he had captured forty thousand mustangs during a lengthy private career and as a BLM subcontractor for fourteen years before the federal act came into effect in 1959.

Velma became convinced that Utter was somehow listening in on her office conversations. Even during the day with people around her, she grew fearful of the large man's presence and intimidating manner. She kept a detailed log of the activity at Utter's office, noting his visitors' physical features and their license plate numbers. She strongly suspected that Utter was planing horses illegally, and over the next fifteen months she played a cat-and-mouse game with him, trying to catch him in the act. Tom McCord, still working at the Reno airport and using his code name, Penelope, reported on the comings and goings of his plane.

Utter's presence in the building continued to be disturbing; several times Velma found herself stuck in the bathroom while he and his chums conversed loudly in the hall outside. Finally, Gordon Harris became fed up with the shady characters frequenting the halls and leaned on the building owner, who evicted Utter in February 1969. Even so, Velma began to carry Charlie's pistol again, and she greeted late-evening callers at the house gun in hand. After a late party, her niece Trudy, Betty Jo's daughter, tried to sneak into Velma's house to spend the night, only to be confronted by two barrels and her frightened aunt. Velma also got an unlisted phone line when she grew tired of repeated threatening calls and hangups.

Utter popped up again the following year when Velma's original outlander, Zeke, reappeared to tell her that Utter had boasted in a local bar that he was going to pull off "a big one" right under Wild Horse Annie's nose. A few days later Zeke produced a crude, hand-drawn map of an elaborate trap being constructed by Utter on private land ten miles from Virginia City. There were about 300 wild horses known to frequent the area. Utter had already introduced thirty or thirty-five freshly branded horses into the herd, so he could claim the entire band was his. He intended to chase them off public land with his plane and into the trap on private land. Michael Pontrelli made an aerial search for the trap, but it was so well hidden he would have missed it if there hadn't been a red pickup truck parked nearby. He and Velma hatched a scheme to secure photos of the actual chase, including the use of the plane. By this point Pontrelli, too, was in Velma's thrall.

Velma called in reinforcements from the days of the first hearing in Virginia City. Tex Gladding, now retired as postmaster, manned a telescope on a peak overlooking the corral. Another outfielder kept watch over the area frequented by the largest herd, and Tom McCord continued to monitor the airport. The Storey County sheriff stood ready with a posse for the arrest. Stanley Routson was prepared to impound the animals, and an Associated Press reporter and photographer were on alert to document the whole event. Velma was never more than thirty seconds from a phone for the first two weeks. Then a leak, apparently from someone inside the posse, caused Utter to lie low. Tensions grew among the watchers and word about Utter's plan filtered out to Virginia City residents. Twice Velma had to head off concerned citizens intent on destroying the trap.

Convinced that Utter wouldn't now take a chance on capturing the horses, Velma decided to turn the presence of the trap itself into a media event. She learned that the owners of the property had not granted Utter permission to build it, and they willingly gave Velma permission to take it apart. She suggested that students from Michael Pontrelli's classes neatly dismantle the trap, carefully pile up the lumber and hardware, and return the site to as near pristine condition as possible. The AP reporter and photographer agreed to be on hand and Velma worked to round up more media. All the arrangements were in place but before she could act, a group of Virginia City residents equipped with chainsaws reduced the trap to "kindling."

After all of her machinations to find a test case for the Wild Horse Annie law, the only people charged were Michael Pontrelli and fifty John Does and fifty Mary Does, representing the unidentified persons involved in destroying the corral. And the charges were laid in a civil suit launched, not by any government department, but by Chug Utter. Velma believed Pontrelli was implicated as a way to discredit her, and she wondered if the destruction of the trap had been done for the same purpose. She expected to be named in the lawsuit herself in short order. Utter sought $2,500 in damages for the demolition of the corral, $2,500 for the cost of building a new one, $50,000 in punitive damages, and $10,000 for losses sustained as a result of "being unable to round up their domestic horses or brand, wean and selectively breed them."[28]

# FOURTEEN

# The Children's Crusade

T HE DESTRUCTION OF the horse trap in the summer of 1970, though not at all what she'd intended, brought Velma fresh media attention. Prime-time television news, radio syndicates, and wire services kept up a steady demand for her comments and for the first time large-circulation women's magazines such as *Cosmopolitan* and *McCall's* paid court. "How sweet the ride on the bandwagon is," she exulted to Pearl Twyne. "And the politicians are quick to smell out a possible campaign boost."[1]

Yet amid her jubilation, Velma often found herself overwhelmed; correspondence piled up and some of it went unanswered. In the previous two years she had been plagued by recurrent colds and bouts of flu, each lasting longer and leaving her weaker. Her doctor urged bed rest but Velma ignored him. Finally, after a particularly severe flu episode, he prescribed a powerful barbiturate, phenobarbital. "Which reduced me to a languorous Camille-type patient who thoroughly enjoyed the rest, sleeping lots, reading a little, and lazily watching the clouds drift by outside my bedroom window," she wrote to Marguerite Henry. "I was so tired and the mixture of 'to hell with everything' drugs kept my conscience from plaguing me."[2] Worried about her health, singer Judy Lynn and her husband, Jack Kelly, paid for a part-time secretary to take care of routine correspondence for a few months, leaving Velma to focus on media and political requests.

One such request came from California. Golden State politicians took note of the widely publicized fact that thousands of Nevada's wild horses ended up in California's slaughterhouses. State Senator Anthony C. Beilenson, who was already preparing an endangered-species protection bill, called on Velma for help in adding wild horses to the list. On August 7, 1970, Beilenson's Bill 128, prohibiting the commercial exploitation of eleven endangered species or subspecies of fish, birds, mammals, amphibians, or reptiles, was amended to include "free-roaming feral horses," effectively ending the importation of wild horses into California for slaughter. Governor Ronald Reagan signed it into law. In the same session, a bill authorizing the killing of wild burros by the state fish and game department was voted down twenty to six.

Velma's delight in these victories was muted by a near-constant undercurrent of fatigue. During Charlie's illness and in the months following his death, she admitted to despondency and occasionally to a lack of energy, but she had never experienced the kind of consuming weariness that began to afflict her. In 1969 she had developed a limp, "a hitch in my git-along," after stepping on a stone and injuring the sole of her foot. Phlebitis, a swelling of the veins in that leg, made her doctor reluctant to operate, so Velma hoped the pain and the lump that developed would just go away. But by the time the California legislation passed, she found walking to be almost impossible on some days.

Velma was also deeply concerned about Michael Pontrelli. The lawsuit brought against him by Chug Utter was proceeding, and two days after it was filed, the University of Nevada notified Pontrelli that his teaching contract would not be renewed because of unspecified "personality problems."[3] Velma felt that what amounted to a dismissal had been orchestrated by university board members linked to cattle interests. She arranged for the ISPMB to pay a one-thousand-dollar retainer to Pontrelli's attorney and started building a war chest by soliciting donations from prominent businessmen sympathetic to the wild horse cause. She threw in fifty dollars of her own money and Gordon Harris matched it. Velma also met with various university deans and department heads in an attempt to persuade them to press for a renewal of Pontrelli's contract.

In June 1970, Senator Clifford Hansen delivered the unwelcome news that he did not intend to pursue his bill in the Senate aimed at clarifying the definition of a wild horse. His proposal would have rectified a serious omission in the 1959 Wild Horse Annie act. He told Velma that his original objective had been to help resolve the Pryor Mountains situation, even though that issue had been settled before he and his staff drew up the proposed bill. His explanation didn't sat-isfy Velma; she noted that Hansen's letter had been copied to William Cheney and Dean Prosser, and she penned "cattle barons!" beside their names. The two were actually employees of cattle barons, Cheney as the executive officer of the Montana Livestock Association and Prosser as the secretary-treasurer of the Wyoming Livestock Associ-ation. Across the bottom she added: "Since it is highly unusual for a Senator or a Congressman to indicate to whom copies are sent I think he is trying to tell me something! I got the message."[4]

Walter Baring told her not to worry; they didn't need Hansen, because wild horses were, thanks to all the media coverage, once again politically hot with prominent and obscure politicians alike. Upward of sixty pieces of federal legislation regarding their protection were in preparation, Baring revealed, and there was plenty of time to put together their own bill incorporating Hansen's draft language. The sudden momentum was gratifying and timely. In the decade since the Wild Horse Annie bill had been signed into law, its gaping holes were plain to see: a vague definition of the wild horse that was open to inter-pretation, and a provision allowing ranchers, or those posing as ranch-ers, to scoop up mustangs while reclaiming their own animals that had mixed with the herd. Above all, no enforcement mechanism existed. Until the trap near Virginia City hit the headlines, there had been no opportunity to ride public sentiment back to the lawmakers in Wash-ington.

The involvement of children in the 1959 campaign had occurred spontaneously, but this time Velma deliberately targeted the nation's youth. She'd been plowing that field since 1966 when Marguerite Henry urged her to focus on the younger generation to ensure the wild horse's survival. Now she stepped up her school speaking engagements and seeded every interview with an exhortation to the young. "The children everywhere are gung ho to get their letters off to Washington. The volume of mail from them is terrific, and they all must be answered with instructions . . . this is a golden opportunity to get support for the bill and as the children tell me, 'Annie we did it once, we can do it again' I can't let them down. Yup, by gum, we did it once and we'll do it again."[5]

Securing passage of a stronger act in the 1970s required a more sophisticated style of lobbying than had prevailed in the 1950s. Velma understood that any new and tougher law would be effective only if those governed by it were willing to tolerate its provisions. She worked assiduously to forge relationships with other users of public land, from recreation and conservation groups to BLM district offices and even the forest service. She looked for a middle ground with the ranchers' associations, her longtime foes. During 1970 and early 1971, with Pontrelli providing scientific backup, Velma met frequently with groups representing stockmen, and she spoke before a gathering of the powerful American National Cattlemen's Association. Her most urgent priority was to negotiate a mutually acceptable definition of wild horses and burros. "We knew that if we didn't, a big can of worms would be opened. . . . Because the wild horses and burros are not native to North America as deer, elk, antelope are native, they can never be considered as protected under the 'Endangered Species Act,' as that applies only to wildlife."[6]

This time Velma expected timely support from wild horse organizations and humane societies across the country, groups that wouldn't wait for the eve of the hearings but signaled their intent to join the ranks during the lobbying phase. Success no longer depended solely on her efforts, and her letters were less frantic, more confident, and better reasoned than they had been in the 1950s. It was a politically mature Velma who conducted this round of the wild horse campaign, and she needed every ounce of her assurance and skill as she found it increasingly difficult to shepherd the half-dozen prominent wild horse groups involved, as well as an equal number of animal-rights organizations.

With so many bills in preparation, offering varying degrees of protection for mustangs and burros, Velma decided to travel to Washington in March 1971. There she would "confer with my liaisons . . . to see which ones we should support," as she wrote to the NMA's John McCormack, a man she genuinely liked despite his affiliation.[7] Though she had been furious at the NMA's shenanigans during the hay lift emergency and startled by its promotion of a breed-related definition of the wild horse, she still didn't want to alienate the organization.

Though she claimed to be considering all the options in her letter to McCormack, Velma had already decided where her endorsement would go. Walter Baring had prepared the strongest bill, carefully vetted by Velma, and Henry Jackson of Washington state had agreed to present a virtually identical version to the Senate. Baring and Jackson were the chairmen of the committees on interior and insular affairs in their respective chambers. Baring had enlisted the chairmen of his subcommittees to cosponsor his bill and Velma intended to ask Alan Bible and Howard Cannon, both U.S. senators from Nevada, to cosponsor Jackson's bill in the Senate.

The various humane societies in Washington pooled their resources to hire "a public relations gal," who booked Velma with every media outlet in town, including the major radio stations and print syndication services. Velma met with fifteen senators to confirm their support and nailed down Cannon and Bible as cosponsors.

While in Washington, Velma attended a fund-raising art exhibition organized by a group of society women from Long Island, New York, in aid of the American Horse Protection Association. Among the exhibits were original works by Frederic Remington and Toulouse-Lautrec. "There's no telling where one will wind up when he grabs a mustang by the tail, is there? But I never thought it would be the social register!" Velma wrote to John McCormack, laying on the slightly rustic persona that was so effective with the national media. "My environment has made me more accustomed to a hitching post than to Emily Post and I'd be more comfortable out in the hills somewhere but guess I can hack a few hours in a receiving line on behalf of our wild ones."[8] The event opened her eyes to the kind of money available to the eastern horse conservation organizations.

The day before she left Washington, Velma awoke with severe chest congestion. "Was beginning to cough that morning, but had a one hour TV show with Cleveland Amory and Hope Ryden. As I sometimes do, I made a deal with 'Our Very Dear Sir Upstairs' that if he'd let me off the hook and keep me from coughing during the hour of the show, I would pay his price later. The price was very high and by the time we reached Chicago that evening, I was about ready to deplane and go to the hospital. Finally got home. Ill for a week. Lost 10 of my 110 pounds."[9]

Heavy smoking, immoderate drinking, and an immune system compromised by postpolio syndrome—then not yet identified—made Velma easy prey for every passing bug. At fifty-nine, she looked more like seventy, with the facial skin on her disfigured side limp and wrinkled and the droop of one eye even more pronounced.

Velma returned to the capital again on April 19 for hearings before the Public Lands Subcommittee of the Committee on Interior and Insular Affairs, House of Representatives. It was a striking contrast to her first appearance in 1959, when she and a lone BLM official were the only witnesses to appear. The sixty draft bills had been whittled down to sixteen and there were more than forty groups and individuals scheduled to speak, among them Hope Ryden, Pearl Twyne, Christine Stevens, Tom Holland, and Michael Pontrelli and his graduate student, Steven Pelligrini.

Behind the front rank of activists were legions of children. Twelve-year-old Trina Bellak of Virginia had read about Wild Horse Annie's drive to strengthen the legislation in one of the horsey magazines she adored. Bellak enlisted two friends to help her raise money for the cause through bake sales. The girls sifted, creamed, mixed, sprinkled, and baked dozens of sweet delights. Traditional brownies and peanut butter cookies, lemon squares made from Mrs. Bellak's favorite cookbook, and Rice Krispie bars from the recipe on the cereal box brought in a steady stream of cash. They hoarded the money from sale to sale until the dollar bills, quarters, dimes, and nickels, all carefully counted and bundled in money wrappers, added up to the surprising sum of three hundred dollars.

Trina took this fortune to the post office, purchased a money order, and sent it to Velma Johnston, adding "Wild Horse Annie" to the envelope just to be certain. When a response from Wild Horse Annie herself arrived, Trina could hardly believe it. Velma explained how the money would be used and added a paragraph about Hobo, how he had helped her through many difficult times. Hobo's brothers and sisters on public land, she wrote, deserved to live a long life, just as he had done.

In early 1971, Miss Joan Bolsinger, a teacher in Roseburg, Oregon, read a *National Geographic* article by Hope Ryden about the wild horse crisis to her class of fourth graders. The children also read Marguerite

Henry's *Mustang* and *Brighty of Grand Canyon*. At the time, the Oregon legislature was debating a bill to establish a state preserve for wild horses. The students were so upset by the plight of the horses that they wrote to all ninety members of the Oregon legislature and traveled to the state capital to attend a hearing. The class deputized ten-year-old Lynn Williams to speak on their behalf. Radio, television, and newspapers picked up on their campaign. The state bill died, but when Congress's hearings were announced, Bolsinger and Williams, again representing the class, decided to make a longer journey.

At the same time, a sixth-grade class across the country in Glen Head, New York, had been selling "Save America's Wild Horses" bumper stickers for a quarter each. They sent $111 in proceeds to the American Horse Protection Association. When the class heard about Lynn Williams's trip to Washington, they asked that the money be used to help with his expenses.

Williams and his classmates had conscientiously reviewed the proposed legislation. "We have been studying the bill HR 5375 which Congressman Baring introduced and we think it is a good one," he testified before the subcommittee.[10]

Another speaker was Congressman Gilbert Gude of Maryland, who had his own bill before Congress. He introduced his eleven-year-old son, Gregory, "who actually is really responsible for me getting involved with this legislation. . . . With your permission I would like him to come forward. He has just a few comments about the bill. He is quite a lobbyist. I don't know whether it is proper for a lobbyist to come in and testify at this point." Chairman Baring responded with a laugh, "I think we are all lobbyists. We will be happy to hear him."

"Lots of people have read about the mustangs," Gregory told the committee. "My Dad and I have gotten about a thousand letters and petitions supporting the bill. We even got a letter from Brazil. . . . One letter was from Natalie Wilkins in Jackson, Michigan, and she wrote: 'Every time the men come to kill the horses for pet food I think you kill many children's hearts. I am a nine-year-old girl and love horses. Until you do something about it you will keep many children very sad.' For Natalie and many others I say: Please approve this bill as soon as possible."[11]

If there was any doubt that the bill would receive serious attention, this children's crusade put it to rest. Henry Jackson, the bill's sponsor in the Senate, reported receiving fourteen thousand letters, nine thousand of them from youngsters. "Frankly [it] took me by surprise," he said of the avalanche of mail. "These letters are eloquent in their simplicity and illustrate the sincerity with which these children have expressed their concern for the wild horses and burros. I might add that they greatly influenced my own decision to introduce one of the bills before the committee today. . . . I must say again that I think we can all agree that the interest of children and young people of our country in connection with this proposed legislation is something that is unique."[12]

Representatives of the Bureau of Land Management were scheduled to speak before Velma and the other wild horse advocates. In 1959 the Bureau had claimed that there weren't significant numbers of "authentic" wild horses grazing on public land and those that existed weren't worth saving. In 1971, its public position was radically different. Director Boyd Rasmussen's statement embraced public sentiment wholeheartedly. "The bills under consideration today vary in their details. However all are designed to insure the survival of bands of free-roaming horses and burros on public lands. The animals have captured the interest and imagination of Americans. Many feel that they are representative of our national heritage and a symbol of the Old West."[13] Rasmussen's comments about preserving and managing wild horses could have been lifted directly from Velma's own statements over the years.

Velma was by now a polished speaker, and if she felt the slightest bit anxious when she rose to testify on April 19, there wasn't a hint. She was, as usual, smartly dressed in a hand-sewn suit of her own design. She began by pointing out that she had asked for language in the original act that would have allowed for the management and control of wild horses. "That recommendation was not followed, nor was provision made for enforcement of the public law other than on a local basis, and it is an accepted fact that in most instances there is a curious reluctance on the part of local officials to enforce a law that might not be the most popular among their more vocal constituents, resulting in a tendency to pretend it isn't there and maybe it will go away."

In a strong, resonant voice, burred from years of smoking, Velma detailed her unsuccessful quest to secure a prosecution under the 1959 law. She recommended that specific police powers be given to the Bureau of Land Management, including the authority to issue citations "upon witnessing violation" or "being informed by a reliable witness" about a violation of the law. She then launched into what she considered the most vital point, a designation of the free-roaming mustangs that would end the circular arguments about what did and did not constitute a wild horse.

"The term 'feral,' meaning a once domestic species of animal that has gone wild, is now used in identifying the wild horses and burros. They must be removed from that category, which is a limbo that is neither 'wild' nor 'domestic' and in which their survival has been threatened and the intent of protection efforts has been lost in the debates on semantics and definitions.

"That is the reason for the proposed legislative terminology 'national heritage species and national esthetic resource.' It would designate a new category that would not be in conflict with present wildlife regulations. Other heritage species such as buffalo and American eagles could then be placed in this category. Any argument that these animals may technically be feral by dictionary definition would negate the special role they have played in our American heritage."

Velma knew her final recommendation would be controversial: a prohibition on the ranching tradition of releasing domestic, branded horses to winter over and breed with wild horse herds. "It is a common practice among some individuals in the western states to turn out branded domestic horses to provide a nucleus for a later round-up—by airplane, which is the only way it is commercially profitable to harvest them. Should he be apprehended, he can claim he is rounding up only his own branded horses and could not help it if a hundred or so wild unbranded horses got mixed up with his own. Or . . . he sometimes allows the domestic releases to produce progeny over a period of two or three years, then gathers everything, including the wild ones, claiming them to be offspring of the original domestic release, in a harvest that provides a marketable commodity which has cost him nothing to raise, either in grazing fees or taxes on them."[14] The livestock associations might have come to accept that some protection of the wild horse was a necessity, but most vehemently opposed this particular provision.

Karl Weikel, the Nevada representative of the American National Cattlemen's Association, complained that ranchers were getting a bad rap. "The wish and will to preserve these national heritage species is common to us all. There remains only to find the best and most practical means of its accomplishment. We of the western range livestock industry live with these animals and have done so for many years. We respect them through our long association and in fact feel a nostalgic kinship with them."[15] Bill McMillan, executive vice president of the same organization, made a plea for sympathy. "Ranchers are not opposed to protection of the wild horses. We've been maligned, but I don't know how to counter it."[16]

Even the pet food industry, seldom heard from on the issue, chimed in later outside the chambers. "We are in favour of preserving the wild horses," stressed Henry Bucklin, president of the Pet Food Institute in Chicago. "We don't need the wild mustangs in our products and our companies aren't participating in wild-horse roundups." While admitting that pet food companies did use horsemeat, Bucklin insisted they were careful to procure only older domestic "nags" from farms.

"How do they know?" Velma snorted after hearing Bucklin's statement. "There just aren't enough old worn-out farm horses to supply the demand for fresh pet food."

On June 29, 1971, a new and improved Wild Horse Annie act passed the Senate with a unanimous vote in favor, and on October 4 Congress approved Walter Baring's bill. The Wild Free-Roaming Horses and Burros Act was on its way to becoming Public Law 92–195.

The newspapers hailed it as the triumph of the children. "Opposition vanishes as some kids gang up to save wild horses," trumpeted the *Wall Street Journal*. "Youngsters inundate Congress with mail. Where are the bad guys? They went that-a-way."[17]

A few weeks later Velma learned that the University of Nevada had not changed its mind about Michael Pontrelli's contract. Happily, though, on November 23, 1971, Judge Frank Gregory dismissed Chug Utter's $65,000 damage claim against Pontrelli "with prejudice." The

*Velma and Walter Baring with congratulations*
*on passage of PL 92–195*

judge declared the lawsuit without merit and ordered the plaintiffs to pay court costs and Pontrelli's legal fees of $673.40 as assessed by the court. The *Nevada State Journal* congratulated Pontrelli and Wild Horse Annie, and hailed the verdict as "a complete victory for their cause."[18]

There was relief of another kind that year. In July, a benefactor provided seed money to start a foundation in support of Velma's efforts, particularly in the enforcement of the anticipated legislation and in educating children. The organization was to be called Wild Horse Organized Assistance (WHOA). Louise C. Harrison, a granddaughter and heir of brewer Adolph Coors, was a passionate animal lover.

In 1955, she and her sisters bought the historic Peck Hotel (renamed Hotel Splendide) in Empire, Colorado, and turned it into a pet-friendly establishment. Guests with dogs and cats were welcomed and a legion of local cats ate dinner at the back of the hotel near a pen holding Ponce de Leone, a burro, and his donkey companion, Shadow. Empire residents routinely dropped off their pets at the hotel on their way to the opera. Over the years, Louise Harrison had funded numerous animal-related organizations.

Harrison pledged fifteen hundred dollars a month for six months to establish an office, hire a secretary (to be shared with the ISPMB), and cover travel, printing, and other expenses. "Every thing about the new foundation would be "top drawer" in Velma's words, with an advisory committee consisting of horse "authorities" as well as advo-cates. "I would sure appreciate it, Ma'am, if I could add the name of Henry to the list," Velma wrote to Marguerite Henry in July 1971. "No work involved. But how impressed the young people would be."[19] The Henrys had recently moved to southern California after Sid suf-fered a serious heart attack. There is no response to this letter in the papers of either woman. Marguerite Henry never sat on the board of WHOA and no record has come to light of any further correspon-dence between them.

After limping along on her sore foot for a year and a half, Velma finally sought treatment. In August an operation removed the lump which had grown in mass to a "good-sized hen's egg . . . over a third of the bottom of my foot. No wonder it hurt!" she wrote to ISPMB board members during her weeks of recovery.[20]

Early in December, Velma was delighted to receive a personal let-ter from President Richard Nixon. "Recently my attention was called to your splendid efforts over the years towards the preservation and protection of wild horses and burros on our public lands. . . . In these days when we are all concerned with preserving and restoring our nat-ural environment, it is especially encouraging to note your dedication to saving these wild animals so that future generations of Americans may have the pleasure of seeing them roaming freely in their natu-ral habitat. You are commended for your outstanding work and this note comes to you with my warmest wishes for the years ahead."[21] She immediately passed the letter to the *Nevada State Journal,* which published it in its entirety.

On December 17, 1971, Nixon signed PL 92–195 into law. While Velma felt that it was a vast improvement over the 1959 legislation, she was disappointed it didn't contain specific funding appropriations to pay for management of the wild horses or for research into their behavior. Still, she reasoned it was the best that wild horse advocates could achieve at the time.

Now that there was a mechanism within the law to act on information and eyewitness accounts, Velma redoubled her efforts to bring a test case before the courts. On February 26, 1973, an opportunity presented itself when an Idaho informant reported that sixty or more horses had been chased by snowmobiles and helicopters near the town of Howe, northeast of Idaho Falls. Several had been shot and seven driven over a cliff, apparently by the snowmobiles. The source didn't know the whereabouts of the survivors, but he told Velma that hog rings had been inserted into their nostrils to subdue them by restricting their air intake. His information was so precise, Velma suspected he might have been involved in the roundup.

Shrugging off weakness from the colds, flu, and bouts of pneumonia that continued to plague her, Velma got to work. She notified the BLM in Nevada and Washington and sent out alerts to her circle of wild horse activists. She contacted wilderness photographer Harold L. Perry and asked him to meet her informant at the site. Tapping WHOA emergency funds, she engaged a helicopter at a cost of eleven hundred dollars to take Perry as close to the scene as possible. The next day, Franz Dantzler, an officer of the Humane Society of the United States, arrived unexpectedly, commandeered the helicopter, and without contacting Velma toured the area with a film crew.

The prime-time network news shows aired the footage and gave Dantzler and his organization full credit for discovering what came to be known as the Howe Massacre. The American Horse Protection Association, allies of the Humane Society, quickly stepped in with press releases, likewise claiming a role for itself and following up with public appeals for money that mentioned neither WHOA nor Wild Horse Annie. Velma was furious. "Nope, I've not made the headlines, lately," she wrote to William Loeb, the publisher of the *Manchester Union Leader* newspaper in New Hampshire. "Sort of got crowded out by that headline-stealing so-and-so that took the credit for WHOA's coup in getting pictures and evidence in the Idaho horse atrocity. But . . . still in there pitching."[22]

Receiving no credit for exposing the Howe Massacre aggravated Velma on a personal level and violated the collegial relationships she'd tried to maintain. She assumed the wild horse groups would do as they had in the past, share information and work together. But now turf boundaries had been drawn, quickly creating a fund-raising crisis. Velma received letters from supporters demanding to know why WHOA hadn't mobilized to support the Idaho horses and wondering if they should redirect donations to more active organizations.

Previously Velma's dealings with the American Horse Protection Association had been through her friend Pearl Twyne, president of the organization. But once the 1971 bill had passed into law, Twyne returned to the cause closest to her heart, a ban on the soring of Tennessee Walking Horses. As Twyne withdrew, Joan Blue, the vice president, became the point person on wild horses for the AHPA. Initially, Velma had cordial relations with Blue, but found her slow to compromise or communicate with the other horse groups, something Velma had always considered critical. She also felt Blue was indifferent to western sensitivities regarding wild horses, cattle, and rangeland; she came across as an eastern do-gooder, and an abrasive one at that. More than once Velma pointed out that Blue had never even seen a wild horse until she came to visit Velma in Reno in 1971.

From the moment the AHPA became involved in publicizing the Howe Massacre, Velma had difficulty finding out what the organization was up to. She had to ask Twyne to fill her in on the AHPA's plans and at least twice she learned that the president of the organization was also ignorant of its activities. During one telephone conversation, Pearl told Velma, "Joan and I had a real set to. We are different personalities. They were criticizing you. I said that you had the same dedication for the wild horses as I have for the Tennessee Walking Horse. . . . That is what I think about Velma."[23]

Joan Blue continued to behave as if Velma and WHOA were of

no consequence. The two women spoke on the telephone occasionally, but their conversations were fractious. Velma was disheartened to
learn that Blue disparaged her behind her back as being weak and too
cozy with the BLM. "I wouldn't slam an outhouse door the way Joan
Blue slams me," she said at one point.

Despite the headwind created by these organizational rivalries,
Velma wasn't ready to hand over the Idaho case to Blue or anyone
else. It was her best chance to bring offenders to justice. Velma
tracked down the surviving horses—twenty-seven in all—to a slaughterhouse in North Platte, Nebraska. At her instigation, a federal
holding lien was placed on the animals to prevent their destruction
or removal. Velma also sent her most recently recruited outlander,
twenty-five-year-old photojournalist Alan Kania, to Idaho to quietly
investigate reports that the local BLM office had actually facilitated
the roundup, and she pressed senior BLM officials to do their own
internal investigation.

In March 1973, a joint BLM and Department of Forestry report
indicated that there were sufficient grounds to file criminal charges,
but the assistant U.S. attorney on the scene refused to do so. After several telephone calls failed to persuade him of the case's merits, Velma
flew to Boise in October to present him with a two-inch-thick port-
folio of evidence. In the words of WHOA's later press release, written by Velma, "We were astounded to have been informed that to the
best of the knowledge of the Assistant U.S. Attorney, no investigation
had been conducted by his department in Boise, and that none of the
witnesses who reported the atrocity to us were interviewed by anyone
from the Justice Department. . . . On what basis then did the Justice
Department arrive at the conclusion that available evidence was not
considered to be sufficient to successfully prosecute?"[24]

In December 1973, the American Horse Protection Association,
along with the Humane Society, began filing civil lawsuits that eventually snagged the horse trader who had the twenty-seven impounded
horses in hand, a number of local Idaho officials and individuals, as
well as the Bureau of Land Management and the Department of Agriculture.

Court cases cost money, and the AHPA wasn't shy about asking for it. One seven-page solicitation stated that the "AHPA now stands alone as the sole organization defending the interests of and waging the fight to force the U.S. Department of the Interior and its Bureau of Land Management to live up to both the spirit and letter of the law already on the books—a law designed to protect the natural resources of America's public lands, and the wild horses that roam them."[25]

One evening in the spring of 1974, Charles Clegg, Jr., Lucius Beebe's lover, telephoned Velma. He and Beebe had sold the *Territorial Enterprise* in 1960, after which the two men spent much of their time in Hillsborough, a suburb of San Francisco, until Beebe died of a heart attack in 1966. But Clegg continued to send money periodically to support Velma's various campaigns. He wanted to know why WHOA and Wild Horse Annie had disappeared from the public eye. "It was most thoughtful of you to call me last evening," she wrote to him diplomatically the next day. "I too am disturbed that we are not mentioned in any of the news releases for our efforts have been unremitting (and dangerous at times). I fear that our supporters might think we have been sitting on our hands, and well they could think so from the lack of mention in the press. This latest one originated in Washington and of course the source would be reluctant to mention that any other organization has been of help.

"When the decision was made by the two organizations in Washington to file the civil suit, I was contacted, as I mentioned to you, and advised that our role would be more effective if we were not to join in the suit but appear as a witness and provide evidence that was sorely needed. I concurred, believing that we would be working together, and sent copies of the pictures we had taken, also promising I would forward any evidence we might come upon. This is the last time I was ever consulted and have had to depend upon what I read in newspapers or in their news bulletins to learn what was going on."[26]

It was the worst possible scenario, one that Velma had long feared: two influential horse organizations at odds with each other. In April, Velma flew to Washington, determined to regain control of the Idaho situation. The morning of her departure she took a hard fall, but felt compelled to go through with her plans. She met with politicians and officials in the capital and attempted to patch things up with the

Humane Society and the AHPA. She left for home after a couple of days, discouraged and sore. The next day, her doctor took a look at her bruises, listened to the rasp in her chest, and sent her to the hospital to recover from broken ribs, a sprained wrist, and pneumonia.

————

IN MAY 1974 Velma resigned from her position with Gordon Harris to devote herself full-time to the horses, believing it was the only option if a successful legal case was to be mounted in the Howe Massacre. "I was close to breaking," she admitted to Alan Kania. "You have noticed it; I'm sure I wasn't doing either commitment well. Tired, harassed, ill, mentally drained. My doctor said it was one or the other, Mr. Harris or the horses. Mr. Harris came in second and for that he will never forgive me. It was a traumatic decision to make from a financial and emotional standpoint. But I could not desert the wild ones. So here I am, taking a chance that WHOA can be built up to enable me to draw a little bit from it . . . just enough to get by on without any insurance benefits which I lost when I quit and which I cannot get on an individual basis. No retirement and not eligible for Social Security, meagre though it is. But as I have always said, my commitment to the wild ones is total."[27]

Gordon Harris sulked during Velma's waning days on the job, even refusing to say good-bye to her or wish her good fortune on her final day. But Velma would have none of it. She marched into his office to give him a hug and a kiss. After that she dropped by regularly and Harris began to feel the prick of his conscience. One day after returning home from the WHOA office, Velma found a letter from her former employer; inside was one hundred dollars for a lifetime WHOA membership and a note. "The world is made up of three kinds of people—those who make things happen; those who watch things happen; and those who don't know what's happening. Go, girl, go! And remember this is the first day of the rest of your life. You belong to the first group so keep on making things happen."[28]

That same month Velma severed another tie when she resigned from the Reno chapter of Executive Secretaries, Inc. "It is with tremendous pride and great pleasure that I look back on the years since we chartered . . . remembering the challenges we've met, the good times shared, the deadlines . . . the teamwork and the dedication, that has been the hallmark of the Reno chapter."[29]

Velma was no longer anyone's secretary and somewhat to her surprise it exhilarated her. "It is almost time to turn out the lights, lock the door and leave for home," she wrote to a correspondent. "I love this quiet time when the others have all departed and I have WHOA's office to myself. It is the first time in my forty-five years as a secretary that an office is truly mine . . . for I have always been someone else's Gal Friday."[30]

Being her own boss made Velma wonder if she should have taken this step much earlier. Although she had been an effective lobbyist and a supremely well-organized administrator, the creation of a self-sustaining organization that enhanced and strengthened her own efforts had eluded her. She once confessed that WHOA needed "a forward thrust that I simply don't know how to go about." She didn't have any kind of support group behind her until the Reillys formed the ISPMB in 1964, and they were only peripherally involved in fundraising and political action. Essentially she had always been a one-woman show, an arrangement that allowed her to control every detail in her immediate orbit but kept that orbit necessarily small.

The failure to develop the larger organization she needed was partly a matter of limited resources. Because she could afford neither the money nor the time, Velma missed important meetings in Washington where she might have fostered a larger network. Pride was also a factor. While she could ask, brazenly at times, for money to support wild horses, asking for herself was another matter. There's little doubt that Louise Harrison would have funded WHOA sufficiently to allow Velma to quit her job and work full-time for the horses back in 1971, if she'd been asked.

Though Velma loved the freedom of being her own boss, albeit a poorly paid one, the struggle to turn a personal crusade into a well-oiled national organization continued. The political infighting with Joan Blue and the American Horse Protection Association left her disconsolate. When she poured out her frustration to Trudy, her normally unflappable mother fanned the flame. "That Joan Blue. She came here and stayed here too, and if I had known! I took her for a ride out around the lake. I think I would have thrown her in the lake if I had known all the problems she'd cause."[31] Velma's distress at losing ground to the AHPA and the behind-the-scenes backbiting spilled over into her closest wild horse relationship at the time, that with photojournalist Alan Kania. When he mildly questioned her about tactics, she snapped at him. "Et tu, Brute? Who's been bending your ear, my friend."[32]

Velma's emotional condition was worsened by arthritis, which afflicted her back in 1974. Her twisted spine and compressed discs were always painful and periodically required traction for relief, but now she was in agony much of the time. The strain began to tell and for the first time spelling and grammatical errors crept into her correspondence.

In mid-1975 Velma suddenly gained fourteen pounds and an EKG pinpointed fluid building around her heart. The doctors told her she was on the verge of heart failure. "I am on slow, slow schedule. No

*Velma at her desk, mid-1970s*

stress, no physical activity. Digitalis to regulate my heart beat. Lots of rest. The medical man says if I adhere strictly in a month or so he can start building me up again. I've been one mighty ill Annie. But so many of my friends wonder how I've been able to go like a bat out of hell all these years anyway. Guess I've been pushing too hard."³³ That June, too ill to travel, she was forced to cancel a long-anticipated trip to Hawaii.

In Idaho the legal proceedings dragged on, and a Department of the Interior investigative report was delivered to the federal Senate Interior Committee. Velma received a copy of the lengthy "For Eyes Only" report and marked virtually every page with underlining, asterisks, exclamation points, and comments. "Convenient!" she scribbled where the transcript of a pivotal bit of testimony ended because the recording tape had broken. The evidence seemed damning and clear, the witnesses credible, and the perpetrators guilty. But no charges were ever laid and only eleven of the twenty-seven remaining horses survived.

In the fall of 1976, Velma discovered she had cancer. She submitted to a debilitating regime of chemotherapy that reduced her to little more than a wraith. She came to loathe the visits to Saint Mary's Hospital every two weeks for treatment. Afterward she was ill for days, had no appetite, and couldn't concentrate well enough to read or write. It particularly upset her that she couldn't answer the children's letters that continued to arrive. By the time she was feeling well enough to function, another round of chemo beckoned. Even Trudy found it hard to be optimistic. She thought her daughter would not have agreed to chemotherapy had she known its effects in advance.

It seemed as if some unsympathetic force was monitoring Velma's health when in 1976 an amendment was tacked on to the Bureau of Land Management Organic Act, an environmental manifesto for the agency. Largely unnoticed by the wild horse community, the amendment allowed the BLM to once again use helicopters to gather wild horses. It was signed into law by President Gerald Ford on October 21, 1976.

In February 1977, just before her sixty-fifth birthday, Velma reduced her role at WHOA to a part-time position. She was now eligible for Social Security and the combination of government benefits plus the reduced pay actually netted more than her WHOA salary had. "So why not save it for the organization?" she reasoned.

Late in May 1977, Velma summoned the energy to attend the graduation ceremonies of her niece, Trudy, when she finished medical school in California. Helen Reilly and her mother went with her. Though there were nurses among her relatives and Velma was proud of having been an executive secretary, she considered her niece to be the first truly professional woman in the family. Shrunken to barely eighty pounds, Velma had energy and enthusiasm for the trip, which encouraged her friends and family about the state of her health. Then, in mid-June, she was admitted to Saint Mary's Hospital as a precaution. On June 27, she died there in her sleep.

"Only so many times you can put on your lipstick and tighten up your girdle," she had remarked a few months earlier. Officially the cause of death was heart failure brought on by the cancer; in fact, it seemed that Wild Horse Annie had just plain worn herself out.

The accolades were quick to come. The *New York Times,* the *Washington Post,* and all the major wire services reported on her death, but the praise that would have pleased her the most appeared in the local press. A full-page editorial in the *Reno Evening Gazette* said she was as "symbolic of the American spirit as the horses she worked so hard to protect. Reading about Velma Johnston, better known as 'Wild Horse Annie,' one often comes across the metaphor, 'Little Old Lady in Tennis Shoes.'" The point invariably was to say that Wild Horse Annie was definitely not one of these.

"Annie's detractors would have undoubtedly preferred her to be weak and sentimental. What they got from Annie was a tough, hard-headed realist who marshalled her facts, set about her campaign to protect wild horses with steely determination and who often had a gun handy for self defence.

"Annie was a legendary character when she lived. And Nevada historians should make certain her legend is kept vivid. Beyond her success in protecting free-roaming creatures, she was a living example of what one person can achieve in the American political process."[34]

In a long list of quotations from friends and colleagues praising Velma, two were especially noteworthy. "For the past several years Mrs.

Johnston has been a good friend of the Bureau of Land Management," said BLM's Nevada director, Ed Rowland. "Although we've had minor disagreements in some areas, she worked very well with us. We've lost a good friend and we'll miss her very much."

In the same story, Belton Mouras, the president and cofounder of the Animal Protection Institute of America, based in Washington, called Velma the "single most potent woman to rise up out of the humane movement of this century."[35] Velma wasn't really one for keeping score but, in light of her contentious relationship with Joan Blue, she surely would have taken some satisfaction at this high praise.

But the good-bye Velma would have most appreciated was penned by her old friend, bookstore owner Bill Rainey. He posted his comments in the window of his shop.

"Wild Horse Annie has been living so long on just heart, bravery and sheer determination that her luck had to run out. Cancer took her down to less than eighty pounds, but she fought back. She seemed to me, these last few weeks, nothing more than two loving blue eyes. I don't think death would ever have taken her if she was awake.

"This country will never see the likes of her again. I learned how one person in these United States can believe in something and win against impossible odds. You don't take on the U.S. government and powerful cattlemen and win when you're one woman with little money, but she did.

"I had just left California when I first met her, almost two decades ago. It was a very difficult time of my life. She gave me friendship and a feeling for this country that is still with me.

"To me she was not the woman who talked with presidents, congressmen, authors and painters. She was the very soul of this state."[36]

# *Epilogue*

V ELMA JOHNSTON'S DEATH left a void in the wild horse protection movement. Though declining health hampered her
throughout the 1970s, she still exerted the only national leadership
among the various advocacy groups. Pearl Twyne had the charisma,
contacts, and expertise to step forward; instead she chose to focus
on her beloved Tennessee Walking Horses. Tom Holland left the
National Mustang Association under a hail of charges and counter-
charges of financial impropriety. Most of the board that served with
him had departed earlier.

Joan Blue, though powerful within animal humane circles, didn't
have the self-control to be a general, especially when virtually all the
troops were volunteers. Emotional, insensitive to others, but quick to
take offense herself, Blue held on to slights and nursed her grudges.

While Helen Reilly took over as chairman of the board of trustees
of Wild Horse Organized Assistance and the leadership of the ISPMB,
she functioned more as a caretaker than an initiator.

Marguerite Henry stepped back into the ring shortly after Velma
died, but not to take over the fight. Two fledgling producers, Marcy
Gross and Ann Weston, approached Henry with the idea of basing a
movie on *Mustang: Wild Spirit of the West*. Henry held the film rights
to her own book but not to Velma's life. She lost no time contacting
Trudy who was thrilled to sign over her daughter's story. There's no
record if Henry paid anything to Trudy, but when Gross and Weston
presented the option to Henry, the author made it clear that no money
was to go to Velma's family as she owned the rights herself. "She wasn't
really charming," Gross said of Henry. "It was a very unpleasant situation."

Nonetheless Gross and Weston forged ahead, sealing the deal, which included Betty White as Velma, with CBS over drinks at the Hotel Bel-Air in Los Angeles. The double Emmy-winning actress, who portrayed sarcastic, man-hungry Sue Ann Nevins on the *Mary Tyler Moore Show,* was so taken with the idea she mentioned it to Johnny Carson on the *Tonight Show* in December 1977.

Helen Reilly and the members of Velma's two organizations were outraged. Reilly fired off a protesting letter to the producers replete with condemnations from wild horse advocates. "It is like a nightmare," bemoaned one. "I have never knowingly put anyone down but she is not the person for that role," complained another.[1]

A series of scripts followed, none of which satisfied CBS executives. Two years later Betty White's star was dimming temporarily and Americans had fallen in love with prime-time soaps like *Dallas* and *Falcon Crest* and *Dukes of Hazzard*–type comedies. There no longer seemed much appetite for a film about a disfigured secretary from Reno, Nevada, fighting to save an American icon, and CBS dropped the project.

Marguerite Henry continued writing and on November 27, 1997, she died at the age of ninety-five, having just completed the manuscript of her fifty-ninth book.

Hope Ryden certainly had the credentials and stature to provide leadership. Her influential 1970 book, *America's Last Wild Horses,* continued to be updated and reissued, and Ryden reappeared frequently on the public stage to champion animal rights, but she never had an interest in being Velma's kind of leader, immersed in the day-to-day work of building and nurturing an organization. At the age of seventy-four, Ryden is still a vocal supporter of wild horse protection.

One potential successor emerged from the 1971 children's campaign. West Virginia–born Trina Bellak and friends had raised three hundred dollars in bake-sale proceeds for the cause and Velma had forwarded her letter to the Bureau of Land Management along with scores of others as evidence of public support. In 1973, fourteen-year-old Bellak was stunned when a letter from the Department of the Interior informed her of the BLM's recently launched adoption program and announced that her donation entitled her to adopt a wild horse. "I can tell you, that mustang occupied my thoughts for a long time," Trina later recalled. "I think I convinced myself that a wild horse would just appear on my doorstep one day."[2]

Bellak idolized Wild Horse Annie and yearned to become an equine veterinarian or a famous mustang trainer. But her life took a detour, first to Tulane University Law School and then to the West Wing of the White House as a legal counsel. Still, the siren call of the wild horses drew her. "Velma changed lives," Bellak said, "even after her death. Because of her, I ended up with the Humane Society of the United States."

A big woman with an enormous smile, Bellak cajoled, harassed, and bullied legislators and bureaucrats in her drive to end the slaughter of horses for human and pet consumption. Nor was she content to be a behind-the-scenes lobbyist; she traveled to abattoirs and rendering plants posing as a meat buyer in order to save wild horses. While at the Humane Society Bellak concluded that important political and legal issues were not being addressed by the various wild horse advocacy organizations, if only because they were beyond the resources of individual groups. Like Velma, she recognized that federal and state legislation had to be constantly monitored and adjusted for changing times and that enforcement agencies needed to be continually reminded of their duty. Bellak also believed strongly that the various wild horse protection groups should concentrate their energies on the development of a comprehensive, national management program that would guarantee the long-term existence of the herds. Ending the hunt of wild horses had been only the first step in preserving them; humane management of the herds in their designated territories was the ultimate objective.

In 2000 Bellak founded the American Horse Defense Fund, intended as an umbrella organization to fulfill the larger vision Velma had articulated. And she might have succeeded in corralling the disparate wild horse advocates and associations for a common purpose, had she not succumbed to cancer and died at the age of forty-seven in 2006.

Despite periods of internal strife after Velma's death, the International Society for the Protection of Mustangs and Burros and Wild Horse Organized Assistance are still active today, as are the National

Mustang Association, the American Horse Protection Association, and the Animal Protection Institute of America. And dozens of new associations, most inspired in one way or another by Velma, sprang up, with the majority focusing on a single herd, adoption program, or even a bloodline such as the Kiger mustangs of Oregon, distinctive horses with close DNA ties to their Spanish Barb ancestors.

As the various groups formed and created alliances, most butted up against the same issue Velma spent a quarter of a century trying to resolve: the contention that there were too many wild horses for the land available to them and the herds were destroying precious rangeland. In the first official horse census of 1971 the Bureau of Land Management concluded that seventeen thousand mustangs roamed free on federal public land. Velma arrived at the same figure, though she had reason to understate the total in order to exaggerate the imminence of their extinction. The BLM may also have deliberately lowballed its estimate to set the stage for subsequent recounts that would create the illusion of sudden overpopulation. Sure enough, in 1974 the BLM warned the Department of the Interior of an imminent population "explosion." The warning sparked an unresolved debate about what constitutes a surplus of wild horses and, if one exists, what should be done about it.

By 1982, the free-roaming wild horse population had swollen to more than fifty thousand, an astounding increase in just eleven years. Various explanations were offered, and certainly the relative absence of airborne mustangers had an impact. Though there were still instances of illegal capture or slaughter on public lands, the BLM had been more vigorous in charging violators under the 1971 law. The BLM also pointed to a remarkable fecundity among the herds, which were apparently increasing by 16 to 20 percent annually. Such a rate of reproduction implied that virtually every mare of breeding age conceived every year and produced a live offspring, that predators were almost nonexistent, and that every mustang lived well into old age—conditions that might occur among domestic animals but seldom exist in nature.

A blue-ribbon panel of experts, assembled in 1982, concluded that the original seventeen thousand figure was "undoubtedly low to an unknown but perhaps substantial degree."[3] The panel commissioned research that discovered the horse census takers had missed from 7 percent of horses in open areas to as many as 60 percent in rough or treed terrain. The panel also theorized that the smaller, quieter helicopters used in 1980 facilitated a more accurate count than the noisy, fixed-wing aircraft engaged in 1971.

One solution to overpopulation was the BLM's wild horse and burro adoption program. It began in 1973 with the herds in the Pryor Mountains and eventually spread to eleven western states. Over the next thirty-seven years more than 180,000 wild horses were placed in private hands. However, the program was and is expensive to maintain, despite a legion of volunteers, and difficult to monitor or police. Furthermore, as well-meaning and eager as the majority of adopters may be, a wild horse, like any wild animal, needs special handling. Training is a challenge even for professionals, and most adopters can't afford or don't have access to trainers with the necessary experience.

The BLM has never had the manpower or money to conduct routine postadoption follow-ups. Early on in the program, the Bureau withheld title to the horses, in an attempt to restrict sale for slaughter. In 1980 it amended the policy to give title after one year. Either way, the BLM had virtually no control over the animals' ultimate disposition once the horses were in private hands.

Those intent on profiting from wild horses have been remarkably resilient over the years, adroitly sidestepping the roundup and slaughter regulations and stricter enforcement. Some within the wild horse protection community estimated that as many as 50 percent of the 180,000 adopted BLM mustangs either had been sold to meat buyers or languished unwanted in their owners' fields. In 1990 the Government Accountability Office, a branch of Congress, tracked the fates of 20,000 adopted horses and discovered that they had ended up, via a number of schemes, with seventy-nine individuals and four native bands. "We found that hundreds of these horses died of starvation and dehydration during the 1-year probation period" and "thousands more went to slaughter after obtaining title from the BLM," the GAO reported. With between 3,000 and 10,000 BLM mustangs adopted annually, the wild horse lobby expanded to make room for another subcategory—groups devoted to rescuing adopted wild horses.

As evidence mounted that slaughterhouses were processing thousands of wild horses every year, and public pressure grew, the BLM changed its contracts again in 2005, imposing criminal penalties should the horses be sold to slaughter. The reaction was telling: Twenty prospective individual adopters and two tribes abruptly canceled their applications to purchase 427 wild horses from BLM holding facilities in Nevada. "A number of these individuals had completed the necessary paperwork, some even had sent checks paying for their animals," noted BLM spokesman Tom Gorey at the time. "However, they still decided not to complete the purchases and backed out."[4]

Since 1981 a small number of "surplus" horses have been finding their way into the mustang gentling programs at the Warm Springs Correctional Facility in Carson City, Nevada, the Cañon Correctional Facilities in Colorado, and the minimum security Wyoming State Honor Farm in Riverton, Wyoming. The projects, a joint venture between the BLM and the state correctional systems, are called wild horse training, but wild human training is equally appropriate. The inmates, most of them greenhorns, gentle the horses, but the horses mentor the convicts, and each mentor is every bit as wary as the men themselves. Though gentling a mustang is a formidable task, the wild horses are like blank slates to the inmates. They have no bad habits learned from years of poor handling by inept riders or harsh and impatient trainers. Similarly, the horses aren't influenced by the inmates' appearance, race, or rap sheets—to them all men are the same: two-legged monsters. In the early days of training, whatever handling mistakes the men inflict on the horses are returned in terrifying measure. It is a staggering responsibility for the chronically irresponsible. Yet, in just three to four months the convicts turn their mustang mentors into saddle horses destined for ranches, show rings, police departments, and the U.S. Border Patrol.

Velma Johnston would have adored the prison programs. After all, Charlie had a bit of the bad boy about him. It would have tickled her to the core that mustangs were contributing to the rehabilitation of men whom society had rejected. In particular, she would have enjoyed thumbing her nose at those who had claimed for so long that the wild horse was a pest with no good use outside a pet food can.

BY THE EARLY years of the twenty-first century it had become clear
to all sides in the debate that adoptions, let alone the inmate training
programs, couldn't begin to solve the surplus of wild horses if, indeed,
one existed. Throughout the 1990s the BLM had been rounding up
ever greater numbers in order to protect rangeland from overgrazing—though there was still little empirical data pinning the blame on
mustangs. By 2001 over ninety-eight hundred wild horses resided in
government holding facilities, originally designed as short-term halfway houses for animals supposedly destined for new homes.

The transformation from abundant and free to abundant and
penned had been facilitated by the 1976 amendment to the Bureau of
Land Management Organic Act, passed when Velma was too ill to man
the battlements. It allowed the BLM to once again use planes and helicopters to gather wild horses in large numbers. Then in 2004, a rider
slipped into that year's Omnibus Appropriations Bill changed the conditions of wild horse management, allowing unadoptable and older
mustangs in captivity to be purchased for commercial use—that is, for
slaughter. This gave the BLM license to sell a large number of these
horses or even euthanize them, though to date the agency maintains
that no horses have met this fate.

It all came to a head in 2008 when the Government Accountability Office released its fourth and most exhaustive investigation of
the BLM's progress in meeting the terms of the Wild Free-Roaming
Horses and Burros law. The GAO concluded what virtually everyone
associated with wild horses, including many staffers within the BLM
itself, already knew. Far more horses than could possibly be adopted
were being pulled off the ranges. The GAO calculated that nearly
thirty-three thousand wild horses were interned in 199 "herd management areas"—basically holding pens—and chewing through over
$27 million worth of hay annually, or nearly three-quarters of the BLM's
wild horse and burro budget.[5] At one time horses spent a few months in
transition; now they could pass their entire lives in what many derided
as government horse motels.

The GAO pointed out another factor contributing to the so-called surplus of horses. In 1971, wild horses roamed on 47 million acres of public land; over the next thirty years their territory shrank to 34 million acres. With 28 percent less land, overcrowding and overgrazing on some ranges was inevitable, regardless of fecundity or survival rates.

Sterilization and contraception programs have been touted over the years as a solution to wild horse overpopulation. Dr. Jay F. Kirkpatrick, director of ZooMontana in Billings, Montana, is currently one of the strongest advocates. He successfully reduced fertility rates among the Assateague Island wild ponies with an immunocontraceptive called PZP. But the cost—twenty-three dollars per horse annually—plus the logistics of locating mustang mares in the wild and getting close enough to administer the drug by dart gun made a large-scale program impractical, in the view of the BLM. Some critics argued that the drug merely delays conception, putting mares at risk of out-of-season deliveries during the worst of winter conditions. Still others pointed out that contraception crossed the line from animal preservation to animal husbandry: How could an animal whose breeding was controlled by drugs be truly wild? Kirkpatrick, who remains a proponent of PZP for western mustangs, told the *New York Times* that objections to artificial contraception or sterilization have more to do with tradition than practicalities. "The problem isn't scientific, it's political and cultural. We're dealing with a cowboy culture. One told me, 'We don't do it this way; we do it on horseback with ropes.'"[6]

Velma had so quickened the nation's sensitivity to the value of wild horses that the threat of mass euthanasia or commercial sale of tens of thousands of mustangs in captivity aroused a legion of lobby groups and outraged individuals. Under intense pressure, the BLM held a public hearing in Reno on the future of the surplus animals in the fall of 2008. Nevada still had by far the largest population of mustangs. Those attending were astonished when BLM official Henry Bazan prematurely announced an audacious solution proposed a few months earlier by Madeleine Pickens, wife of billionaire oilman T. Boone Pickens. She had offered to adopt every single horse in long- and short-term holding and set the animals free on a million-acre sanctuary she intended to purchase somewhere in the West, most likely eastern Nevada. It was odd for him to jump ahead of the negotiations, but Bazan, nearing retirement, wanted, in the words of a colleague, "the opportunity to do something right. It was not the intent of Congress in 1971 to let wild horses keep piling up in holding facilities."[7]

While Pickens was a longtime thoroughbred horse owner and breeder and a dedicated supporter of the Humane Society on a multitude of animal-welfare issues, she hadn't previously been prominent in the wild horse movement. Subsequent reports excitedly quoted Pickens talking about children camping out in teepees and waking up to see wild herds thundering by in the distance. Her vision might have seemed a little fanciful, but Pickens drew attention to a conundrum. The system now recognized and celebrated wild horses, but it threatened their viability by restricting them to a diminishing domain. Penning ever-growing numbers was hardly a reasonable management solution.

Hailed as "Wild Horse Madeleine" by one news reporter and dubbed "Mustang Madeleine" by *Town and Country* magazine, Pickens, with tousled mane, permanently bronzed skin, and fabulous wealth, could easily have been dismissed as a headline-seizing, celebrity do-gooder. But she soon attracted supporters for her plan and mounted an impressive protest against the possible sale, slaughter, or lifetime penning of thousands of wild horses. Less than six months after the Reno meeting, Pickens had formed the National Wild Horse Foundation, met with senior BLM officials and members of Congress and the Senate, presented a management plan to the Bureau, and compiled authoritative statistics to counter the perennial argument that wild horses were consuming forage necessary for domestic livestock. She established a social-networking system, capable of reaching thousands in a matter of seconds with bulletins, background details, and a persuasive call to action. Visitors to her website found the details of current legislation, a primer on how to lobby politicians, suggested wording for correspondence, and the voting history on related issues for all House and Senate members. It was a cornucopia of information and incentives made possible by modern technology, personal wealth, and genuine zeal. But those with long memories could glimpse in the background of Pickens's assault on Congress and the BLM the methods and determination of a woman more than thirty years in her grave.

By August 2009, nearly eight thousand emails on the subject had been sent to the newly appointed secretary of the interior, Ken Salazar.

It appeared that no one could turn back the Pickens juggernaut. But the BLM had a long and successful history of jousting, both in the public eye and behind the scenes. A year after the announcement and following dozens of meetings in Washington, Pickens, with the help of retired BLM range conservationist Lee Otteni, had adjusted her plan to focus on only the eleven thousand horses in short-term holding, which were costing the BLM millions to maintain and feed. "A cow brings in four cents a day to the taxpayer on public land," said Otteni, "and the horses in short-term holding cost $5.75 a day to feed. On the range they cost zero money. I'm not a mathematician but I'm being screwed as a taxpayer."[8]

Pickens intended her proposal to be a part of a long-term, viable management strategy for wild horses on public land, but such a plan appeared to be as far out of reach in 2009 as it had been half a century earlier. She reluctantly recognized that her adopted herd would have to be sterilized in order to function as an ongoing destination for horses who would otherwise live out their days in some form of captivity. While she received support from across America some horse advocates feared emptying the holding facilities would simply provide license to the BLM to fill them up again with more captured wild horses.

Others, whose primary interest was protection of the land and not the horses, waded into the range wars. They maintained the only solution was to remove all nonindigenous species, including cattle, sheep, and horses, from public land entirely, especially in Nevada where damage was rapidly becoming irreversible. One of those, ironically, was Tina Nappe, Gus Bundy's oldest daughter. She acknowledged that her father's extraordinary and unheralded photos "started the whole thing off," but now thinks they weren't a good thing. Though Nappe has followed in her father's footsteps with her longtime involvement in the Sierra Club, she is among an emergent group of range stewards who believe that wild horses, let alone cattle and sheep, do not belong on public land if native flora and fauna are to survive.

Pickens didn't intend to take full financial responsibility for the horses, though she estimated her plan would save the government

$800 million over ten years. She requested that the five-hundred-dollar annual per-head allotment, the cost of caring for horses in long-term facilities, be diverted to her sanctuary. The BLM maintained that such a move would require the consent of Congress.

As Pickens wound her way through the bureaucratic labyrinth, national attention focused once again on the Pryor Mountains, where Velma achieved her first political triumph following the passage of the 1971 act. The Pryors, she had hoped, would become the template for management of wild horse herds and preserves throughout the West. Instead, the Pryor horses have existed in a tenuous state on the thirty-two thousand acres originally set aside for them. Since 1968 the BLM has removed six hundred horses in order to maintain what the agency considered an ideal number of between eighty-five and one hundred twenty animals. Lee Otteni wryly noted that ranchers who supported the removals to save grazing for their livestock, found themselves trying in vain to urge their animals to the higher plateaus in summer to reach the areas where the horses foraged. In an eerie reprise of Lloyd Tillett's words back in 1965, Otteni pointed out that, "Horses range much higher than cattle and in rougher terrain. They don't get as sore-footed as a cow."[9]

Each roundup, or gather, as the BLM now prefers, sparked protests of more or less magnitude but opposition flared in earnest in September 2009. This time the lightning rod was not a grizzled rancher thumbing his nose at bureaucracy but an author and filmmaker who had devoted herself to cataloguing the lives of the Pryor horses, most particularly the herd led by Cloud, a stallion of the palest hue. Ginger Kathrens, with two Emmy Award–winning documentaries to her credit, had turned Cloud into an equine celebrity among wild horse enthusiasts. In late 2008, the BLM announced a gather to reduce the Pryor horse numbers by removing some permanently and treating mares with the birth control drug PZP. Kathrens raced into battle with a host of volunteers behind her. After failing to derail the BLM's plan she argued, in a video released on the Cloud Foundation website, that if the horses had to be taken off the range the BLM should wait until the spring when the animals, including still suckling foals, would not have to be driven long distances from the high country. When the roundup actually took place Kathrens turned to what she did best, documenting the impact of a late-season airborne chase on the wild horses. In the corrals she filmed a foal staggering to reach its mother on hooves badly bruised from a long, terrified run across rocky terrain. As with the Gus Bundy photos, the footage accomplished what no words could.

The BLM abruptly released a number of the horses, including the stallion Cloud, who frantically raced around trying to herd together his harem of mares as well as their foals. The Cloud Foundation declared victory while the BLM claimed that capturing, then releasing horses had been the plan all along.

Though the sands beneath wild horse management and advocacy have shifted frequently in the decades since Velma Johnston's death, the very issue which motivated her to champion the wild horse still remains as the greatest threat to their existence—airborne pursuit. Velma campaigned tirelessly against it for a quarter of a century because it was a brutal method of rounding up horses in the wild. She also maintained that airborne roundup was just too easy and too tempting a practice to leave in the hands of a government agency which was not created to manage, let alone conserve, the American wild horse. Velma believed that if BLM agents could effortlessly round up wild horses, for reasons both real and imagined, they would. And they have.

If the BLM was barred from using airplanes and helicopters, it would have been forced to ponder carefully taking horses out of the wild willy nilly. Today blanket roundups are increasingly common, even of herds in remote areas where their existence presents, as far as can be determined, little or no competition to livestock or wildlife. Some, of course, maintain that if airborne roundups had not been reestablished in 1976, a year before Velma's death, the overpopulation of wild horses would have inflicted catastrophic damage to Western ranges. And that raises another issue Velma Johnston strove to resolve over the years: the lack of independent scientific research relating to range management and wild horses. It is a problem that endures and one that encourages futile bickering about how many wild horses the various ranges can support in concert with other users of the land. Within the BLM corridors, low-, mid-, and high-level bureaucrats alike privately confess in one form or another, "We don't really know what we're doing when it comes to the wild horses. It isn't based on science, but we keep doing it because that is what we've always done."

As long as the BLM faces a multitude of local and issue-specific fires kindled by hundreds of advocacy groups, there will be no foundation on which to develop a national solution to wild horse management. This situation seems to play into the BLM's hands, but that assumes the Bureau is the primary spoiler in efforts to maintain and manage an important aspect of American heritage, rather than a victim of budgets, inertia, and history. The BLM is also squeezed by the same people who, in one way or another, have guided much of its action since the early days of the Grazing Service—livestock ranchers and, more recently, hunters.

The absence of a single, strong national wild horse organization, based in Washington, staffed by the politically astute, and led by someone with a vision and legal canniness actually hampers the BLM. The agency wastes a great deal of time relating to too many groups and individuals—well meaning though they are. A partnership with the BLM and a national wild horse organization might be possible. Velma always thought so. But it may be that the fate of America's wild horse is, and always has been, in the wrong government hands. This, then, is the next debate. The sooner it begins the sooner the saga begun by a secretary from Reno, Nevada, will come to a conclusion.

---

THERE IS NO doubt that if Velma Johnston hadn't looked into the back of that livestock truck in 1950 and vowed to do something about what she saw, there wouldn't be any wild horses left to fight about today. The debate Velma fostered about America's last mustangs isn't over and her dream of a sustainable management plan isn't yet in place. But in the end what is truly important about Wild Horse Annie isn't just the preservation of a historical legacy but the affirmation of that quixotic American idea that an individual can and should make a difference.

# ACKNOWLEDGMENTS

KEVIN HANSON OF Simon & Schuster Canada belongs in our forever grateful file for recognizing the great story encompassed by the
life of Velma Johnston. Beside him go horse-loving Samantha Martin
and Susan Moldow of Simon & Schuster in New York for agreeing with
him. Alison Clarke, also with Simon & Schuster Canada was always so
cheery and supportive. You provided much-needed encouragement
during those all-too-frequent periods when writer confidence fails.

Jan Walter proved to be a superb editor who guided the manuscript
with deft hands, great ideas, and a kind red pencil.

Many of Velma's family members assisted us with their recollections, most especially Roy Larson, Jack McElwee, Dr. Trudy Larson,
Judy McElwee, Loreene and Bob McElwee, Mary Popish, Linda Har-
rell, and Charlie's sister June Allen. We are indebted to Tom McCord
for adding important information about Velma and Charlie's early life
together and to Gordon Harris, Jr., for his memories of his father's
office and the people who worked there. Also to Steven Pelligrini for
bringing into sharp focus the excitement of the early days in Velma's
fight to save the mustangs.

While it was impossible to write this story without being critical of
the BLM, there are dozens of current and past employees who offered
great insight into how the agency has evolved through many interesting and difficult eras. Thank you all.

Though only a small aspect of their story made it into this book,
the inmates and staff of the wild horse training programs at the Cañon
City Correctional Facility in Colorado and the Warm Springs Correctional Facility in Carson City, Nevada, provided an extraordinary view
of how mustangs have changed the lives of men thought to be irre-
deemable. Much thanks to Hank Curry, Tim Bryant, Mike Holmes,
Jack Palmer, Brian Hardin, and Guy McEnulty. We also appreciate the

candor of the many inmates we spoke with as they gave us glimpses into experiences difficult to imagine let alone understand. More on the Colorado program is contained in the remarkable documentary film *The Wild Horse Redemption,* produced by Terence McKeown and directed by John Zaritsky. Thanks also to Bob McKeown for "discovering" the story through a conversation with Alison.

We wish we could thank her in person, but the late Trina Bellak provided a candid assessment of the wild horse situation before she died in 2006, far too young. There are many other knowledgeable and dedicated mustang advocates, among them Ginger Kathrens, Karen Sussman, and Cathy Barcomb. Hope Ryden generously provided photographic and research materials collected over the years and gave us a great deal of valuable information.

We are particularly grateful to and admiring of Tina Nappe, Gus Bundy's daughter, for her recollections and candid discussions about whether wild horses and domestic livestock belong on public land. She is a stalwart among the army of citizens dedicated to protecting public land.

Archival records have been central to the telling of Velma Johnston's life. Without the records in private hands as well as major holdings in the Denver Public Library; University of Minnesota; Nevada State Archives; University of Nevada, Reno; Arizona Historical Society; and smaller holdings in a host of other places, these kinds of stories would not be possible. Thanks to those who save things, donate things, and look after them forever. We also are grateful to archivist Joyce Cox of Reno who was instrumental in the fact-checking.

There were so many tears in the writing of this book. Our beloved Toby, a fearsome-looking German shepherd with a heart of gold, died, as did Fogerty, David's wonderful trail horse. And as we edited this manuscript, Alison's mother, Patricia, passed away also. She was a lover of all things equine her entire life. Their bodies are gone but their spirits remain.

The gestation of Velma's story spanned a far longer time than we usually take for a book. Our youngest daughter, Quinn, left high school and nearly finished university in the process, and our oldest, Claudia, with some help from Jeff Perry, gave us a grandson, Jack, who now loves horses as much as we do. Thanks for surviving all the grumps and grouches.

Many friends heard the story of Wild Horse Annie (probably far too often) over the years. Thanks Barry Flatman, Jeanne Beker, Anne Francis, Margie Taylor, and especially dear friends Susan Nesbitt and Don Proudlove for lending your ears. And to Fiona Griffiths and Peter Griffiths, say hurrah, you won't have to ask, "How's the book going?" until the next one. Thank you for not giving up.

# NOTES

## Notes on Sources

For readability we have very occasionally altered spelling, punctuation, and order in the quotes used throughout this book.

We consulted a wide variety of archival sources, large and small, for material relating to Velma Johnston and the history of wild horses. There are vast and fascinating collections that touch on every aspect of the wild horse in America. There are only a handful relating to Velma but, fortunately, what exists details almost every aspect of her life after 1950. Here are the sources we found most useful in assembling her story.

### Primary Sources

Alan J. Kania Collection (AJKC), Denver Public Library, Western History/ Genealogy Department.

Arizona Historical Society: In addition to print material there is the wonderful photographic collection of Charles Herbert with thousands of images of the West.

Glenbow Museum, Calgary, Alberta: There is only a small amount of material relating directly to Velma Johnston, but the archives here are an excellent source for western Canadian history, especially ranching, horses, and First Nations.

Marguerite Henry Collection (MHC): Kerlan Collection, the Children's Literature Research Collection, University of Minnesota.

National Cowboy & Western Heritage Museum, Oklahoma City, Oklahoma: Most particularly the Donald C. and Elizabeth M. Dickinson Research Center.

National Cowgirl Museum & Hall of Fame: Fort Worth, Texas—Women are underrepresented in most archival collections about the West, both past and present. This is a great source of material that views the Western experience through female eyes.

Nevada State Archives and Library.

Private Family Collection (PFC): This material has not yet been donated to a library or archive but likely will be in the near future.

Public Lands Foundation Archives, BLM National Training Center, Phoenix, Arizona: Documents and material relating to the history of the Bureau of Land Management.

University of Nevada Reno Library, Special Collections: A wealth of material about Nevada and the Oral History Program is particularly interesting. This is also the repository for Gus Bundy's magnificent photos.

Velma B. Johnston Collection (VJC), Denver Public Library, Western History/Genealogy Department: An excellent source containing not only extensive letters but also scientific and government reports as well as speeches, scrapbooks, and photo albums.

## Books

There are far too many books on our shelves and in libraries that provided useful background material in the writing of Velma Johnston's life to list here, but this summary highlights some of the most interesting.

Amaral, Anthony. *Mustang: Life and Legends of Nevada's Wild Horses*. Reno: University of Nevada Press, 1977.

Bennett, Deb. *Conquerors: The Roots of New World Horsemanship*. Solvang, Calif.: Amigo Publications, 1998.

Berger, Joel. *Wild Horses of the Great Basin: Social Competition and Population Size*. Chicago: University of Chicago Press, 1986.

Coolidge, Dane. *Old California Cowboys*. New York: E. P. Dutton and Company, 1936.

Dines, Lisa. *The American Mustang Guidebook*. Minocqua, Wis.: Willow Creek Press, 2001.

Dobie, J. Frank. *The Mustangs*. Boston: Little, Brown and Company, 1952.

Harbury, Martin, and Ron Watts. *The Last of the Wild Horses*. Toronto: Key Porter Books, 1984.

Henry, Marguerite. *Mustang: Wild Spirit of the West*. New York: Macmillan Publishing Co., 1966.

Idell, Albert, ed. *The Bernal Diaz Chronicles*. New York: Doubleday, 1956.

Orndorff, Richard L., Robert W. Wieder, and Harry F. Filkorn. *Geology Underfoot in Central Nevada*. Missoula, Mo.: Mountain Press Publishing Co., 2001.

Ryden, Hope. *America's Last Wild Horses*. Chester, Conn.: Lyons Press, 1970.

Scanlan, Lawrence. *Wild About Horses*. New York: HarperCollins Publishers, 1998.

Smith Thomas, Heather. *The Wild Horse Controversy*. New York: A. S. Barnes and Co., 1979.

Steele, Rufus. *Mustangs of the Mesas.* Los Angeles: Press of Murray and Gee, 1941.

Stillman, Deanne. *Mustang: The Saga of the Wild Horse in the American West.* New York: Houghton Mifflin Co., 2008.

Stong, Phil. *Horses and Americans.* New York: Garden City Publishing Co., 1946.

## Abbreviations Used in the Notes

AJKC: Alan J. Kania Collection

BV: Bill Vincent

CS: Christine Stevens

GB: Gus Bundy

LH: Louise Huhne

MH: Marguerite Henry

MHC: Marguerite Henry Collection

PFC: Private Family Collection

RO: Robert O'Brien

TG: Tex Gladding

TM: Tom McKnight

TS: Tim Seward

VJ: Velma Johnston

VJC: Velma B. Johnston Collection

WB: Walter Baring

ONE: VELMA

1. Some sources note date as 1884.

2. Murray, Bill, "I'm On My Way To Reno" (RCA Victor, 1910).

3. Velma Johnston to Marguerite Henry, undated answers to Henry's questions, n.d., circa 1965, Marguerite Henry Collection (hereafter MHC), Elmer L. Andersen Library, University of Minnesota Libraries, Minneapolis, MN, Box MF 2630.

4. In some family recollections and correspondence Joe's horse is also referred to as Baldy.

5. *Los Angeles Times,* August 9, 1916, cited in "What Ever Happened to Polio?" Smithsonian Museum of Natural History, http://american history.si.edu/polio/index.htm (consulted by the authors in 2008).

6. VJ to "Turnbull," 1967, VJC, Box 1 FF7.

7. Alan J. Kania interview with Mrs. Trudy Bronn, April 26, 1980, Velma Johnston Collection (hereafter VJC), Denver Public Library, AV Box 12.

8. Alan J. Kania interview with Mrs. Trudy Bronn, April 26, 1980, VJC, AV Box 12.

9. Ibid.
10. Marguerite Henry's notes of interviews with VJ, MHC, Research, Box MF 2630.
11. VJ to MH, n.d., circa 1965, MHC, Box MF 2630.
12. Ibid.


TWO: CHARLIE

1. VJ to Phyllis, August 29, 1959, VJC, Box 1 FF2.
2. VJ to MH, n.d., circa 1965, MHC, Box MF 2630.
3. VJ to Phyllis, August 29, 1959, VJC, Box 1 FF2.
4. VJ to Mary Lea Turcott, October 10, 1972, VJC, Box 1 FF29.
5. Hole, Rita S., "Do You Need Your Job?" *Good Housekeeping,* September 1932, 24–25.
6. VJ to MH, October 21, 1965, VJC, Box 2 FF27.
7. VJ to MH, n.d., circa 1965, MHC, Box MF 2630.


THREE: THE DOUBLE LAZY HEART RANCH

1. VJ to John McCormack, VJC, February 21, 1971, Box 2 FF33.
2. De Azara, Félix, *Voyage dans l'Amérique Méridionale depuis 1781 jusqu'en 1801* (France: Dentu, 1809). English translation by Walckenaer, Charles Athanase; Haenke, Thaddäus; and Cuvier, Georges. Digitized version, October 23, 2007, Google Books.
3. Judy McElwee, interview with the authors, April 2005 and May 2005.
4. Authors' interview with Tom McCord, May 2005.
5. VJ to MH, February 8, 1966, VJC, Box 1 FF11.
6. VJ to MH, October 21, 1965, VJC, Box 1 FF11.
7. Ibid.
8. VJ to MH, January 19, 1966, MHC, Box MF 2630.
9. Alan J. Kania interview with Mrs. Trudy Bronn, April 26, 1980, VJC, Box 4 FF41.


FOUR: THE ROAD TO RENO

1. Dobie, J. Frank, *The Mustangs* (Boston: Little, Brown and Company, 1952), 72.
2. James, Will, *Cowboys North and South* (New York: Scribner's, 1926), 200.
3. Goldsmith, Walter, "Wild Horses and Outlaws," *Western Horseman,* November–December 1944.

4. Amaral, Anthony, *Mustang: Life and Legends of Nevada's Wild Horses* (Reno, NV: University of Nevada Press, 1977), 56.

5. "A Horseless Horseman," *Sunset Magazine,* May 1914.

6. Barnum, Charles, "Trapping Wild Horses on the Nevada Plains," *Denver Republican,* January 14, 1912.

7. Barnum, Charles, "How I Trap Wild Horses," *Sunset Magazine,* August 1908.

8. "A Horseless Horseman," *Sunset Magazine,* May 1914.

9. Wyman, Walker D., *The Wild Horse of the West,* 126.

10. Trachtman, Paul, *The Gunfighters* (Alexandria, VA: Time-Life Books, 1974), 199.

11. Ibid., 201.

12. Wyman, Walker, op. cit., 139.

13. July 7, 1939, letter by Archie D. Ryan, cited in Wyman, Walker, *The Wild Horse of the West,* 163.

14. McKnight, Dr. T. L., "Feral Livestock in America," *University of California Publications in Geography,* vol. xvi, University of California Press, 1964.

15. VJ to MH, January 17, 1966, PFC.

## FIVE: A LAW OF OUR OWN

1. Authors' interviews with Roy Larson and Jack McElwee, 2005 and 2009.

2. VJ to MH, MHC, November 11, 1965.

3. Abbott, Clifton, "Wild Fortune," *True: The Man's Magazine,* January 1948.

4. Ibid.

5. Keas, Chas. H. "Corralling Wild Horses with a Helicopter," *Western Horseman,* August 1952.

6. Letters to the Editor, *Life,* July 25, 1938.

7. VJ to MH, MHC, November 11, 1965.

8. Based on $1.00 of unskilled income in 1951 valued at $12.45 in 2006. Samuel H. Williamson, "Five Ways to Compute the Relative Value of a U.S. Dollar Amount, 1790 to Present," www.MeasuringWorth.com, 2008. Price per pound in 1952 roughly six cents according to BLM stats.

9. VJ to MH, MHC, November 11, 1965.

10. Rocha, Guy, "Seeing Justice in Virginia City," Historical Myth a Month series, myths # 30 & 142, Nevada State Library and Archives, October 2007.

11. O'Brien, Robert, "The Mustangs' Last Stand," *Reader's Digest,* December 1957.

12. VJ to Tex Gladding (hereafter TG), June 9, 1952, VJC, Box 2 FF1.

13. Minutes of the Storey County Commissioners Report, June 6, 1952.
14. Harvey, Ann, "An Interview with Edward Daniel Gladding," Oral History Program, University of Nevada, 1984.
15. Minutes of the Storey County Commissioners Report, June 6, 1952, VJ to MH, August 3, 1965, VJ to MH, November 11, 1965, both PFC.
16. Johnston, Velma, "Transcription of Storey County Meeting," VJC, Box 3 FF12.
17. VJ to MH, n.d., PFC.
18. Editorial, Lucius Beebe, *Territorial Enterprise,* June 13, 1952.
19. Elizabeth W. Richards, Storey County, County Clerk and Treasurer, to VJ, December 13, 1965.
20. VJ to MH, August 3, 1965, PFC.
21. Johnston, Velma, "From Court House to White House," n.d., PFC.
22. Ibid.
23. Editorial, Lucius Beebe, *Territorial Enterprise,* February 12, 1955.
24. "Saddle Chatter," *Nevada State Journal,* February, 27, 1955.
25. VJ's press release, February 16, 1955.
26. VJ to MH, November 11, 1965, PFC.
27. Journals of the Assembly and Senate 1864–1965, in Records of the Nevada State Legislature, Nevada State Legislature Archives, Carson City, NV.
28. VJ to MH, November 11, 1965, PFC.

### SIX: MOCCASIN WALKING

1. VJ to TG, VJC, March 11, 1957, Box 1 FF1.
2. Ibid.
3. VJ to MH, August 31, 1965, PFC.
4. VJ to Robert O'Brien (hereafter RO), August 11, 1957, Box 1 FF1.
5. Interview with Mr. Stoddard at his home, June 6, 1957. VJC, Box 3 FF8.
6. Ibid.
7. Ibid.
8. Interview with Arne Bailey, August 9, 1957, VJC, Box 3 FF8.
9. VJ to RO, August 11, 1957, op. cit.
10. VJ to Mrs. Zelda R. Smith, August 2, 1957, VJC, Box 1 FF1.
11. Ibid.
12. VJ to RO, August 11, 1957, citing *Las Vegas Sun,* March 13, 1957.
13. Ibid.
14. Authors' interview with Tom McCord, 2005.
15. VJ to RO, August 11, 1957.

## SEVEN: MRS. JOHNSTON GOES TO WASHINGTON

1. O'Brien, Robert, "The Mustangs' Last Stand," *Reader's Digest,* December 1957.
2. Ibid.
3. Ibid.
4. VJ to TG, December 9, 1957, VJC, Box 1 FF1.
5. Ibid.
6. Ibid. Velma, intent on missing no opportunities, also cooked up a scheme to lobby the post office for a commemorative mustang stamp. The stamp never came into being but it showed the extent she was willing to go to bring the wild horse plight into the public eye.
7. Evans, K. J., "Walter Baring: The Paradoxical Politician," The First 100 series, *Las Vegas Review-Journal,* http://www.1st100.com. Also published (Las Vegas: Huntington Press, 1999).
8. VJ to Sid Henry, May 4, 1966, PFC.
9. VJ to Tim Seward, August 3, 1959, VJC, Box 1 FF6.
10. VJ to WB, December 11, 1957.
11. Ibid.
12. VJ to TG, February 7, 1959, VJC, Box 1 FF1.
13. VJ to Robert O'Brien, March 10, 1958, VJC, Box 1 FF2.
14. VJ to TG, February 7, 1959.
15. VJ to WB, January 7, 1958, VJC, Box 1 FF2.
16. VJ to WB, February 27, 1958, VJC, Box 1 FF2.
17. VJ to TG, March 28, 1958, VJ to TG, January 20, 1958, VJ to WB, February 27, 1958, VJ to WB, December 11, 1957, VJC, all Box 1 FF2.
18. VJ to WB, February 27, 1958.
19. VJ to Louise Huhne (hereafter LH), April 2, 1958, VJC, Box 1 FF3.
20. VJ to TG, January 20, 1958.
21. Huhne, Louise, "Scoundrels, Horses and One Woman," *Revue* (English translation), December 1958, VJC, Box 7 Item 1.
22. VJ to LH, April 2, 1958.
23. VJ to RO, March 10, 1958, VJC, Box 1 FF9.
24. Extension of Remarks of Hon. Walter S. Baring, Congressional Record—Appendix, July 16, 1959.
25. VJ to RO, March 10, 1958.
26. VJ to TG, January 20, 1958.
27. VJ to LH, April 2, 1958.
28. VJ to TG, January 20, 1958.
29. "Mustang Murder," *True,* June 1958.
30. Stevens, Christine, press release, n.d., The Dwight D. Eisenhower Library.

31. VJ to LH, April 12, 1958.
32. VJ to H. M. Mason, Jr., November 11, 1957, VJC, Box 1 FF1.
33. VJ to H. M. Mason, Jr., April 2, 1958, VJC, Box 1 FF1.
34. H. M. Mason to VJ, April 8, 1958, VJC, Box 2 FF32.
35. Author's Agreement, Fawcett Publications, Inc., November 11, 1957, VJC, Box 6.
36. Tom McKnight (hereafter TM), to VJ, October 21 and November 19, 1958, VJC, Series 2, Box 1 FF46.
37. TM to VJ, November 26, 1958, VJC, Series 2, Box 1 FF46.
38. TM to Gus Bundy (hereafter GB), November 19, 1959, VJC, Series 2, Box 1 FF46.
39. GB to VJ, November 29, 1959, VJC, Series 2, Box 1 FF46.
40. VJ to TM, November 22, 1959, VJC, Series 2, Box 1 FF46.
41. H.R. 2725, 86th Congress, 1st Session, January 19, 1959.
42. VJ to TG, February 7, 1959, VJC, Box 1 FF4.
43. *Sports Illustrated,* May 1975.
44. Ibid.
45. VJ to WB, April 17, 1959, VJC, Box 1 FF4.
46. VJ to Christine Stevens, June 15, 1959, VJC, Box 1 FF5.
47. VJ to WB, May 11, 1959, VJC, Box 1 FF4.
48. VJ to Howard Cannon (Senator), June 15, 1959, VJC Box 1 FF5.
49. Ibid.
50. Ibid.
51. VJ to Christine Stevens, June 15, 1959.
52. VJ to Howard Cannon, June 15, 1959.
53. Taylor, Jock, "Eastern Humanitarians Upset over Cruelty to 'Beautiful' Wild Horses," *Reese River Reveille,* June 17,1959.
54. Ibid.
55. VJ to WB, June 24 and July 2, 1959, VBJ, Box 1 FF5.
56. VJ to WB, July 2, 1959.
57. Ibid.

EIGHT: IT'S A HELL OF A GOOD DAY

1. Eleazer, Frank, "Newsmen in Washington See Wild Horse Annie Without Shootin' Irons," UPI, July 15, 1959.
2. Extension of Remarks of Hon. Walter S. Baring, Congressional Record— Appendix, July 16, 1959.
3. Ibid.
4. Extension of Remarks of Hon. Walter S. Baring, Congressional Record— Appendix, July 21, 1959.

5. Koterba, Ed, "Wild Horse Annie," United Feature Syndication Inc., July 21, 1959.

6. Committee on the Judiciary Report, House of Representatives, 86th Congress, 1st session. Report No. 833, p. 4.

7. VJ to WB and Tim Seward (hereafter TS), July 21, 1959, VJC, Box 1 FF5.

8. Committee on the Judiciary Report, House of Representatives, op. cit.

9. Ibid.

10. VJ to WB and TS, op. cit.

11. VJ to the Editor, *Time,* July 27, 1959, VJC, Box 1 FF5.

12. VJ to TS, August 3, 1959, VJC, Box 1 FF6.

13. VJ to WB, August 3, 1959, VJC, FF6.

14. VJ to WB and TS, July 21, 1959.

15. VJ to Phyllis, August 29, 1959, VJC, Box 1 FF6.

16. VJ to WB, August 24, 1959, VJC, Box 1 FF6.

17. VJ to Phyllis, op. cit.

18. Terry Simmons to the President, July 24, 1959, the Dwight D. Eisenhower Library, G.F. 140-F. Ellen Kaminski to Mr. President, July 15, 1959, the Dwight D. Eisenhower Library, G.F. 140-F.

19. VJ to Eugene L. Conrotto, September 8, 1959, VJC, Box 1 FF6.

20. Loeb, William, *Manchester Union Leader,* September 12, 1959.

21. VJ to Yvonne M. Spiegelberg, September 17, 1959, VJC, Box 1 FF6.

22. VJ to LH, August 11, 1959, VJC, Box 1 FF6.

23. VJ to Phyllis, August 29, 1959.

24. VJ to Dean (last name illegible), September 13, 1970, VJC, Box 1 FF22.

25. VJ to MH, May 28, 1965, PFC.

26. VJ to Dean, op. cit.

27. VJ to Duane, December 14, 1971, VJC, Box 1 FF27.

28. VJ to MH, May 28, 1965, PFC.

## NINE: THE LADY IN THE GREEN COAT

1. Alan J. Kania interview with Mrs. Trudy Bronn, April 26, 1980, VJC, Box 4 FF41, and Marguerite Henry, "Do You Know Wild Horse Annie?" MHC.

2. Ibid.

3. Mershon, Helen L., "Horse Interests Spur Author," *Oregon Journal,* November 9, 1965.

4. Sutton, Elizabeth, L., "Marguerite Henry," obituary, Misty of Chincoteague Foundation Inc., www.mistyofchincoteague.org, consulted by authors in 2009.

5. Henry, Marguerite, "This Is Your Newsletter," # 4, PFC.

6. In 2001, *Misty of Chincoteague* was eighty-fifth on *Publishers Weekly* All-Time Best Selling Paperbacks list with 2.5 million copies sold to that point. *Brighty of Grand Canyon* sells twelve thousand a year and a new version of *Misty* published in 2006 has sold eighty thousand copies.

7. Mooar, Brian, "'Misty' Author Marguerite Henry Dies at Age 95," *Washington Post,* November 27, 1997.

8. VJ to MH, "First Day of Summer," 1965, PFC.

9. VJ to MH, November 8, 1966, PFC.

10. VJ to the Henry Family, January 19, 1966, PFC.

11. Henry, Marguerite, "This Is Your Newsletter," #7, PFC.

12. Ibid.

13. Ibid.

14. VJ to MH, April 2, 1965, PFC.

15. Ibid.

16. VJ to MH, April 20, 1965, PFC.

17. VJ to MH, May 5, 1965, PFC.

18. VJ to MH, April 2, 1965, PFC.

19. Ibid.

20. VJ to MH, April 20, 1965, PFC.

21. MH to VJ and Mrs. Bronn, April 11, 1965, PFC.

22. Ibid.

23. VJ to Avis Swick, November 29, 1965, MHC, Box MF 2630.

24. MH to VJ, n.d. attached to August 31, 1965 from VJ, PFC.

25. VJ to MH, August 31, 1965, PFC.

26. MH to VJ, n.d., attached to October 8, 1965, letter VJ to MH, PFC.

27. MH to VJ, n.d., circa mid-June 1965, PFC.

28. Henry, Marguerite, "This Is Your Newsletter," #7, PFC.

29. VJ to MH, October 13, 1965, PFC.

30. Ibid.

31. Ibid.

32. MH to VJ, circa October 1965, PFC.

33. VJ to MH, November 3, 1965, PFC.

34. MH to VJ, circa November 1965, PFC.

35. MH to VJ, circa November 1965 (different letter from the one cited in note 34).

36. Avis Swick to VJ, November 17, 1965, MHC.

37. MH to VJ, December 1965, PFC.

38. MH to VJ, December 1965, PFC.

39. VJ to MH, January 17, 1966, PFC.

40. VJ to MH, May 4, 1966, PFC.

TEN: OUT OF COLD STORAGE

1. VJ to MH, January 19, 1966, PFC.
2. VJ to MH, January 17, 1966, PFC.
3. VJ to MH, n.d., attached to MH to Gertrude, August 3, 1966, PFC.
4. VJ to MH, February, 21, 1966, PFC.
5. Ibid.
6. Ibid.
7. MH to VJ, June 29, 1966, PFC.
8. VJ to MH, April 28, 1966, PFC.
9. MH to VJ, April 18, 1966, PFC.
10. MH to VJ, n.d., attached to VJ to MH, May 4, 1966, PFC.
11. VJ to MH, May 4, 1966, PFC.
12. VJ to MH and Sid, June 13, 1966, MHC, Box MF 2630.
13. VJ to MH, October 6, 1966, PFC.
14. Ibid.
15. Henry, Marguerite, *Mustang: Wild Spirit of the West* (Chicago: Rand McNally, 1966), back jacket review quotations.
16. Ambler, Barbara, "New Books for the Young Reader," *New York Times,* January 15, 1967.
17. VJ to MH, January 19, 1967, PFC.
18. Henry, Marguerite, *Mustang: Wild Spirit of the West* (New York: Simon & Schuster, 1992), 76.
19. Henry, Marguerite, *Mustang: Wild Spirit of the West* (1966), 190.
20. Henry, Marguerite, "This Is Your Newsletter," # 8, PFC.
21. Henry, Marguerite, "This Is Your Newsletter," # 7 and 8, PFC.
22. MH to VJ, n.d. attached to VJ to MH, March 27, 1967, PFC.
23. VJ to MH, January 19, 1967, PFC.
24. VJ to MH, March 4, 1967, PFC.
25. Ibid.
26. Ibid.
27. VJ to MH, March 16, 1967, VJC, Box 1 FF7.
28. VJ to MH, February 1, 1967, and March 4, 1967, PFC.
29. Henry, Marguerite, "This Is Your Newsletter," # 4, PFC.
30. MH to Glenn W. Faris, April 2, 1967, MHC, Box MF 2630.
31. MH to VJ, circa early April 1967, PFC.
32. VJ to MH, April 20, 1967, PFC.
33. MH to VJ, circa early April 1967, PFC.
34. Ibid.
35. VJ to MH, April 26, 1967, VJC, Box 1 FF7.
36. VJ to MH, June 6, 1967, PFC.

37. MH to VJ, n.d., MHC, Box MF 2630.
38. Ibid.
39. VJ to MH, June 6, 1967, PFC.
40. Ibid.

### ELEVEN: THE BATTLE OF THE PRYOR MOUNTAINS

1. Remsberg, Charles, "One Man's Fight to Save the Mustangs," *True*, April 1967.
2. Ibid.
3. Ibid.
4. Ibid.
5. Ibid.
6. VJ to MH, April 12, 1966, VJC, Box 1 FF7.
7. Reverend Schweiger interview with Ginger Kathrens, May 23, 2005, www.thecloudfoundation.org.
8. VJ to MH, October 28, 1966, VJC, Box 1 FF7.
9. Remsberg, Charles, op. cit.
10. VJ to MH, March 16, 1967, VJC, Box 1 FF7.
11. GB to Bill Vincent (hereafter BV), May 25, 1967, and BV to GB, June 5, 1967, PFC.
12. VJ to GB, June 1, 1967, PFC.
13. GB to VJ, June 3, 1967, PFC.
14. BV to GB, June 5, 1967, PFC.
15. VJ to BV, June 8, 1967, PFC.
16. Douglas S. Kennedy to GB, June 26, 1967, PFC.
17. GB to VJ, June 29, 1967, PFC.
18. VJ to William C. Sanford, July 3, 1967, PFC.
19. "Bundy's Wild Horse Photos Added to Cowboy Hall of Fame Display," *Nevada State Journal*, December 1967.
20. Stillman, Deanne, *Mustang: The Saga of the Wild Horse in the West* (New York: Houghton Mifflin, 2008).

### TWELVE: A PERFECT STORM

1. VJ interview with Stanley Routson, July 12, 1967, VJC, Series 5, Box 3 FF8.
2. "Mustangs Blinded by Shotguns," *Las Vegas Nevadan*, August 13, 1967.
3. Cited in Ryden, Hope, *America's Last Wild Horses* (Guilford, CT: Lyons Press, 1999), 227.
4. Statement of Shirley G. Robison before FBI Special Agent Robert Lee, February 10, 1967, VJC, Series 10, Box 6 FF13.

5. Ibid.

6. VJ to Helen and John Reilly, February 22, 1967, VJC, Box 1 FF7.

7. VJ to MH, March 4, 1967, VJC, Box 1 FF7.

8. VJ to Ann, February 22, 1967, VJC, Box 1 FF7.

9. Cited in "Trial Report," p. 4, VJC, Series 10, Box 6 FF13.

10. VJ to MH, March 4, 1967, VJC, Box 1 FF7.

11. VJ to MH, July 17, 1967, VJC, Box 1 FF7.

12. VJ to MH, August 7, 1967, VJC, Box 1 FF7.

13. VJ to Christine Stevens (hereafter CS), March 8, 1968, VJC, Box 1 FF7.

14. VJ to MH, August 30, 1967, VJC, Box 1 FF7.

15. VJ to Pat Stafford, October 3, 1967, Box 1 FF7.

16. "Pryor Mountain Horses Without Sponsor," BLM Press Release, June 16, 1968, MHC, Box MF 2630.

17. VJ to Lynn Augustine, February 25, 1968, VJC, Box 1 FF8.

18. VJ to CS, March 8, 1968, VJC, Box 1 FF7.

19. Ryden, Hope, "The Battle to Save the Pryor Mountain Wild Horses," June 9, 2005, address at Bighorn Canyon National Recreation Area Visitor Center, Hope Ryden's personal papers.

20. Ibid.

21. Ibid.

22. Ibid.

23. VJ notes, September 4, 1969, VJC, Series 5 Box 3 FF 14.

24. Kroll, Jack, "Hairpiece," *Newsweek,* May 13, 1968.

25. Ryden, Hope, "The Battle to Save the Pryor Mountain Wild Horses," op. cit.

26. Hansen, Clifford (Senator), to BLM, August 13, 1968, cited by Hope Ryden, "The Battle to Save the Pryor Mountain Wild Horses," op. cit.

27. Ryden, Hope, "America's Last Wild Horses," op. cit., p. 255.

28. VJ to MH, August 26, 1968, VJC, Box 1 FF13.

29. VJ notes of meeting with Gerald H. Brown, September 5, 1968, VJC, Series 5, Box 3 FF14, and VJ to Lynn Augustine, September 6, 1958, VJC, Box 1 FF8.

30. Ibid.

31. Ibid.

32. Ibid.

33. "Wild Horse Refuge Established in Pryor Mountains," BLM Press Release, September 12, 1968, MHC, Box MF 2630.

34. Ibid.

35. Ibid.

### THIRTEEN: TRAPPED

1. Michael J. Pontrelli to VJ, May 21, 1968, VJC, Series 3, Box 2 FF39, and VJ to CS, June 25, 1968, VJC, Box 1 FF11.
2. ISPMB Bulletin, December 1968, Alan J. Kania collection (hereafter AJKC), Box 7.
3. VJ to Marguerite and Sid, November 13, 1968, PFC.
4. Ibid.
5. James R. Hall to Duane Sonnenburg, Memorandum, December 3, 1968, MHC, Box MF 2630.
6. James R. Hall to Pryor Mountain Wild Horse Management Committee, April 30, 1969, VJC.
7. Ibid.
8. Ibid.
9. ISPMB Bulletin, December 1968, op. cit.
10. VJ to MH, May 12, 1969, PFC.
11. VJ to MH, June 29, 1969, PFC.
12. "Scorecard," *Sports Illustrated,* December 14, 1964.
13. VJ to MH, June 29, 1969, PFC.
14. "Advisory Committee Urges Management Plans for Montana Wild Horse Herd," Department of Interior, News Release, June 20, 1969.
15. June 21, 1969, *New York Times.*
16. "Our Public Lands," Department of the Interior report, September 15, 1969.
17. Wambolt, Carl L., "Statement on the Pryor Mountain Wild Horse Range," Montana State University, September 29, 1971, VJC, Series 6, Box 4 FF15.
18. National Mustang Association, incorporation documents, VJC, Series 3, Box 2 FF37.
19. VJ to Donna L. Carman and Louise Wernike, March 22, 1970, VJC, Box 1 FF20.
20. ISPMB Bulletin, April, May, June 1969, AJKC.
21. VJ to Alan Kania, March 8, 1970, VJC, Box 1 FF19.
22. ISPMB, July, August 1969 newsletter, Vol. 8, No. 2, AJKC.
23. VJ to Howard Caudle, September 10, 1969, VJC, Box 1 FF18.
24. VJ to John McCormack, August 24, 1969, VJC, Box 1 FF17.
25. VJ to Hope Ryden, October 10, 1969, VJC, Box 1 FF18.
26. VJ to John and Helen Reilly, March 8, 1968.
27. VJ to MH, March 8, 1968, PFC.
28. "A Week of Successes for Wild Horse Buffs," *Nevada State Journal,* December 5, 1971.

## FOURTEEN: THE CHILDREN'S CRUSADE

1. VJ to Pearl Twyne, January 1969, VJC, Box 1 FF16.
2. VJ to MH, February 1969, VJC, Box 1 FF16.
3. University of Nevada Reno, board of directors minutes, September 30, 1970, University of Nevada Special Collections.
4. Clifford P. Hansen (Senator) to VJ, June 15, 1970, VJC, Series 3, Box 2 FF27.
5. VJ to MH, May 6, 1970, VJC, Box 1 FF20.
6. VJ to Mr. Chauck, May 15, 1971, VJC, Box 1 FF25.
7. VJ to John McCormack, March 8, 1971, VJC, Box 1 FF24.
8. Ibid.
9. VJ to MH, March 29, 1971, PFC.
10. Hearings before the Subcommittee on Public Lands of the Committee on Interior and Insular Affairs, 92nd Congress, April 19 and 20, Congressional Record pp. 197, 142.
11. Statement of Master Gregory Gude, Hearings before the Subcommittee on Public Lands of the Committee on Interior and Insular Affairs, op. cit.
12. Large, Arlen J., "Opposition Vanishes and Some Kids Gang Up to Save Wild Horses," *Wall Street Journal,* April 19, 1971, and Hearings before the Subcommitte on Public Lands of the Committee on Interior and Insular Affairs, op. cit.
13. Statement of Boyd L. Rasmussen, Hearings before the Subcommittee on Public Lands of the Committee on Interior and Insular Affairs, op. cit., p. 31.
14. Statement of Mrs. Velma B. Johnston, Hearings before the Subcommittee on Public Lands of the Committee on Interior and Insular Affairs, op. cit., p. 90.
15. Statement of Karl Weikel, Hearings before the Subcommittee on Public Lands of the Committee on Interior and Insular Affairs, op. cit., p. 118.
16. Large, Arlen J., op. cit.
17. Ibid.
18. "A Week of Successes for Wild Horse Buffs," *Nevada State Journal,* December 5, 1971.
19. VJ to MH, July 17, 1971, PFC.
20. VJ to Howard Caudle, August 10, 1970, PFC.
21. "A Week of Successes for Horse Buffs," op. cit.
22. VJ to William Loeb, May 22, 1973.
23. Transcript of telephone conversation, Pearl Twyne and VJ, July 9, 1974, VJC, Series 5, Box 3 FF26.

24. WHOA News Release, November 1973.

25. "AHPA Launches Emergency Fund Drive," American Horse Protection Association, Inc., December 1974.

26. VJ to Charles Clegg, Jr., May 14, 1974, VJC, Box 1 FF40.

27. VJ to Alan Kania, May 27, 1974, VJC, Box 1 FF40.

28. VJ to Mary Lea Turcott, May 26, 1974, VJC, Box 1 FF40.

29. VJ to Directors of the Board, Executive Secretaries, Inc., May 15, 1974, VJC, Box 1 FF40.

30. VJ to Marce, August 14, 1974, VJC, Box 1 FF42.

31. Alan J. Kania interview with Mrs. Trudy Bronn, April 26, 1980, VJC, Box 4 FF41.

32. Alan J. Kania to VJ, May 17, 1974, AJKC, Box 13.

33. VJ to Alan Kania, April 29, 1975, AJKC, Box 13.

34. Editorial, *Reno Evening Gazette,* July 11, 1977.

35. "Wild Horse Annie Dies in Reno: Mustang Protection Her Life Work," *Nevada State Journal,* June 28, 1977.

36. Rainey, William, III, "The Very Soul of Nevada," *Reno Evening Gazette,* July 11, 1977.

### EPILOGUE

1. Helen Reilly to Marcy Gross and Ann Weston, December 20, 1977, MHC.

2. Trina Bellak interview with the authors, February 2005.

3. "Wild and Free-Roaming Horses and Burros," Department of the Interior, Final Report 1982, Hope Ryden private papers.

4. Young, Samantha, "427 Wild Horses Seeking New Homes," *Las Vegas Review-Journal,* October 31, 2005. The foal sale program was also canceled in April 2005.

5. "Bureau of Land Management: Effective Long-Term Options Needed to Manage Unadoptable Wild Horses," Government Accountability Office, October 9, 2008.

6. Robbins, Jim, "As Wild Horses Breed, a Voice for Contraception," *The New York Times,* April 21, 2009.

7. Interview with BLM officials, September 2008.

8. Author interview with Lee Otteni, September 14, 2009.

9. Ibid.

# INDEX

*Page numbers of photographs appear in italics.*

Wild horses *(continued)*
  protection under Public Law
    92–195, 248
  Pryor Mountains horses, 185–95,
    207–19, 220–29, 271–72
  refuge at Nellis Air Force Base, 169
  refuges for sought, 225
  release of captured animals, by
    Velma and Charlie, 64–67,
    69–71, 80
  slaughterhouses/rendering plants,
    61, 84
  stallions competing for mares,
    223–24
  stallions taking mares, 34–35, 52,
    60–61
  sterilization/contraception
    programs, 268

  survivors of Little Big Horn, 186
  as symbol of the West, 74, 87, 212,
    246
  systematic elimination of, first,
    56–57
  Utter's horse trap, 238–39, 241
  Utter's illegal killing of, 235–38
  World War I demand for, 6
Wild ponies (of Chincoteague), 149
Wilkins, Natalie, 245
Williams, Lynn, 245
World War I, 5, 6, 57
Wright, James C., 124–25, 129
Wyman, Walker D., 50, 52, 58
Wyoming Livestock Association,
  241

Young, Roy, 89

# ABOUT THE AUTHORS

David Cruise and Alison Griffiths began writing together in 1983 and are the authors of seven bestselling books, including *Fleecing the Lamb, Lords of the Line, Net Worth, On South Mountain, Vancouver: A Novel,* and *The Great Adventure.* They live on a small farm in southwestern Ontario with their horses.